The Meaning and Culture
of *Grand Theft Auto*

The Meaning and Culture of *Grand Theft Auto*

Critical Essays

Edited by NATE GARRELTS

McFarland & Company, Inc., Publishers

Jefferson, North Carolina, and London

LIBRARY OF CONGRESS CATALOGUING-IN-PUBLICATION DATA

The meaning and culture of Grand theft auto : critical essays /
edited by Nate Garrelts.
    p.   cm.
Includes bibliographical references and index.

ISBN-13: 978-0-7864-2822-9
softcover : 50# alkaline paper ∞

1. Grant Theft Auto games—Social aspects.   2. Video
games—Social aspects.   I. Garrelts, Nate.
GV1469.35.G738M43 2006
794.8—dc22   2006023510

British Library cataloguing data are available

Cover art ©2006 Digital Vision

Manufactured in the United States of America

McFarland & Company, Inc., Publishers
 Box 611, Jefferson, North Carolina 28640
 www.mcfarlandpub.com

For Beth and Winton

Contents

An Introduction to Grand Theft Auto Studies

Nate Garrelts

Pogo is just what the video game industry was looking for. A
cutesy character in a platform puzzler. 10/10.
—*Joy-Stuck.net* (qtd. *on pogothemonkey.com*)

The public discourse on digital games is a tangle of political rhetoric, reactionary responses, and game journalism; it is as passionate as it
is negligent. But the public discourse is not the only discourse on digital
games; academics have been studying this new medium since its invention. With the explosion of academic interest in digital games at the
beginning of the twenty-first century, academic discourse on games has
just now begun spilling into the public discourse with an ever-increas-
ing number of books, journals, interviews, and testimonies centered on
academic inquiries into the medium. Though there are some exceptions,
the academic conversation is informed and critical but not often accessible to the general public or even other academics—digital game studies span several disciplines and draw upon diverse sets of theories, each
with a complicated vocabulary. This collection of essays was compiled to
help academic game studies bridge the boundaries of academia to speak
directly to the gaming public and other interested parties—including
politicians, journalists, review boards, and parents. To this end, the essays
in this collection study the immensely popular and controversial Grand
Theft Auto series, with a particular emphasis on *Grand Theft Auto III
(GTA3)*, *Grand Theft Auto: Vice City (GTA:VC)*, and *Grand Theft Auto: San
Andreas (GTA:SA)*.

Part One is aptly titled "Grand Theft Auto v. The Power-Go-Round." Obviously, the games in this series are significant not just because they are popular among players, but because they have also given rise to a host of fears, lawsuits, legislative proposals, and other public reactions. The series has entered culture in such a way that it is embraced by adult players because it empowers them in various ways, and, at the same time, the games have become an icon for child endangerment and are continually used by politically minded individuals and organizations to further their agendas.

The first few essays in this part sketch out a scenario in which game developers like Rockstar are trying to make adult oriented games and at the same time are faced with new forms of censorship. The essays talk about the depictions of race and violence in Grand Theft Auto games, the pleasure of the carnivalistic gameplay, and the significance of satire in the series. At the end of this part, it is argued that the way we think and talk about digital games was fundamentally altered following the release of *Grand Theft Auto III*.

Part Two, "A Grand Theft Auto Way of Life," approaches the games as they might be studied absent the controversy; the essays in this part study how players meaningfully and purposefully play Grand Theft Auto games. The authors in this part reflect on the elements of daily life that are represented, including the connection between gamespace and real space, and the many ways that players mediate the symbols in a game with their minds, computers, and controllers.

Aside from strategy guides and other popular texts, this is the first academic book to focus explicitly on a single game series, and there are several advantages to this approach. Because of the popularity (and notoriety) of Grand Theft Auto games, readers have ample incentive to wade through some of the theoretical complexity. Additionally, because of profound overlaps in game content, the analysis of one game in the series is often easily transferred to several other games in the series without further qualification.

In effect, this means that readers need knowledge of (or easy access to) only one of the primary games under discussion. For teachers at the college level who want to briefly introduce upper level undergraduate or graduate students to game studies, they can do this with one game and one book. Of course, because each essay is working from a different theoretical perspective, some of the essays contradict one another in typical academic fashion. This reflects the complexity and difficulty of digital game studies and the fact that this collection thoroughly engages its object of study.

From Hot Cars to Hot Coffee

In many ways this collection is both a serious digital game studies text, exemplifying several approaches for studying the medium, and a compliment (sometimes backhanded) to the visionaries at Rockstar Games—the publisher of the *GTA* games that are the focus of this analysis. Rockstar is a coming together of people with strong personalities, unique talents, and a vision for what the digital game medium can be. Despite the fact that there are certain employees commonly associated with the founding of Rockstar, the company tries hard to avoid singling out any one person. It recognizes that the project of making a game is monumental and involves thousands of hours of work from each individual involved. With a network of employees that spans the globe,[1] no one individual can take credit (or blame) for a Grand Theft Auto game; the series is a manifestation of their collective vision. Whatever the game title, Rockstar has managed to entertain audiences and provoke politicians, not always with dignity but surely with style.

The gameplay presented to players in the first *Grand Theft Auto (GTA)* game, released in 1997, provided an overall outline for later games in the series to follow. The original *GTA*, developed by DMA and published by BMG Interactive, allowed a player to direct the player-controlled character in the game to freely explore a town named Liberty City. While directing the character to answer the telephone would activate missions, a player could also choose to have the character complete side missions that were activated by having the character enter certain designated vehicles. After the character earned enough money through committing various crimes, the other cities of Vice City and San Andreas were unlocked. Of course, players could simply choose to have the character explore and interact with the game world instead of working to unlock new areas. As with future games in the series, the character was permitted to steal cars and other vehicles and drive anywhere in the city, while music and commercials played on the in-game radio. A character was also permitted to assault other characters in the game, including police officers, with weapons ranging from pistol to flamethrower. And as in other games, if the character was witnessed by the police while acting in a violent manner, the character's wanted level would go up and the police or other law enforcement agencies would begin pursuit. Although most of the core elements of gameplay were present in the first *GTA* and its expansion packs, this game did not generate the fervent controversy and praise bestowed upon later games in the series; the same was true of the futuristic sequel, *Grand Theft Auto 2.*[2] With their top-down 2D perspective and simple graphics, the chasm between these first Grand Theft Auto games and reality was significant. And as with other media, the more the audience was forced to imagine the controversial content the less public guardians had to say. Of course, this would all change with the next iteration of the series, *Grand Theft Auto III (GTA3)*, which was published in 2001 by Rockstar Games.

With the introduction of *GTA3*, there were some significant changes in the platform that permitted this release in the series to stand out. To begin, whereas earlier games in the series were produced for the Playstation and PC, *GTA3* debuted on the PlayStation 2 (PS2), a futuristic black box that could display 66 million polygons per second at a resolution ranging from 256 × 224 to 1280 × 1024 ("Under the Hood"). Utilizing this hardware, *GTA3* made the move from a top-down 2D game to a real-time 3D game, a shift which Laurie Taylor argues in her essay "From Stompin' Mushrooms to Bustin' Heads: *Grand Theft Auto III* as Paradigm Shift" is the root of much of the debate over Grand Theft Auto games. True to the series origins, there is only one nameless and silent player-controlled character. At the beginning of this game a player is presented with a cut-scene that shows this character and his girlfriend, Catalina, after robbing a bank. Catalina shoots her nameless boyfriend and leaves him for dead, and he is then arrested for the robbery. After recuperating and on his way to prison, he escapes along with an explosives expert named 8-Ball. It is at this point that the player gains control of the nameless character and is free to have him explore the world of Liberty City, or be sucked into a life of crime with the help of 8-Ball, which reveals the embedded gangster narrative of *Grand Theft Auto III*. However, at any time a player can choose to stray from the narrative or abandon it totally in favor of arresting criminals, putting out fires, or a number of other activities—including those activities that were permitted in the earlier games in the series.

The follow-up to *Grand Theft Auto III*, contrary to the past precedent, was not *Grand Theft Auto IV*. Instead the game was named *Grand Theft Auto: Vice City* (2002), which hinted that the 3D games were having a conversation with the first game in the series and possibly creating a miniseries based on the levels presented in this first game. *Grand Theft Auto: Vice City*, which is a prequel to *Grand Theft Auto III*, is set in 1986, and through its iconography resembles the Miami of *Scarface* and *Miami Vice* (Bogost and Klainbaum). The lone player-controlled character, Tommy Vercetti, is a criminal with mob connections. As a player learns from cut scenes, Vercetti's back-story is gruesome. He was released from jail after serving time for committing multiple murders. Upon his release, he is asked by Sonny Forelli to establish drug operations for the "family" in Vice City. At this point a player has the option of interacting with the game in such a way as to reveal the complex narrative, which takes Vercetti on a path of *Scarface*-esque crime, or simply to explore and interact in the world of the game. At the end of the narrative it is revealed that Sonny Forelli was the cause of most of Vercetti's woes, including Vercetti's imprisonment for murder at the beginning of the game. As with previous games, a player can have the player-controlled character explore and interact within this city, which means driving a variety of '80s inspired vehicles and listening to '80s music.[3]

The series matured significantly in 2004 with the release of *Grand Theft Auto: San Andreas*, which takes place in the fictional state of San Andreas in 1992 (as opposed to a single city in the original *Grand Theft Auto*). Instead of belonging to the Italian mafia, a player adopts the identity of Carl Johnson (CJ) a former gang-banger and member of the Grove Street Families who escaped the gang life and moved to Liberty City. Unfortunately, upon hearing of his mother's murder, CJ is forced to return to San Andreas, where he is harassed by police officers and framed for murder. At the same time, CJ works with his old gang mates to retake the city from gangs like the Ballas. The game ends with massive riots, the death of crooked police officer Tenpenny (after a Rodney-King-style acquittal), and CJ going outside to continue exploring the neighborhood.

In this game, a player is presented with all of the previously defining elements of a Grand Theft Auto game adapted appropriately for the time. But there is more of everything, from the environments to the types of interactions that are possible in the environments. San Andreas is massive when compared to Liberty City and Vice City, which is fitting as San Andreas is comprised of the three cities of Los Santos, Las Venturas, and San Fiero. For the first time in the series, a player can choose to shape the player-controlled character, CJ, by having him exercise, eat food, go shopping, get tattooed, or any number of other activities. To this, CJ's body responds appropriately, if he eats too much and doesn't exercise he gains weight, which means that his stamina is decreased and he runs slower. Depending on the way he grooms himself, different types of women will desire him. Moreover, CJ is capable of learning to become a better driver, shooter, pilot, etc., by practicing. CJ can also go on dates with women and engage in a soft-porn sex mini-game if the game is modified by a player to make this option available. The modification, which is referred to as the "Hot Coffee" mod, requires an original release of the game for the PC/PS2 and game hacking software. It is not easy to access this content without research and technological savvy.[4]

Part One: Grand Theft Auto v. The Power-Go-Round

Digital games are play spaces for adults, and this has been the case since the dawn of digital gaming. Whether one is talking about Steve Russel and Alan Kotek's *Space War*, which was developed as a student project at MIT, or Nolan Bushnell's *PONG*, which debuted in a bar, digital games have from the beginning been aimed at older audiences. According to the Entertainment Software Association's most recent data, the average player of digital games is now thirty years old and is no longer strictly male, if it ever was. Moreover, eighty-nine percent of rentals and game purchases made by children happen under the supervision of a parent, which means one can be hopeful that parents are aware of their child's gaming habits ("Essential Facts"). It is within this context that the more recent Grand Theft Auto games, the primary focus of this collection, emerged. These games are targeted at this mature audience; Rockstar Games, the publisher of the series, has made this argument and the demographics support this claim. The first section of this book aims to understand how these adult games have entered society and give some insight into the controversies that surround them.

In the first essay in the collection, "Spilling Hot Coffee? Grand Theft Auto as Contested Cultural Product," Aphra Kerr studies the digital games industry and "the transnational production network and core business strategy behind the GTA games within wider trends." Kerr frames the social significance of GTA games as "a conflict between multinational cultural corporation(s) and local political, cultural and social actors" resulting in "a struggle for freedom of speech versus new forms of censorship." Kerr's essay is followed by Mark Finn's "Political Interface: The Banning of *GTA3* in Australia," which historicizes "the 2001 decision by the Office of Film and Literature Classification to refuse classification to *Grand Theft Auto III* (*GTA3*)." According to Finn, the "high-profile" nature of the case especially spoke to "the curious absence of an adult classification for games in Australia" and highlighted the perverse ways in which "traditional media regulators deal with highly interactive content."

In an effort to protect children, U.S. Senators Hillary Clinton and Joe Lieberman proposed the Family Entertainment Protection Act in late 2005. According to Senator Clinton's official website, the act attempts to regulate digital games at the point of sale, which will in turn empower parents. Clinton "acknowledges that video games are fun and entertaining and does not support any limitations on the production or sale of games to adults" ("Senators Clinton"). Yet, because major retailers like Wal-Mart and Best Buy have such a profound influence on the market, and because this legislation singles out digital games media, some consider this legislation (and proposals like it) a new form of censorship that is simply not warranted. Besides the fact that digital games are already less accessible to consumers than other forms of media because of the cost of the hardware and software, anyone who has ever actually played a digital game knows that the animated sexual and violent depictions, among other controversial content, still pales in comparison to the virtually real depictions of other less regulated media like film and television. Court rulings in some states have already said that similar legislative acts were unconstitutional, especially because the evidence that links children, video games, and violence is not compelling ("Court Rulings").

Indeed, MIT professor Henry Jenkins highlights the farce perpetuated by segments of the media and some politicians, saying that there is a gap "between the public's perception of video games and what the research actually shows." According to Jenkins the research to date[5] has only proven that "violent play leads to more violent play." David Gauntlett, a professor of media and audiences, has also examined the research conducted to measure the effects of mass media on people, particularly research that aims to understand the relationship between any media and violence. According to Gauntlett, instead of studying a problem and trying to find the causes, media effects studies begin by assuming that media is the cause and set about proving or disproving this. Sadly, the "basic question of why the media should induce people to imitate its content has never been adequately tackled." Moreover, he finds that many studies are "selective" in the media they choose to criticize and acts of "violence which appear on a daily basis on news and serious factual programs are seen as somehow exempt." Even Senator Clinton has supported legislation to "create the first-ever coordinated research center devoted to revealing the impact of media on our children. This center would focus particularly on the impact of media on infants, an area that is widely not understood, and on the growing link between television viewing and childhood obesity" ("Fighting Culture").

Of course one doesn't need a scientific study to show that sex, violence, strong language, and other adult themes are not appropriate for children because these do not reflect the values of our society that we want to impart to children. So the challenge, as with all media, is to keep controversial content out of the hands of children while at the same time protecting the civil liberties we all also value. If the game industry had its way, the discourse would shift from legislation to empowering parents. For example, a spokesperson for Rockstar was quoted as saying "We support any effort to empower parents to control what their kids consume, but we also want to strike a balance so that the average video game player, who is not a child, is able to continue to play the games that they enjoy" (Walker qtd. in Hernandez). The Entertainment Software Rating Board (ESRB), responsible for rating games in the United States, has an "OK To Play?" initiative that they actively promote in gaming magazines and at stores to assist parents in making decisions. There are also parental controls on the next generation game consoles that help parents regulate the games that can be played on the console.

Whether legislators are right or wrong, the digital game is simply not the most logical media to begin legislating. So one must investigate other factors that influence this decision. Ultimately, many of the contributors in this collection point out that this controversy and legislation is about ideology and power as much as it is a general concern for the welfare of children and society.

In perhaps the most cutting and critical essay in the collection, "Virtual Gangstas, Coming to a Suburban House Near You: Demonization, Commodification, and Policing Blackness," David Leonard indicts politicians, the public, and the game industry for their bias and complacency. As Leonard paints it, the criticisms of GTA for violence are not fair, not because the game is innocent, but because the logic by which opponents arrive at this position is skewed by ideology and new racism. The most resonating insight is Leonard's awareness that previous games in the GTA series "never resulted in national debates and cries for governmental intervention" nor did ideologically sanctioned games like *America's Army* and *Socom.*

Given our familiar cultural proclivities for violence: we tolerate, even relish, violence, that confirms our ideology of good triumphing evil and abject other forms of violence (of course the prevailing ideology posits each of these roles).

No, this debate was stimulated because in games like *GTA:SA* the violence is committed by young men of color. According to Leonard, "race contributes to both the societal condemnation and widespread popularity of these games." He argues "that both the game itself and the various receptions replicate such practices reducing blackness to a sign of criminality, hypersexuality, and cultural/moral chaos" which prompts both "regulation/state intervention" and celebration. The distressing reality Leonard exposes is that "celebrations and demonizations of blackness jointly facilitate the hegemony of new racism, which in the end maintains color lines and white privileges, whether manifesting in the perpetuation of the prison industrial complex or systematic poverty that reared its head in wake of Hurricane Katrina."

Tanner Higgin locates the controversy over the Grand Theft Auto games in a "recurring cycle of paranoia and misunderstanding of media."

In his essay "Play-Fighting: Understanding Violence in *Grand Theft Auto III*," Higgin does not dismiss the game as nonviolent. On the contrary he points to the way that the game by design encourages violent behavior that "de-mythologizes the outside world." In other words, it lays bare the ideology that organizes Western society, and this violent gameplay is thus both "satiric and cathartic."

David Annandale, who dissects *GTA:SA* in his essay "The Subversive Carnival of *Grand Theft Auto: San Andreas*," takes up a similar line of theorizing. For Annandale, "the game transforms huge swatches of American culture and society into ridiculous caricatures ... the game is a digital incarnation of Mikhail Bakhtin's concept of the carnivalesque." Gameplay thus takes on the form of "unauthorized rebellion" and the more it is denounced in society the more powerful it becomes.

Thus, what pundits deride in GTA games as gratuitously violent gameplay, many academics see as a critical commentary on the absurdity of modern life. Such readings are not surprising, as John Fiske argues, through the process of "excorporation" members of a subordinate group often use the resources produced by a dominant group, i.e. the culture industry, to produce popular culture (15) which "is relevant to the immediate social situation of the people" (25).[6] Thus, Fiske proposes that we focus both on the products of the culture industry and the ways that people appropriate these products (20). This is the method we must take with digital games: they are industry-produced products, loaded with significant sound and images that are continually being remade as people play them. The agency of gameplay is discussed in several essays included in the second section of the book.

While the previously mentioned essays highlight the ideological nature of gameplay through some intellectual gymnastics, reading the satirical nature of the games is much more a surface endeavor. Indeed, my favorite aspect *GTA3* and the games that have followed it is the often-sardonic advertising and talk shows featured on the in-game radio stations. Among the most cutting, self-reflexive advertisements is one for a *Pogo the Monkey* video game. Pogo, who has springs for legs, is billed by the advertiser as a "new friend for everyone," and this is substantiated by a girl who exclaims "I love you Pogo, you bounce!" According to the advertisement, players help Pogo escape from the genetics lab where he is kept, fend off cosmetics researchers, save Timmy from a well, and eventually become president of the United States. For these acts, Pogo is rewarded first with gold coins, but these later give way to greater rewards like diamonds and cars. The advertisement promises that the game is something "kids are sure to stare at for hours!" Of course, the game is also complimented by an assortment of children's toys and stereotypical gendered products, such as ties for men and "chocolates and hygiene products" for women. More information, literarily, is made available at the advertised website, pogothemonkey.com. On this real-world website the critique is foregrounded even more with comments like "Teach kids to win things" and "Teach kids to kill and covet money."

Obviously, this fictional game is satirizing game culture. Seemingly benign games, which reflect the tropes and conventions of media culture and prevailing ideologies, are marketed to the general public along with a slew of ephemeral products. Violence and capitalist themes, carefully disguised in a cute cartoon format, are celebrated instead of critiqued. At the same time, this game, *Pogo the Monkey*, is reflecting the very real challenges facing players in the world outside of the game which in the context of the game the monkey is justified in fighting against. In essence, Rockstar's Grand Theft Auto series deprives audiences of this comfortable façade to better reveal the absurdity and atrocities of the real world—literary parallels can be drawn to the works of William Burroughs and Kurt Vonnegut.

This satire is the subject of "Grand Theft Video: Running and Gunning for the U.S. Empire" by Dennis Redmond. In an upbeat, yet critical essay, Redmond applauds the series for "uproarious satire" that gave "the world the comic relief it desperately needed" during a period of "nightmarish political regression."

In rejecting the children's characters and fantasy elements that were prevalent in their competitors products and instead targeting a mature adult audience, *GTA3* and later games in the series advanced the cultural scope of the medium. At the same time, when *GTA3* was released it was a game like none other because it combined the best aspects of several different game genres into one highly graphic 3D world with flexible rules. When compared to the other games of the time, and the significant games of the past, it was this achievement that stands out and continues to make Grand Theft Auto games popular.

The last essay in Part One, "From Stompin' Mushrooms to Bustin' Heads: *Grand Theft Auto III* as Paradigm Shift" by Laurie N. Taylor, marks the release of *GTA3* as the beginning of a new paradigm in digital gaming. According to Taylor, "*GTA3* emerged at a point in gaming history where games had not yet matured as much as their players." When presented with graphic, adult oriented content "the public's perception of gaming as a child's form" was challenged and this "ignited large-scale controversy over video games and violence." The end result was a fundamental change in the way we thought and talked about digital games.

Part Two: A Grand Theft Auto Way of Life

The essays in the second part address the Grand Theft Auto games not as controversial cultural artifacts but as a symbolic media that players actively and purposefully engage.

This part begins with the essay "Everyday Play: Cruising for Leisure in San Andreas" by Timothy Welsh. For Welsh the "quotidian elements" in *Grand Theft Auto: San Andreas,* things such as eating and getting haircuts, are significant because they allude to established "cycles of daily life" yet do not demand the same attention; the consequences for not eating, sleeping, or exercising are not dire as they are in the world outside the game. In effect, these elements contribute to the reality of *GTA:SA* and at the same time create "the illusion that one has escaped everyday life and all the responsibilities and monotony it entails."

The amount of space to be explored and interacted with has steadily increased in GTA games, and this space too is symbolic. In early digital games the environment for interaction created in the limitless space of the virtual was denoted by a handful of colors, usually one to simulate the ground and one to simulate the sky. Of course in some digital games space is still denoted by color, or unchanging background images. However, with the increased technological capabilities of modern hardware these spaces are increasingly complex and filled with ambient objects such as mountains, buildings, flags, and chairs, and their primary function is to combine to create different environments within a digital game. For example, for many people the image of a couch is the defining object of a living room environment. When a couch is joined with paintings, a television, and reclining chair the living room environment is even more solidified.

Instead of focusing on the typical elements that we think define environments, in his essay "Cruising in San Andreas: Ludic Space and Urban Aesthetics in Grand Theft Auto," Zach Whalen emphasizes the "surfaces and paths" that define the relationship between the artificial Los Santos and the real Los Angeles. Moreover, he tries to discern the multiple overlaps between space that is designed to re-present and space that is designed for play.

As Whalen mentions throughout his essay, many of us have come to know significant aspects of reality and places like Los Angeles through the sounds and images of mass media. Postmodern theorist Jean Baudrillard has argued that we are now living in an age of simulacrum in which the media creates reality and not the other way around. Although a reference to the physical world can often be found in this media, it is increasingly the case that the simulation itself is referring to another simulation—what Umberto Eco has referred to as neo-television. Even something as real as reality television is populated not by real people, but by real media personalities like Paris Hilton. Because of the original referent is so far removed from media, and our experience is largely constructed by the sounds and images in the media, many of us are living in completely simulated worlds of fantasy.

Ian Bogost and Dan Klainbaum, in their essay "Experiencing Place in Los Santos and Vice City," argue that digital games have effectively exploited our simulated existence and that games like *Grand Theft Auto: Vice City* and *Grand Theft Auto: San Andreas* are able to create a profound reality not by realistically recreating the city of Miami but instead by recreating a *Miami Vice* version of the city. In short, the new culture of digital games is yesterday's adult media culture recycled. And by recycling the right images, narratives,[7] and sounds,[8] digital games have been able to efficiently present "realistic" space. For Bogost and Klainbaum, the significance of GTA games are that they are both "a critique as well as an affirmation of the influence of media on people in the developed world."

Gameplay is an act that is motivated by several factors and influenced by, among other things, a player's ability to interpret and negotiate the signs presented in the gaming situation, and this is a significant factor in the previous two essays. In "Positioning and Creating the Semiotic Self in *Grand Theft Auto: Vice City* and *Grand Theft Auto: San Andreas*," John A. Unger and Karla V. Kingsley study the ways that players interact with the symbolic domain of two GTA games. Unger and Kingsley are particularly interested in understanding "the relationships between signs and cognition, how these relationships develop," and their research draws on theorists such as Vygotsky and Bakhtin, among others. By actually studying players as they play and interviewing them after they play, they uncover some of the complex ways in which "players create and respond to utterances" and work "within specific and general semiotic domains that overlap with the sociocultural histories of past utterances and other semiotic domains."

Players do not make the initial conditions of their character's existence in GTA games—that is unless one considers the case of "modding" a digital game (using programs to alter the content of a game).[9] In "Against Embedded Agency: Subversion and Emergence in *GTA3*," Cindy Poremba proposes "one cannot always assume the author/game designer has control over the boundaries in which player agency unfolds" and because of this proposes that "narrative agency cannot follow an embedded structure."

Continuing this line of inquiry, Wm. Ruffin Bailey's essay "Inviting Subversion: Metalepses and Tmesis in Rockstar Games' Grand Theft Auto Series" highlights the many ways that players have entered into a "nuanced dialog" with the games and developers. The ultimate effect being that players become complicit in "coauthoring their experience." The history of game modding combined with Baily's speculations on concealed contents in video games, such as the "Hot Coffee" sex mini-game, signals a greater significance to the series: "Grand Theft Auto has developed the idea of potential texts in ways unlike any other composition, and is uniquely experimenting with digital media in ways other designers are only beginning to understand."

As the Grand Theft Auto series has progressed it has become less and less predictable how a player will play a game. In many games, the act of playing the game has become an act of choosing which content will surface—choosing which media culture will re-surface. The book closes with David Parry's "Playing with Style: Negotiating Digital Game Studies," an essay as much about the Grand Theft Auto games as it is about the future of digital game studies. According to Parry the "analytic frameworks" used by game studies to discuss digital games often "divide gamer from game, treating the subject (gamer) and object (game) as discretely separable concepts." For Parry, it is "never really possible to speak strictly of the game; instead, one must always speak of gameplay" and what "is really important" is an understanding of the restless negotiation of the digital game interaction, one in which the GTA series serves as a paradigmatic example."

The Definitive Analysis

To be sure, Rockstar has imbued the Grand Theft Auto series with both reality and social agency without abandoning the gameplay qualities that make these games so successful and entertaining. Drawing on popular media and dominant ideologies as a source for centrally important game content, Grand Theft Auto games have escaped the fantasy of popular images and have dived head-first into brutal reality. As some argue, players who wallow in this postmodern spectacle by hedonistically consuming the sounds and images of GTA are privy to a heightened sense of reality outside of the game world. For others, this spectacle simply reifies already present stereotypes or promotes undesirable behavior. Thus, digital game studies must continually acknowledge that what appears to be simple fun or gratuitous violence might be engaging culture and society in several different ways. If we want to study this, we must understand what players are given to interact with and the myriad ways in which players and game cultures make sense of, embrace, reject, and appropriate this content. Moreover, because digital games are so vast and change based on how a person plays, we are obligated to not settle for our first, second, or even third analysis. If after careful analysis we are led to jettison Grand Theft Auto games from our culture, let it be. Until then, let us not be guided by reactionary and emotional propaganda.[10]

Acknowledgments

Many friends, colleagues, and students helped me as I compiled this collection. I would like to thank Jeremy Martin, Vince Samarco, Janice Wolff, Lori Kranz, Don Bachand, and the students in ENGL212 and ENGL203. I am especially indebted to my wife, Beth, who was, as usual, both patient and supportive throughout this project.

Notes

1. To date developers include Rockstar North (Edinburgh), Rockstar Leeds, Rockstar London, Rockstar San Diego, Rockstar Toronto, Rockstar Vancouver, and Rockstar Vienna. With the exclusion of Rockstar London, which was established by Rockstar Games, all of these development houses existed under other names and authorities before coming in to the Rockstar fold.

2. Other games in the Grand Theft Auto series have been released for portable gaming devices. Versions of *GTA* and *GTA2* were developed for the Gameboy Color. More recently, *Grand Theft Auto Advance* (2004) was published for the Gameboy Advance and *Grand Theft Auto: Liberty City Stories* (2005) was published for the PlayStation Portable.

3. While *GTA3* included quality voice acting from actors such as Joe Pantaloni and a diverse playlist of songs and commentary, the list of voice actors in *GTA:VC* is even more impressive. Tommy Vercetti, for example is voiced by Ray Liotta. Vercetti's sometimes partner, Lance Vance, is voiced by Philip Michael Thomas of *Miami Vice* fame. With the addition of Gary Busey, Dennis Hopper, and Jenna Jameson, the voice acting is superb. The voice acting in *GTA:SA* is also superb with contributions from stars like Samuel L. Jackson, James Woods, Ice-T, and Peter Fonda.

4. The "Hot Coffee" farce is significant largely because it provided the impetus for the current cultural debates on video games.

5. While some have countered that the military does use digital games to train soldiers, according to Jenkins such simulations are used "as part of a specific curriculum" with real consequences. Indeed, Saginaw Valley State University was recently awarded a grant to develop a crisis intervention training program that utilizes simulator technology. When I asked to participate in the project, I cited my background in digital game studies as a potential asset—I was directly corrected. The chamber was not a game to be played but a simulator designed for training. Given the seriousness with which police officers brandish the replica pistols, I am now convinced that motive makes a difference.

6. De Certeau cites the example of indigenous peoples who mixed their native religion with Christianity in order to preserve their religion during colonization. Their usage of Christianity was not an unthinking consumption; instead, "their usage of the dominant social order deflected its power, which they lacked the means to challenge; they escaped it without leaving it" (xiii).

7. Among other media references, the agents in *Grand Theft Auto: Vice City* are a mixture of images and object functions from *Miami Vice* and the film *Scarface*, which itself was a remake of a 1932 film. Like Tony Montana in *Scarface*, the player-controlled character escapes to Miami after being released from jail—both were convicted murderers and both can do little more with their hands than kill. Even the names

Tommy and Tony sound alike. Early in the game players are introduce to a character named Lance Vance, a light skinned black man who looks like Tubbs from *Miami Vice*, which is appropriate because the character is voiced by the man who played Tubbs on the series. The agents in *San Andreas* are also clearly based on popular media personalities. Notably, one character named Lance "Ryder" Wilson strongly resembles the late '80s rap artist Eric Wilson, otherwise known as Easy-E. Perhaps it is a stretch, but when one thinks of the nickname "Ryder" the term "Easy" seems to come to mind. Of course, this overlap would come to mind considering that a hippie character named "Truth" is voiced by *Easy Rider* star Peter Fonda.

　　8. Uniquely, the game series found a way to make the soundtrack, which is typically non-literal, literal by having each vehicle in the game equipped with a radio that plays period-specific music. In *GTA:VC*, players can hear artists popular during the time like 2 Live Crew, Michael Jackson, and David Lee Roth. During nonmusical moments, as with real radio, PBS employees beg for support and motivational speakers hoc products.

　　9. While deliberating about the nature of authorship in digital environments, Janet Murray discusses this issue in *Hamlet on the Holodeck* (152).

　　10. I am especially concerned with the ESRB request that the industry as a whole begin preemptively protecting game content against mods that may "undermine" ratings. This new form of censorship is like laminating the pages in a book to prevent people from drawing dongs in the margins.

Works Cited

"Court Rulings and Legal Briefs." *Entertainment Software Association.* 6 Jan. 2006 <http://www.theesa.com/facts/industry_self_reg.php>.
DeCerteau, Michel. *The Practice of Everyday Life.* Berkley: U of California P, 1988.
Entertainment Software Review Board (ESRB). 24 Feb. 2006 <http://www.esrb.org/esrbratings_guide.asp>.
"Essential Facts about the Computer and Video Game Industry." *Entertainment Software Association.* 6 Jan. 2006 <http://www.esa.org>.
"Fighting the Culture of Sex and Violence in the Media." *Senator Hillary Rodham Clinton.* 29 Nov. 2005. 6 Jan. 2006 <http://clinton.senate.gov/issues/children/>.
Fiske John. *Understanding Popular Culture.* Boston: Unwin Hyman, 1989.
Gauntlett, D. "Ten Things Wrong with the Effects Model." *Newmediastudies* (1999). 6 Jan. 2006 <http://www.newmediastudies.com/effects1.htm>.
Grand Theft Auto. New York: BMG Interactive, 1997.
Grand Theft Auto III. New York: Rockstar, 2001.
Grand Theft Auto: San Andreas. New York: Rockstar, 2004.
Grand Theft Auto: Vice City. New York: Rockstar, 2002.
Hernandez, Raymond. "Clinton Urges Inquiry Into Hidden Sex in Grand Theft Auto Game" New York Times.
Jenkins, Henry. "Reality Bytes: Eight Myths about Video Games Debunked." *PBS: The Video Game Revolution.* 6 Jan. 2006 <http://www.pbs.org/kcts/videoplayerevolution/impact/myths.html>.
Murray, Janet H. *Hamlet on the Holodeck: The Future of Narrative in Cyberspace.* Cambridge: MIT P, 1997.
Pogo the Monkey. 2001. 6 Jan. 2006 <http://www.pogothemonkey.com>.
"Senators Clinton, Lieberman Announce Federal Legislation to Protect Children from Inappropriate Video Games." *Senator Hillary Rodham Clinton.* 29 Nov. 2005. 6 Jan. 2006 <http://clinton.senate.gov/news/statements/details.cfm?id=249368&&>.
"Under the Hood." *Sony.* 2002. 21 January 2003 <http://www.us.playstation.com/hardware/PS2/415007657.asp>.

PART ONE : GRAND THEFT AUTO v. THE POWER-GO-ROUND

1. Spilling Hot Coffee?
Grand Theft Auto as Contested Cultural Product

APHRA KERR

Grand Theft Auto (GTA) games are highly successful in terms of sales, and their content is part of an explicit business strategy that aims to exploit the latest technologies and platforms to develop games aimed at adult game players in certain markets. By all accounts this has been a highly successful strategy with the GTA franchise selling more than 30 million units across platforms by 2004, even before *Grand Theft Auto: San Andreas (GTA:SA)* was launched in late 2004 (Take-Two Interactive 2004). The latter was the top selling console game in the United States and in the top ten in the United Kingdom in 2005. At the same time games in the GTA series are arguably the most maligned of game products in many markets, attracting much negative commentary and numerous legal actions in the United States. This chapter argues that the GTA case demonstrates a key tension within the cultural industries between the need to maximize sales globally and the need to conform to, or be seen to conform to, local distribution, social and moral systems. At the same time the story demonstrates that despite the widespread rhetoric of free trade and the dismantling of state sanctioned censorship systems in the United States, most parts of Europe and Australia, the censorship of cultural products continues and is perhaps a less overt, but nonetheless, highly political, socially negotiated and nationally specific process.

GTA games are produced by a network of companies in the United Kingdom and in the United States. While the games continue to outsell other games in the United States, the United Kingdom and Ireland in particular, the content and increasing realism of the most recent games provoke a strong and largely negative discourse from powerful stakeholders like politicians, parents and the media in those same countries. The resulting discourse revolves around different perceptions of risk, particularly to minors, of adult interactive media content and of the openness of game content and technology. Despite the fact that the industry is largely self-regulated these perceptions have, in some contexts, forced voluntary regulatory bodies to intervene and censor both the content and the distribution of GTA games.

The reaction to the release of *Grand Theft Auto: San Andreas (GTA:SA)* in late 2004 provides a case in point. Regulators in most countries gave the game their most mature age rating, ranging from 18+ in Europe to Mature/17 in the United States, and the game achieved a very high level of sales, particularly in the Christmas market. Commentators however reacted negatively to the perceived graphic realism of the violent content and the dominant media discourse focused on the potential effect this type of content might have on children if they played the game. By July 2005 the discovery of the hidden "Hot Coffee" sex mini-game in *GTA:SA* resulted in a revival of the negative discourse this time focused on the effect of interactive sexual content on minors and the ability of the producers to exploit the digital nature of games to effectively hide content from regulators. Politicians, academics and numerous lobby groups contributed to the debate. In the United States regulators eventually reclassified the game as Adult/18 (effectively removing it from most main street retail outlets) and Australian legislators, having no adult/18 classification, withdrew classification for the game (effectively banning it). In Europe, regulators stood by the original rating. Of interest here is firstly, the attempt and perceived need by the developers to smuggle/hide content from the regulatory bodies; secondly, the varying reactions of stakeholders in different countries to realistic violence and to sexual content in digital games; and finally, the contrast between responses from regulatory bodies in the United States and Australia to those in Europe.

One way to approach the conflict surrounding GTA games is to examine it as a struggle for freedom of speech versus new forms of censorship. Another is to view it as a conflict between multinational cultural corporation(s) and local political, cultural and social actors. In fact it is both and in this chapter we will focus on the struggle between multinational cultural corporations in the games industry and local actors in the United States and the United Kingdom primarily. The chapter will firstly explore the structure of the digital games industry and secondly, locate the transnational production network and core business strategy behind the GTA games within wider trends. Finally, the chapter will look at how this strategy is challenged and negotiated by local institutions, discourses and politics.

Understanding the Digital Games Industry

With a few notable exceptions, very few academic texts have been written examining the structure and dynamics of the digital games industry and most tend to focus on the industry in one country or on a particular company (Sheff 1993; Williams 2002; Alvisi, Narduzzo et al. 2003; Aoyama and Izushi 2003). Similarly the latest publications in game studies omit any investigation of the structures and dynamics of the digital games industry (Raessens and Goldstein 2005). Notable exceptions to this are the books by Kline, S. et al. (2003) and Kerr (2006). This neglect is somewhat surprising given that the digital games industry operates internationally, is estimated to be worth approximately $20 billion globally and both rates of growth and revenues compare favorably to more established media industries in many markets (ESA 2004; OECD 2004).

Digital games have rapidly corporatized and professionalized from the early 1970s to the present. In the terms of Raymond Williams' (1981) four modes of cultural production, it is clear that the industry has moved away from, for the most part, artisinal production, and towards corporate professional production whereby the source of game ideas lies either with a development company or with a publisher.[1] The vast majority of games are now developed by what are called in-house studios or "first party" development companies, fully owned by publishers. Much development is also done by second party development companies who are hired to work on a game concept developed by a publisher. Few of the top selling games are developed by and originate with an independent development studio. Indeed, the trend over the past five years has been towards greater consolidation between publishers and between publishers and developers. In addition, many publishers now own their own distribution companies (Kerr and Flynn). Indeed in order to understand the digital games industry one must understand the powerful role that the publishers play in terms of commissioning, producing, marketing and distributing digital games (Cornford).

Another key aspect of the digital games industry is that it is made up of at least four different segments or sub-sectors. The conventional approach divides the industry into three segments based on the major technical platforms on which games are played: console, handhelds and PC (Williams). Each of these segments has their own dynamics and while companies may operate across segments most developers decide to specialize in one or two. Top games are often released exclusively on certain platforms and only later are they "ported" or translated onto other platforms. This segmentation is applied widely in industry reports and using this approach it is clear that in terms of sales, console game currently significantly outsell games sold for other platforms and constitute anywhere from 57 to 78 percent of total global software sales (DataMonitor 2002; Deutsche Bank 2002; Spectrum Strategy Consultants 2002). At present the main consoles are Sony's PlayStation 2 (PS2), Microsoft's Xbox 360 and Nintendo's Gamecube (GC). Some reports group games for handhelds such as the GameBoy Advance (GBA) and Sony's PlayStation Portable (PSP) with the other console platforms.

Interestingly, not all markets have the same affinity for console games. While such games dominate in Japan, with almost 94 percent of total sales, this falls to 80 percent in the United States and 55 percent in Europe (Spectrum Strategy Consultants 10; ESA). Europe is by far the largest market for sales of PC games, at 47 percent, followed by the United States at 35 percent (Spectrum 11). Sales of games on other platforms form only a small portion of total revenues currently. However, one UK report estimates that the mobile games market in Europe, the United States and Japan was worth £73m in 2001, with Japan constituting over half of this total (15). They predicted that the mobile games market would double in value by 2005. Other sources claim that online gaming will increase dramatically as broadband becomes more widespread, and point to the growth of online games in South Korea where they constitute over 60 percent of the total domestic game market (KGDI 2004).

While there is a strong complementary relationship between hardware and software in the games industry the diversity of relationships between developers and the market, the development of new platforms like interactive television and mobile phones and the development of new genres of games like massively multiplayer online games (MMOG) pose quite a challenge to the conventional division of the industry. Elsewhere I have developed a slightly different market segmentation of the digital games industry that can be usefully applied in this context to situate and understand GTA games and the GTA story. This segmentation focuses on the key differences in the power of the key actors, in the degree of openness in the hardware and software system, in how they fund, make and maintain their games and how they sell and distribute their games. Kerr (2006) identifies four distinct segments: standard single and multiplayer closed console games, standard single and multiplayer open PC games, MMOGs, and single and multiplayer open mini games. Table 1.1 summarizes the main segments and their key characteristics.

	Market Concentration or Number of Companies	Technology	Production Process	Retail Model/ Interaction with Players
Segment 1 Standard Console & Handheld Games	oligopoly	closed	upfront investment by publishers mainly, average dev. time < 2 yrs., dev. team of 12–40 people	shops and advertising /limited interaction with players
Segment 2 Standard PC Games	numerous	open	upfront investment both by publishers and self-pub., updates released online after launch, average dev. time < 1 yr., dev. team of 12–20 people	shops and intermittent updates online/ intermittent interaction with players
Segment 3 MMOG	numerous	open	upfront and continuous development, funded by publishers and self-pub., average dev. time < 2 yrs., dev. teams vary with success < > 100 people	shops/ continuous interaction with players online
Segment 4 Mini-Games	numerous	varies	upfront investment, numerous intermediaries, average dev. time < 3 mos., average dev. team of < 10 people	advertising, pay per play, pay per download, sponsorship/ intermittent relationships with players online

Table 1.1. Key segments of the Digital Games Industry.

GTA games can be situated both in segments one and two but I believe their origin in the more open segment two and their move into segment one is highly significant in relation to recent controversies. Segment one is clearly the most significant in terms of market share at the moment in the United States and in the United Kingdom, and therefore is very attractive to game developers. However, segment one is also controlled by a small number of very large corporations and therefore gaining access to this market is not easy. Segment one is often described as an oligopoly with three platform developers involved in both hardware and software production: Nintendo, Sony and Microsoft, alongside a relatively small number of independent publishers, including Rockstar Games/ Take-Two, publishers of Grand Theft Auto games.[2] While one might describe the segment as an oligopoly there is strong competition between the major players in this segment with the three major companies attempting to vertically integrate and control everything from hardware production to software and distribution.

Another significant feature of segment one in terms of understanding the GTA story is the fact that standard console games are designed to work on a small number of proprietary, closed and non-compatible technological systems with a lifecycle of four to five years. The hardware manufacturers work hard to create security systems that cannot be modified by third parties and will not play games developed for rival platforms. Of course these are arbitrary and contingent security systems given that all game systems are based on digital technologies and code, but nevertheless both console and handheld devices and the majority of games developed for them attempt to erect technical barriers to prevent game players and other companies accessing their platforms. These technologies are upgraded entirely every four to five years and often changed so fundamentally that they impose not only an extra cost on the consumer but also pose a significant challenge to developers who must attempt to harness the particular technological strengths offered. Thus each generation of platform technology brings a significant qualitative difference in standard console games, not only in terms of graphical quality but also in terms of other features like online capabilities, storage space and interface devices. This closed approach to technology also means that there is limited scope for the average game player to modify commercial products or to produce their own.

In addition to the technology barriers the major players have developed certain business strategies aimed at protecting market share and preventing competitors from developing standard console games. Thus while games can be "ported," from one platform to another the main platform developers go to great lengths to control the flow and quality of content onto their system and to sign exclusivity deals to ensure popular games only appear on their platform. Thus, Take-Two signed an agreement with Sony so that *Grand Theft Auto: Vice City* and *Grand Theft Auto: San Andreas* appeared exclusively on the PS2 initially and only later were the games ported to the PC and the X-Box. Across all the platforms in this segment independent publishers/developers must pay a license fee on every game sold to the platform developer, which is estimated to add $7 to $10 to the total cost of a console and handheld game. In addition, all the platform developers impose stringent quality control, known as Technical Certification Requirements (TCRs), on publishers/developers before they will allow a title to be released on their platform. Both the technological and the business strategies help to offset production and marketing costs and help to maintain a relatively high price for standard console games.

The core business strategy adopted by the platform manufacturers in the console segment are to sell their hardware as a "loss leader" in order to build market share and to rely on the sales of software to make their profits (Alvisi, Narduzzo, and Zamarian 2003). This pricing strategy is similar to that adopted by manufacturers of razors, who sell their razors at a loss but make their money back on the sale of razor blades. If the platform developer succeeds in building a large installed base then they can make generous profits on their software and in turn reduce the cost to the consumer of their hardware, which should in turn spur sales of software. Thus, while market share is dependent upon the sale of consoles, consoles sales are directly related to the number of high quality titles available for the console. This provides an incentive to make some games "exclusive" to certain platforms. Companies like Microsoft and Sony, while leaders in technology development, had initially no tradition in game development and thus relied heavily on outside developers and publishers to deliver content. The relationship between GTA games and Sony is an important element of the GTA story.

Standard console games are sold at a premium price through specialist and non-specialist shops and are generally distributed on write only DVDs or cartridges and packaged in boxes or jewel cases. While retailers currently constitute an important stage in the value chain an interesting development is the growth of console games with online functionality, which may in time open up a more direct retail channel. To date both Sony and Microsoft have launched networks to support online multiplay—PS2 Network Gaming and Xbox Live—allowing users to play against other players online and to download additional game content. The continued development of online functionality may ultimately lead to a different retail and production model in this segment and perhaps reflect more the ongoing support and development evident in the MMOG segment. However, at the moment the segments remain quite distinct and no GTA game has thus far had an online element although multiplay has been a feature of handheld versions.

Segment Two includes standard single and multiplayer PC games but not MMOGs. In contrast to segment one this segment has a much smaller market share, particularly in Japan and the United States, but is still significant in Europe. While this might prove a disincentive for some developers, for others, the smaller market share is outweighed by the cheaper development costs, smaller teams required to deliver a game and the openness of the underlying technology. Indeed many small and start up developers develop standard PC games initially while they are building internal competencies and a profile. In this segment developers do not have to pay a license fee or royalties to the platform manufacturer and this is reflected in a cheaper retail price than console games. They are also not tied into four–five year technical lifecycles and arguably the rate of, for example, graphical improvement in PC games is much faster than in console games. The downside of this openness is that there is greater competition. Williams (2002) notes that there were 4,704 PC titles available in 1998 compared to 44 for the Nintendo 64 and 399 for the PlayStation. PC games are generally sold as boxed CDs through specialist and non-specialist retail outlets but publishers and developers release upgrades and patches, i.e. software that fixes bugs, online.

An important aspect of the PC game market is that one needs a very high specification computer to play many of the AAA titles, and many PC game players are very technically competent. Given that the underlying technologies are widely available and relatively open they are more susceptible to modification and hacking than console based games. Indeed many PC developers and publishers openly cultivate the game development and modification skills of their game players by releasing tools and profiling "mods" developed by game players on their websites (Søtamaa 2004). One could argue that the relationship between developers and PC game players is qualitatively different than between developers and game players in the console segment and that the culture of hacking and modification is a key part of the standard PC games segment and certainly of those GTA games which have been developed as standard PC games.

The History and Production of GTA Games— Going Adult and International

Console games are seen as a key children's leisure time activity. From Pac-Man to Pokemon and from Ratchet to Rayman the major "stars" in this industry have tended to be comic book fantasy characters aimed at teenage and younger children. The early console and handheld systems were designed to appeal to young people given their design and choice of colors and input/output devices. However when Sony entered the market and launched the original PlayStation (1994) and PlayStation 2 (2000) they made a concerted effort to broaden the games market beyond children and teenagers. The PS2 in particular was marketed as an "entertainment system" and its launch campaign which included a David Lynch directed television advertisement with the tagline "The Third Place" was clearly aimed at young adults (Kerr 2003).

A shift was also perceptible in game content and given the complementary relationship between hardware and software in segment one this is no surprise. While most in-house games developed by Sony still focused on the general audience slowly the company began to publish a range of third party titles that might appeal to older teenagers and to adults. First, there was Lara Croft and her curvaceous figure (initially released in 1996 on PlayStation). Then some first person shooters (FPS) were ported from PC, such as *Quake III: Revolution* (2001) and *UnReal Tournament* (2001). Standard multiplayer PC games like *CounterStrike* (2000), which pitted terrorists against anti-terrorists and *Half-Life* (1998), which sees top secret experiments go wrong in a research laboratory, spawned a strong late teenage and older gamer culture and eventually made it to the PS2. FPSs were joined by games with more sexual themes and nudity like *Leisure Suit Larry* (1997, PC) and *BMX XXX* (2002, PS2). Around the same time the first GTA game appeared on PlayStation.

The first GTA game appeared on the PlayStation and the PC in 1997 and the most notable thing about the first iteration was that the player got to play a bad guy. The trademark graphics, violence and sexual content were less evident. Of course, the PlayStation was much less powerful than today's consoles and the graphical quality would be incomparable to what a player experiences today given that it was in two dimensions and with a top down perspective. Thereafter all GTA games appeared on the PlayStation, the PC and later the X-box. Some of the games have been ported to the Gameboy Advance but the screen size and limited capacity of the storage device limits the aesthetics and gameplay on that platform.

GTA:III was the first three-dimensional version of the game and its production coincided with the development of the PS2 and the move to increase the age demographic of the PS2 market. Since then each GTA game has attempted to better harness the graphical capabilities of the PS2 and its storage capacity. The latest GTA games have appeared exclusively on the PS2 and in the years between major releases the games are ported to other platforms and to PC, clearly to increase sales and to maintain a profile. Much of the porting to other platforms is outsourced to other development teams so that the core Rockstar North development team can begin to develop a new title. Table 1.2 lists the different GTA games from 1997 to the present, their release dates, the platforms on which they were released, and their ratings.

The developer, Rockstar North; the publisher, Rockstar Games/Take-Two; and Sony, as owner of the PlayStation 2 (PS2) and the PlayStation

Title	Platform (Year)	ESRB (U.S.)	PEGI (Europe)	OFLC (Australia)
GTA	PS (1997) PC (1997)	Mature (17+), Animated Blood, Strong Language	18+, Violence	MA 15+, Medium Level Animated Violence, Adult Themes
	*GBC (1999)		*16+, Violence (Finland=15+, Violence)	*M, Low Level Violence, Adult Themes
GTA2	PS (1999) DC (1999) PC (1999)	Teen (13+), Animated Violence, Strong Language, Suggestive Themes	18+, Violence	MA 15+, Medium Level Animated Violence, Adult Themes
	*GBC (2000)	*Teen (13+), Mild Animated Violence		
GTA3	PS2 (2001) Xbox (2002) PC (2002)	Mature (17+), Blood, Strong Language, Violence	18+, Violence	MA 15+, High Level Animated Violence (Censored Release= MA 15+, Medium Level Animated Violence)
GTA: VC	PS2 (2002) Xbox (2003) PC (2003)	Mature (17+), Blood and Gore, Strong Language, Strong Sexual Content, Violence	18+, Violence	MA 15+, Medium Level Animated Violence
GTA: Advance	GBA (2004)	Mature (17+), Blood, Sexual Themes, Violence	16+, Violence	MA 15+, Medium Level Animated Violence, Adult Themes
GTA: SA	PS2 (2004) Xbox (2005) PC (2005)	Mature (17+), Blood and Gore, Intense Violence, Strong Language, Strong Sexual Content, Use of Drugs	18+, Violence and Bad Language	MA 15+, Medium Level Animated Violence, Medium Level Coarse Language
GTA: LCS	PSP (2005)	Mature (17+), Blood and Gore, Intense Violence, Strong Language, Strong Sexual Content, Use of Drugs	18+, Violence	MA 15+, (Restricted) Strong Violence, Strong Coarse Language

Table 1.2. Timeline of GTA games, 1997–present. Sources: <http://www.pegi. info/index.html> and <http://www.esrb.org> and <http://www.oflc.gov.au>.

Portable (PSP) are the principle actors, but other companies are contracted when necessary and CapCom publishes the games in Japan. Despite its sunny locales and bikini clad babes, GTA games are made by a development company based in the rather less than sunny Edinburgh, in Scotland. Formerly called DMA Design (established in 1989 in Dundee, Scotland) the company was bought by Gremlin Interactive in 1997 but left when Gremlin was bought by French publisher Infogames in 1998. DMA went on to sign a publishing deal in 1999 with Rockstar Games, a division of Take-Two Interactive, who proceeded to release *Grand Theft Auto 2* for the PC, PlayStation and Dreamcast. DMA was subsequently bought by Rockstar Games/ Take-Two Interactive and renamed Rockstar North. Acquisitions by publishers of development companies are increasingly prevalent in the games industry and helps publishers to maintain control over key brands and the creatives who develop them (Kerr and Flynn 2003). Interestingly, the lead designer and founder of DMA Design, David Jones left the company in the same year to found another development company, Real Time Worlds.

GTA games appear initially on Sony's console, due to an exclusivity deal with Sony, and subsequently on other consoles, handhelds and the PC. Take-Two, its publisher, is based in New York and is comprised of a number of wholly owned subsidiary publishing and distribution companies, illustrating that the company is following the wider industry trends towards vertical integration. Rockstar Games is their premium game publisher that publishes games like *Grand Theft Auto, Max Payne* and *Midnight Club.* However it has two other publishing companies: The Gathering, which publishes more mid-priced products for console, PC and handhelds; and Global Star which publishes "bargain" products across all platforms. Finally, Take-Two owns its own distribution company in the United States, Jack of all Games.

Take-Two also employs over 500 developers in companies mainly in the United States, Canada, the United Kingdom and Austria with peripheral and accessory manufacturing in Hong Kong and marketing and sales offices elsewhere around the world, including Sydney and Auckland (Take-Two Interactive). In 2003 the company's revenues exceeded $1 billion with net income of $98 million. In that year *GTA:VC* on PS2 accounted for almost 37 percent of all sales. Over 70 percent of total sales were in the American market. More recently *GTA:SA* topped the all format sales charts in the United Kingdom and the United States in 2004, even though it was only released in early Dec. in both markets. The Entertainment Leisure Software Publishers Association (ELSPA) in the United Kingdom also notes that the fastest selling titles in that market are *GTA:III, GTA:VC* and *GTA:SA* pointing to some interesting "geocultural" or perhaps "geo-linguistic" similarities between the two markets (Hesmondhalgh 2002). The games are less popular in Japan however pointing to some interesting political economic, social and cultural differences in that market.

In its annual report Take-Two writes that Rockstar Games "has forged a unique niche with its titles which utilize sophisticated game play, humor and immersion." It talks of the GTA franchise as a "blockbuster" and notes that *GTA:VC* "would rank as the 22nd top grossing movie of all time" if game sales were compared to box office proceeds (Take-Two Interactive 2–3). Later in the report it notes that the company has "pursued a growth strategy by capitalizing on the widespread market acceptance of video game consoles and the growing popularity of innovative gaming experiences that appeal to more mature audiences" (12). Academic researchers largely agree. While some have questioned the representation of women and ethnicity in the games, most see the GTA series as an example of an innovative open-ended game (Frasca).

Indeed GTA games defy generic definition in that they are action games that include racing and shooting. The player's avatar can take control of any vehicle in a game, including helicopters, boats and motorbikes, and any number of objects can be used as weapons as the player attempts to take on the role of a petty criminal who tries to complete a number of missions in order to work his way up the ladder of the criminal world in one of three fictional American cities; Liberty City, Vice City or San Andreas. Of course, one does not necessarily have to complete the missions and part of the pleasure of playing a GTA game is exploring the open endedness of the game and the potential for more ludic orientated play. The potential to play the games in different ways allows for a wide range of game play experiences and player choice. This fact undermines some of the effects discourse which various protractors draw upon and which we will look at in the next section.

The most recent GTA games are visually distinct in their use of retro graphics and lurid colors (bright pink arrows etc.), which somewhat complicates discussions which focus on the graphic "realism" of the games. These games are not socially realistic or even visually realistic in conventional terms although it is clear that there have been great graphically improvements as compared to pre–*GTA3* games. The games are also widely praised for their use of humor and music. While in a car the player can change radio stations from Esperantoso to Wildstyle to K-Chat and play hits from the 80s interspersed with purposefully made radio commercials. The games also draw upon and reference a range of existing cultural texts. *GTA:VC* for example recalls the iconic 1980s television series *Miami Vice* in everything from the setting to the dress, the cars and the music and combines this with classic gangster films themes and characters voiced by actors like Ray Liotta, Denis Hopper and Burt Reynolds. *GTA:SA* by comparison is set in 1992 in three cities on the west coast of the United States loosely modeled on Los Angeles, San Francisco and Las Vegas.

Global Product, Local Conflict—Rating and Regulating GTA

In the Republic of Ireland in December 2004 the main current affairs program on terrestrial public service television, *Prime Time*, ran a twenty minute piece on *GTA:SA*. The item opened with a video showing how someone could kill a prostitute in the game and was followed by a discussion with a representative of a parent's organization and a representative from ELSPA. The discussion focused on the potential impact of the game on minors and the need to regulate both the content and the circulation of violent games. The ELSPA spokesperson noted that console manufacturers and publishers in Europe ascribe to the Pan-European Game Information (PEGI) System that adds an age rating and content descriptor to every game. Applied in most Western European countries, except Germany, this system has been in place since 2003 and had given *GTA:SA* an 18+ rating signaling its adult orientated and violent content.

By July 2005, the discovery of the "Hot Coffee" mod for the PC and later the PS2 version of the game changed the focus from violence to sex when it was discovered that a simple game modification could unlock a hidden sex scene in the PC version of the game. Despite initial claims that a third party added the whole scene, the subsequent discovery of the scene on the write-only DVD of the console game indicated that this was not the case. This led Senator Hilary Clinton in the United States to call for stricter regulation of games and Australian legislators to consider banning the product outright (Hernandez and Schiesel). By late July 2005, following an investigation and disturbed by what was perceived as deliberate subterfuge, the Entertainment Software Ratings Board (ESRB) in the United States changed it original rating from Mature/17 to Adult Only/18. This resulted in many mainstream retail outlets in America removing the game from their shelves. Rockstar responded by discontinuing manufacturing the existing version of the game and the new version, without the sex scene, was again given a Mature rating. An ESRB press release stated:

Going forward, the ESRB will now require all game publishers to submit any pertinent content shipped in final product even if is not intended to ever be accessed during game play, or remove it from the final disc. Furthermore, the ESRB calls on the computer and video game industry to proactively protect their games from illegal modifications by third parties, particularly when they serve to undermine the accuracy of the rating.

What is interesting in this story is firstly that the game developers hid such a scene in the game in the first place knowing that it would probably not be found by game ratings boards but suspecting perhaps that game players would unlock it, particularly in the PC version of the game where both the technology and gaming culture almost demand such modifications. This approach to third party intervention recalls creative efforts by writers to smuggle contentious ideas into literature in countries with strict censorship regimes in the early twentieth century. It highlights, as Müller notes, that regulation and censorship can result in artists trying to avoid or criticize censorship aesthetically in their work. Secondly, the story shows that a range of stakeholders above and beyond the regulatory body may play a role in the censorship process and in the United States. The reaction to the "Hot Coffee" mod prompted politicians, the media and a range of academics and other interest groups to exert pressure on the regulator and the company. The discourse particularly focused on the "sexually graphic images hidden in the game" which could "fall into the hands of young people" (Hernandez and Schiesel). The discourse drew upon a strong media effects tradition but ironically this discourse also meant that the scene circulated widely on the internet and became accessible on a wider range of channels than had been originally intended.

Finally, the response of the regulators in the United States to this discourse is noteworthy. Digital games in the United States and in Europe are rated by industry-established bodies (i.e. ESRB and PEGI) and thus games are essentially self-regulated. Self-regulation is a system where the state refrains from interfering because it is presumed that the market and other parties will serve to regulate on the basis of an agreed code of conduct. In the United States the ESRB effectively intervened following a period of intense negative publicity to censor the content and circulation of *GTA:SA*. In the United Kingdom and Ireland where again the industry is self-regulated and there is no legislative framework within which to censor games a degree of co-regulation between state film and video censors and the industry exists (McGonagle 30). In both these countries the distributors forward over 18 games and some over 16 games rated under the PEGI system to the film censors who check the accuracy of the rating with regard to their statutory goal to protect children from harmful or violent content. The censors may refuse to certify a game or request cuts. In 2004 the Irish film censor's office received complaints about two games, *Manhunt* and *The Punisher.*[3] It received queries as to the suitability of the GTA games for younger children but no complaints about the 18+ rating.

The *GTA:SA* story demonstrates that censorship is alive and well in free trade liberal democratic countries and while the job of game censor may not exist censorship may operate in less direct and explicit ways. Further, context of consumption is clearly important in terms of understanding the different reactions and interventions in different countries. For the author, this is obviously a struggle involving a number of actors who are attempting to cope with and understand the increasing visual realism and interactivity of digital games on the one hand and the adult and mature nature of digital games on the other. Historically, GTA games on PC and PS2 received a mature 17+ rating in the United States, an 18+ rating in Europe and 15+ in Australia. The same games ported onto early handheld consoles like the Gameboy Color and the Gameboy Advance received a lower age rating due to the lower level of animation and storage available on that platform. More recently, handhelds like the PSP have moved more towards the graphical and storage capacity of the PC and console versions and thus received more adult ratings. Table 1.2 demonstrates the varying rating and descriptions given to GTA games by the American, the European and the Australian regulatory bodies.

Recent GTA games are clearly aimed and marketed at game players over the age of 18, an increasing segment of the game market according to recent surveys (ESA). The games contain varying degrees of violence but the most contentious aspect of the game for regulators is the potential for sexualized violence, i.e. against prostitutes, and the depiction of sexual activity. While the player can ignore this potential (or refrain from the arduous task of modifying a game to unlock hidden scenes), it is videotapes of someone attacking and killing a prostitute in the game which are discussed in detail by the Australian Office of Film and Literature ruling on *GTA:III* and videotapes that were shown on Irish television in 2004. What is interesting is that watching videotapes of decontextualised scenes from a game is a qualitatively different experience to playing and interacting with a digital game and one which most game players do not experience. Much of the theoretical work in game studies is concerned with the differences between the cut scenes in a game, which one watches, and the interactive segments of a game which one plays and with the role of the game player in the formation of the gameplay experience. Unfortunately, it would appear that most commentators only experience games as scenes which they watch and this leads to games being analyzed and assessed in terms of films and videos rather than in their own terms, as games.

Part of the problem it would appear is that most rating systems are not designed to rate games in the first place and particularly not adult orientated games. For example, Australia had no mature rating for games until very recently and so games deemed too mature for 15+ were refused classification (Finn). Both *GTA3* and *GTA:VC* games were refused classification in Australia because they were deemed to contain "sexualised violence" which was not covered by the classification system. The games were subsequently released in an edited form. However, it appears that people were able to hack these censored versions to unlock the censored content. Interestingly, initial reports indicate that *GTA:SA* was originally released uncut in Australia. Germany, the only European country to maintain its own rating system, censors the GTA games for blood. In Japan the Computer Entertainment Supplier's Association (CESA) has recently introduced new retail controls to stop the sale of adult orientated games to minors and the organization is developing a voluntary rating system in line with PEGI (Fahey).

In this chapter, I have argued that in order to understand the GTA story one must place it in the context of a wider shift within the digital games industry to target and develop content for more mature adult audiences. This shift is particularly stark in segment one which has traditionally been largely associated with games for children and which shifted dramatically with the entry of Sony in the 1990s and more latterly Microsoft in this decade. These relative newcomers to the industry have had a powerful shaping particularly on segment one, and their desire to grow market share in the United States and the United Kingdom has meant that adult orientated content, making deals with developers and publishers who can provide it, and the development of more powerful and proprietary gaming technologies to display this content are now key elements of their business strategies. These strategies are in sharp contrast it would seem to the strategies adopted by Nintendo, the other major player in this segment.

Over the past seven years Rockstar North, as developer, and Rockstar Games, as publisher, have developed increasingly sophisticated and adult standard console games which appear exclusively on Sony's PS2 technology. These games are aimed primarily at the American and the British markets and while sales have been very high in both markets the reaction of regulatory bodies to the negative public discourse has been quite different. In the United States the discovery of sexual content particularly in the "closed" console games has attracted the attention of a range of actors whose discourse of strong effects, security and protection of minors led the self-regulation body in the country to intervene both in terms of the games content and distribution. In Europe and particularly in the United Kingdom and Ireland public discourse focused more on the potential for "sexualised violence" in the game but regulatory bodies did not appear to feel under the same pressure to change the classification of the game or the need to limit its circulation. This may be related to the stronger tradition of more open PC games in Europe or it may signal a more fundamental difference in cultural politics between Europe and the United States. Regardless, it would appear that while certain cultural products may be produced by a transnational network of companies the reception and circulation of these cultural products may have less to do with "geo-linguistic" proximity and more to do with locally contingent political, social and cultural processes.

Notes

1. Raymond Williams (1981) identified four modes of cultural production based on the relationship and distance between the artist and their clients and the origin of the creative idea. These were artisinal, post-artisinal, market professional and corporate professional.

2. An oligopoly occurs when a market is dominated by a few large suppliers.

3. Information gathered in discussion with the film censor and the European project Co-Regulatory Measures in the Media sector. See <http://www.hans-bredow-institut.de/forschung/recht/co-reg/>.

Works Cited

"2005 Sales, Demographic and Usage Data." Essential Facts about the Computer and Video Game Industry. *Entertainment Software Association.* 20 July 2004. <hhtp://www.theESA.com>.

Alvisi, A., A. Narduzzo, et al. "Squint-Eyed Strategies for Success: PlayStation and the Power of Unexpected Consequences." *Information, Communication and Society* 6.4 (2003): 608–627.

Aoyama, Y. and H. Izushi. "Hardware Gimmick or Cultural Innovation? Technological, Cultural and Social Foundations of the Japanese Video Game Industry." *Research Policy* 32 (2003): 423–444.

Cornford, J., R. Naylor, et al. "New Media and Regional Development: The Case of the UK Computer and Video Games Industry" *Restructuring Industry and Territory: The Experience of Europe's Regions.* Ed. A. Giunta, A. Lagendijk and A. Pike. London: Stationery Office, 2000. 83–108.

DataMonitor. "Global Electronic Games." London: Datamonitor Corporation, 2002.

Deutsche Bank. "The Video Games Industry: Game Over or Extended Play?" Frankfurt: Deutsche Bank, 2002.

ESRB. 12 Jun 2005. Jan 2006 <http://www.esrb.org/about_updates.asp#12-6-05>.

"Essential Facts About the Computer and Video Game Industry." *Entertainment Software Association.* 20 July 2004. <hhtp://www.theESA.com>.

Fahey, R. "CESA Introduces Age Controls for Japanese Game Retailers." 21 July 2005. <http://www.gamesindustry.biz/content_page.php?aid=10237>.

Finn, M. "*GTA3* and the Politics of Interactive Aesthetics." 20 July 2005. <http://www.dcita.gov.au/crf/papers03/finn7paperfinal.pdf>.

Frasca, G. "Sin Sin City: Some Thoughts about *Grand Theft Auto III*." *Game Studies* 3.1 (2003). <http://www.gamestudies.org>.

Hernandez, R. and S. Schiesel. "Clinton Urges Inquiry Into Hidden Sex in Grand Theft Auto Game." *New York Times*: B.3.

Hesmondhalgh, D. *The Cultural Industries*. London: Sage, 2002.

"Industry Sales and Economic Data" 2003 Consumer Spending Poll. *Entertainment Software Association*. 8 August 2003 <http://www.theesa.com/pressroom.html>.

Kerr, Aphra. "Girls Just Want to Have Fun." *Strategies of Inclusion: Gender in the Information Society*. Ed. N. Oudshoorn, E. Rommes and I. van Sloten Trondheim. Centre for Technology and Society NTNU, 2003. 211–232.

_____. *The Business and Culture of Digital Games: Gamework/Gamplay*. London: Sage, 2006.

Kerr, Aphra, and R. Flynn. "Revisiting Globalisation through the Movie and Digital Games Industries." *Convergence: The Journal of Research into New Media Technologies* 9.2 (2003): 91–113.

KGDI. "The Rise of Korean Games: Guide to Korean Game Industry and Culture." Korean Game Development and Promotion Institute. 2004.

Kline, S., N. Dyer-Witheford, et al., *Digital Play. The Interaction of Technology, Culture and Marketing*. Montreal: McGill-Queens' UP, 2003.

McGonagle, M. "Co-operative Regulatory Systems in the Media Sector in Ireland." European Commission. Brussels: Directorate Information Society, 2005.

Müller, B. "Censorship and Cultural Regulation: Mapping the Territory." *Censorship and Cultural Regulation in the Modern Age*. Amsterdam: Rodopi, 2004. 1–31.

OECD. "Digital Broadband Content: The Online Computer and Video Game Industry." Paris: OECD, 2004.

Raessens, J. and J. Goldstein, Eds. *Handbook of Computer Game Studies*. Cambridge: MIT P, 2005.

Sheff, D. *Nintendo's Battle to Dominate an Industry*. London: Hodder and Stoughton, 1993.

Søtamaa, O. *Playing it my Way? Mapping the Agency of Modders*. Internet Research 5.0. University of Sussex, UK. 2004.

"Statement by ESRB President Patricia Vance regarding Grand Theft Auto: San Andreas Modification (July 8th, 2005)." *ESRB*. 19 July 2005. <http://www.esrb.org/about_news.asp>.

Take-Two Interactive. " Take-Two Interactive Software, Inc. 2003 Annual Report." New York: Take-Two, 2004.

Williams, D. "Structure and Competition in the U.S. Home Video Game Industry." *The International Journal on Media Management* 4.1 (2002): 41–54.

Williams, R. *The Sociology of Culture*. Chicago: U of Chicago P, 1981.

2. Political Interface:

The Banning of *GTA3* in Australia

MARK FINN

Although not strictly a turning point in the history of video games in Australia, the 2001 decision by the Office of Film and Literature Classification (OFLC) to refuse classification to *Grand Theft Auto III* (*GTA3*) represents a significant moment in the regulation of games in this country. While certainly not the first game to be banned in Australia, *GTA3* was clearly the most high-profile, having already achieved huge sales and critical acclaim prior to its removal from retailers' shelves. The banning of such a high-profile title worked to focus attention on the curious absence of an adult classification for games in Australia but also brought to the fore several deeper issues about how traditional media regulators deal with highly interactive content. This chapter will provide a detailed analysis of both the banning of *GTA3* in Australia and the debate that followed, as well as explore some of the broader implications for the regulation of interactive content.

All books, magazines, films, videos, DVDs, music CDs and computer games in Australia are regulated by the Office of Film and Literature Classification, through its administration of the National Classification Code. When assessing content, the OFLC is guided by Section 11 of the Classification Act, which states that content must be classified in terms of:

a) the standards of morality, decency and propriety generally accepted by reasonable adults; and
b) the literary, artistic or educational merit (if any) of the publication, film or computer game; and

c) the general character of the publication, film or computer game,
  including whether it is of a medical, legal or scientific character; and
d) the persons or class of persons to or amongst whom it is published or
  is intended or likely to be published [Commonwealth of Australia].

Any company wishing to publish or distribute a game in Australia must apply in writing to the OFLC for assessment by the Classification Review Board, with the procedure for assessing computer games outlined under Section 17 of the Act. According to this Section, applications for assessment must be accompanied by a copy of the game (Section 17.1.cb), with any potentially contentious material being highlighted by a statement outlining the particulars of the material and a separate recording of that material (Section 17.2).

It is commonly assumed that this was the process followed for the release of *GTA3* in early November 2001, but as is the case with many titles, *GTA3* was actually released prior to official classification through a special provision in the Classification Act. As is the case with all software titles released in Australia, the game carried an official OFLC rating, stating that the game had been classified as "MA 15+" and that it contained "high-level animated violence." However, while the rating carried the official OFLC stamp, it was in fact the result of an internal classification, done by staff at the game's distributors, Take-Two Interactive (Ellingford). Given its immense workload, it would have been physically impossible for the OFLC to classify all the content submitted to it in time to meet commercial deadlines, so Section 18.3 of the Act allows companies to assess their own content according to official guidelines using in-house reviewers trained by the OFLC. In this way a game could be released prior to "official" classification by following the procedures set out in the Act:

If the applicant is of the opinion that the game would, if classified, be classified G, G (8+), or M (15+), the applicant may also submit with the application:

a) an assessment of the computer game, signed by or on behalf of the
  applicant and prepared by a person authorized by the Director for
  this purpose, including:
  I. a recommended classification for the game; and
  II. consumer advice appropriate to the game; and
b) a copy of any advertisement that is proposed to be used to advertise
  the game [Commonwealth of Australia].

In the case of *GTA3*, the OFLC took exception with the classification made by Take-Two Interactive's in-house reviewers and immediately ordered the game to be withdrawn from sale on November 6 (IGN).

Whereas Take-Two's reviewers had classified the game as MA15+, the OFLC argued that the game clearly exceeded the limitations of this rating. In a telephone conversation between the OFLC and the Managing Director of Take-Two, James Ellingford, the OFLC argued that the game permitted characters to engage in what it termed "sexualised violence," and as such was not suitable for teenage gamers. The primary concern here was the ability of players to hire prostitutes within the game world and then, if they chose to, kill them, although such acts were not part of the game's mission-based structure.

Take-Two Interactive responded under Section 43 of the Act, notifying the OFLC of its intent to appeal the decision. At a Classification Review Board meeting held on December 11, 2001 the company presented its case for why the ban should be lifted, citing 35 separate points in its defense (Ellingford). Take-Two's defense was conducted along two main lines, with the first being that the original OFLC decision had not been based on the official classification code it was supposed to administer. While the code used to classify the game stated that "any depiction of sexual violence or sexual activity involving non-consent of any kind" would be refused classification, at no point did it refer to a notion of "sexualised violence." Furthermore, Take-Two argued that while the term "sexual violence" has a specific and recognized meaning in peer-reviewed psychological literature, "sexualised violence" has no such status (Ellingford).

The company's second line of defense centered on the game itself, and in particular on the way in which events occurring in the game world could be interpreted. While admitting that the game was inherently based upon the committal of violent acts, Take-Two disputed that there was a direct connection between the ability to hire a prostitute in the game and any violence that was then done to the prostitute. According to Take-Two Interactive, the fact that no violence can be perpetrated while the prostitute is in the car with the protagonist undermines the notion of "sexualised violence" in that there is a clear point of disconnection between the depiction of sexual activity (as indicated by the car's rocking motion) and any violence that follows (Ellingford).

The Classification Review Board made no direct response to Take-Two's contention that the classification code contained no direct reference to "sexualised violence," instead focusing on the need for a glossary of terms to be established ("40th Meeting"). However, the Review Board's response to Take-Two's arguments about the reading of the prostitute scene was much more expansive, although again they did not offer any direct response to the applicant's position. Instead, they provided a more detailed overview of the section of gameplay in question:

> In one scene, of which the Review Board took particular note, the gamer
> stops to pick up a sex worker.... She agrees to get into the car and the
> gamer drives onto a grassed, treed area. The car begins rocking and
> exhaust fumes are emitted in increasing amounts. The Review Board took
> this imagery to be a suggestion of sexual activity.
> After the sex worker leaves the car the gamer first drives off, then changes
> his mind and pursues her through the trees. A circle of white (which Ms.
> Baird for the applicant stated was a spotlight from a helicopter) appears
> on the ground. The sex worker is run over by the car and she is spread-
> eagled in the circle of light/white.
> The sex worker then recovers and starts walking away. The gamer then
> leaves the car and accosts her by beating her repeatedly until she is prone
> on the ground and surrounded by red fluid. The gamer then takes the
> sex worker's money. This scene, from when she leaves the car until when
> the gamer returns to the car after assaulting her for the second time,
> takes over two minutes.

The Review Board made it clear that it was the connection between violence and sexual activity that represented the most contentious aspect
of the game. According to the Board, "this juxtaposition gave the attack
greater impact than if the two images had been widely separated by other
game play" ("40th Meeting"). For this reason, the Review Board felt that
the OFLC was correct in its original decision to refuse classification for
GTA3, adding that the level of violence depicted in the game "was unsuitable for a minor to see or play" ("40th Meeting").

With the rejection of the appeal, Rockstar Games decided to take
the expensive and unprecedented step of modifying the game's original
code, altering it to prevent players from hiring prostitutes. In this way the
developers were able to circumvent any possibility of the "sexualised violence" the OFLC was concerned about, but also creating a special "Australia only" version of the game that was substantially different to that sold
elsewhere. With the offending content neutralized, the OFLC reassessed
the game and issued a MA 15+ rating, allowing it to be once again offered
for sale from February 15, 2002 (Monnox). This was more than two
months after its original release, and meant that the game had been pro-
hibited from sale throughout the lucrative Christmas retail season.

As the overview presented above demonstrates, the decision to
refuse classification to *Grand Theft Auto III* was based on a specific interpretation of the game's mode of operation, one that seemed to simultaneously assert and deny the fundamental elements of computer game
play. On the one hand, the decision seems to imply that the ability for
players to make decisions within the game world is precisely what makes
games more harmful than other media, a sentiment clearly expressed in
the Review Board decision:

> The Ministers are concerned that games, because of their "interactive nature" may have greater impact, and therefore greater potential for harm or detriment, on young minds than film or videotape ["40th Meeting"].

At the same time, the decision also seems to imply that players are not able to freely make choices within the game structure, that the murder of the prostitute described above was somehow an inevitable outcome of gameplay. In fact, the ability to hire prostitutes within the game world is not actually referred to in any of the literature published by the game's creators or publishers, and for most gamers knowledge of the feature came from word of mouth or Internet gaming sites. Furthermore, at no point in the game does hiring a prostitute actually advance the story-driven part of *GTA3*; its presence in the game exists primarily as an in-joke created by the programmers, albeit a tasteless and potentially offensive one. As such, any player who knows about the feature is presented with a choice as to whether or not they proceed with hiring a prostitute, a fact that seems to have been overlooked by the Classification Review Board.

    GTA3 is not the only Rockstar game to have refused classification in Australia, and a brief examination of the 2003 decision regarding *Manhunt* serves to help unpack the reasons why games such as these concern Australian regulators so much. Like *GTA3*, *Manhunt* was actually released with a MA 15+ rating, with the consumer advice "High Level Animated Violence." What is unusual about the release of this game was the fact that the head of the OFLC took the unusual step of publicly announcing that the game met the requirements for classification under the Code. According to a press release posted on the OFLC website,

> The Classification Board formed the view that the content of game did not exceed a strong viewing and/or playing impact. Des Clark, the Director of the Office of Film and Literature Classification, said "The Classification Board has strictly applied the Guidelines for the Classification of Film and Computer Games in arriving at this decision, and has found that *Manhunt* sits firmly within the MA15+ classification" [Office of Film and Literature Classification].

    Despite this assertion, calls by the Western Australian Attorney General, Michelle Roberts, prompted the federal Attorney General to call for a review of the rating. A Classification Review Board was subsequently formed and met on September 20, 2004 to review the game. After hearing evidence from Take-Two Interactive, the Review Board made the unusual move of postponing their decision until the members had been able to play the game (or have it demonstrated to them) in their own homes ("Meeting Report"). After a further 8 days of deliberation, the

Review Board announced that the game would be refused classification, banning it from sale in Australia. A press release issued by the Western Australian Attorney General Roberts stated that she believed the decision to be "a big win for the Australian community," and added that "as the mother of teenage children [she] was appalled at the sickening level of violence contained in the game and that its rating made it accessible to many young people."

Whereas "sexualised violence" was the main concern with *GTA3*, the sheer degree of general violence and its duration were the main issues with *Manhunt*. With respect to the former, the Review Board expressed particular concern about the way the game tended to linger on the gory details of a kill, with the disembowelment of the character of the director singled out for mention. In terms of duration, the Review Board was concerned about the ability of players (and indeed, of other characters) to continue killing long after the victim had expired, with the Convenor of the Board killing a character and allowing the action to continue for a further five minutes and thirty seconds ("Meeting Report"). The Review Board's concerns with the game was neatly summarized in the following paragraph:

> The impact of specific interactive game play scenes ... and the ability to "kill" characters in the game for an unlimited period with the accompanying detail of gore of smashed heads, blood splatter and in some scenes dismemberment was of high impact. As such, the material was beyond that which minors should be allowed to play.

This is perhaps the most important paragraph in the entire decision document, and demonstrates several key elements that help explain why games such as *GTA3* continue to be problematic for Australian regulators. Most importantly, the paragraph clearly identifies interactivity as a major point of concern, a view that is not consistent with much of the recent literature on games. In fact, such discourse seems to refer back to a comparatively simplistic effects-based model, which belies the complexity of player-game interaction.

Games do produce undeniable effects, and these effects are the primary reason players enjoy them. Several studies have indicated that players experience physical changes such as an increased heart rate (Griffiths and Dancaster) or the release of neurochemicals such as Dopamine (Koepp et al). Others have taken this evidence and attempted to extrapolate a psychological causality from it, with writers such as Tamborini et al, Zillman and Weaver and in particular, Anderson proposing a direct causal relationship between violent games and violent behavior and/or attitudes. Although not explicitly stated, it appears that those responsible for regulating games in Australia support this view. Words such as "impact" and "effect" permeate classification decision documents, and as such indicate an underlying belief that games have the potential to produce negative psychological effects in players. Indeed, the review documentation for *GTA3* indicates that members of the Review Board themselves felt that the game was having a detrimental effect on them:

> The Review Board watched one and a half hours of game play in total. Whilst this was time consuming, and had some negative impact on most of those viewing the game, such that Ms. Baird asked at the end of the viewing "Can we please have a break?" and two of the applicant's representatives left the room during the screening, it was considered that such viewing would not be an unrealistic period for an average gamer to be sitting at the console playing the game, and should represent a reasonable experience of a skilled player ["10th Meeting"].

The belief in effects demonstrated here reflects a wider popular view, perpetuated at least partially by sensationalist stories of game-related crime in the popular press. However, this popular perception is not supported by scholarly research, with several prominent writers demonstrating the methodological and theoretical problems with effects based research (for examples, see Sefton-Green, Gauntlett, and Heins and Bertin). In this respect, a recent paper by Jeffrey Goldstein is particularly useful, in that it provides an articulate overview of the key criticisms made of effects-based games research.

According to Goldstein, critiques of effects-based games research can be divided into three main categories, with the first relating to the artificiality of the methodological procedure used by many studies of this kind. In keeping with the established tradition of media effects research, many of the studies that investigate the effects of video games utilize a laboratory-based protocol, with volunteers playing a game for specific period of time and then having the psychological effect of that play measured through a variety of techniques. Goldstein, however, questions the validity of this entire procedure, arguing that the artificial experience created by the experiment automatically invalidates the results. As the author explains,

> In laboratory experiments, no one plays. Being required to play a violent video game on demand is no one's idea of an entertainment experience. It is like being forced to listen to someone else's favorite music; it sounds like noise.
> Almost no studies of violent video games have considered how and why people play them, or why people play at all. Experimental research does not recognize the fact that video game players freely engage in
> play, and are always free to stop. They enter an imaginary world with a

playful frame of mind, something entirely missing from laboratory studies of violent video games.

In addition to this, Goldstein also questions the definitions of "violence" and "aggression" that effects based research tends to use, arguing that it is important to differentiate between the types of aggression and violence that occur in video games and that which occurs in real life. More importantly, Goldstein argues that games provide players with a set of audio and visual cues that constantly remind them that they are playing a game:

> The same features that inhibit an opera audience from rushing the stage to prevent murder are present in video games. There are physical cues to the unreality of a game's "violence," including the willing suspension of disbelief, the knowledge that you have control over events, and can pause at will or stop playing altogether. In video games, there are sound effects, scorekeeping, a joystick or keypad in your hand, and often playmates commenting on your performance, which simply involves streaming pixels at imaginary creatures on a two-dimensional screen.

This notion of in-game cues that break the suspension of disbelief in a game is especially relevant to any discussion of *GTA3*, in that realism appears to be one of the chief concerns expressed by the Classification Review Board. According to the decision documentation,

> The game is one which is violent throughout and which depicts some detail of criminal behaviour. The animation and graphics are realistic. The game retains some almost "cartoon-like" characteristics, although it is possible to become very involved in the game play to the extent that some might consider it harmful ["40th Meeting"].

While *GTA3* does attempt to generate a sense of realism in terms of its visual design, and in particular it physics model, this realism is constantly and unavoidably undermined by the very things that make it a game. Like almost every video game, *GTA3* is based on achieving a specific set of goals within a set of constraints, with details of both continually displayed on screen. The main character's health status and other information are continually displayed at the top right of screen, and a dynamic map indicating the character's position in the game world occupies the bottom left. A more detailed version of the map is available by briefly suspending play, which the player has to frequently refer to in order to complete the game's missions. This, combined with the frequent cutscenes used to progress the game's narrative make playing *GTA3* quite a disjointed experience, and very different to the suspension of disbelief that characterizes other entertainment forms such as film or television.

The "unrealism" of *GTA3* is further enhanced through the way this particular game is constructed, especially through the title's audio track. Every time a player enters a vehicle they immediately encounter one of the game's numerous radio stations, with the actual content seemingly being selected at random. This introduces a further disjointing element to the game, and is further emphasized by the fact that the game has no real incidental music; aside from the radio the only sounds are environmental sound effects. Perhaps more importantly, the radio stations themselves tend to undermine any pretence of realism through their satirical content. Almost all the radio stations featured in the game are aimed as some kind of social commentary, including some advertising spots that satirize gaming itself. In some respects, this kind of self-referential content works as *anti-realism*, constantly reminding the player that they are dealing with a fictional universe.

Goldstein's final set of concerns about effects-based games research relates to the notion of causality that a majority of these studies propose. As the author explains, claims of causality is usually made on the basis of specific psychological measurement tools, but these tools themselves can often be seen as flawed. Specifically, many of the studies infer aggression from measures that have only a tangential relationship to aggression as it is commonly understood. As an example, Goldstein cites one study by Anderson and Dill in which students were asked to perform a word recognition test after playing a violent video game for three fifteen-minute sessions, with the speed with which they recognized "aggressive" words supposedly indicative of increased levels of aggression.

Such dubious connections between video game violence and real world aggression are at the heart of the decision to refuse classification to *GTA3* in Australia, but also point to a wider issue concerning the place of games in contemporary society. The alleged connection between violent content and anti-social behavior is not limited to video games, and has been made in relation to almost every form of media at one time or another. Indeed, as O'Hehir demonstrates, the controversy over *GTA3* bears a striking resemblance to a 1948 Canadian case where two young boys killed a passing motorist, supposedly as a result of the violent crime comic books they had read. Like the 1948 outcry over comic book violence, the discourse surrounding the banning of *GTA3* was based firmly on notions of child protection, a point made clear by the Classification Review Board's summation in the 40th Meeting report:

> In considering all the evidence before it, it was the decision of the Review Board that Grand Theft Auto III contained material which, on a cumulative basis and given the high degree of flexibility and control by the gamer who could increase the already serious levels of violence, was unsuitable for a minor to see or play. The description of Mr. Gertsmann

as the game having been "written specifically for an adult audience and it
definitely isn't for kids" was one held by all members of the Review Board
who participated in the review.

Statements such as this reveal an underlying assumption that video games
in general, and hence *GTA3*, are primarily a children's form of entertainment. However the evidence does simply not support this. A recent
report on video games in Australia found that the average age of gamers
in Australia is 24 (Brand 6). This is in line with research from overseas
that indicates that in America 36 percent of players are 18 to 35, while
19 percent are over 36 (Interactive Digital Software Association).

The notion that games are seen as a childrens' form of entertainment is further reinforced by the Australian classification system itself,
which has an adult rating for every form of audio-visual content except
games. Despite the fact that the federal government had recently introduced amendments to the classification system designed to unify
classification guidelines for different forms of content, the federal Attorney General still felt it necessary to single out games for special attention:

> The Government takes the issue of violence in films, computer games and
> publications very seriously. We will continue to ensure games with violent
> content are banned in this country or strictly regulated in a manner that
> supports informed decision-making by consumers, particularly parents'
> [Ruddock].

The result is a classification system that clearly discriminates against adult
players, and simultaneously places regulators in a difficult position. Without the benefit of a full-spectrum classification regime, bodies such as
the OFLC and the Classification Review Board are forced to either allow
controversial content to be given a rating which allows persons 15 years
old and over to access it, or refuse classification entirely, and like most
classification bodies they tend to err on the side of caution. This point
is actually made quite clearly by the Classification Review Board in their
decisions regarding both *Manhunt* and *Grand Theft Auto III*, with the
Board noting that a refused classification rating would not have been
issued if an "adults only" rating was available. This indicates that the
impasse on an "R" classification for Australia originates with the policy
makers rather than the regulators themselves, an idea that has been supported in several informal discussions between the author and senior
games industry representatives.

The apparent desire by OFLC members to have an R classification
for games is mirrored by the gaming public, as indicated by the creation
of several online petitions calling for the introduction of an "R"

classification for games in Australia, with one <http://www.petitiononline.com/oflcr18/petition.html> containing over 3100 individual signatures (Lewis). Although petitions such as this are unlikely to bring about a change in policy, their creation does point to the existence of a significant section of the community who feel their needs are not being adequately met by current procedures. This is supported by Brand's research, which indicates that 88% of those surveyed felt there should be an R classification for games (Brand 57). Perhaps more disturbingly, the same survey revealed a remarkably low level of understanding about the current classification system, with only one-third of surveyed players and one-fifth of non-players being aware that there was no adult rating for games in Australia (Brand 52).

At the most basic level, classification exists at a nexus between several powerful groups, with politicians, lobby groups, games developers and distributors, the media and gamers all having something to gain, and in some cases, much to lose. The case of *GTA3* serves as an interesting case study precisely because it mobilized many of these groups around a single piece of software. As it now stands, the classification system is arguably causing enough confusion to ensure that unsuitable content is falling into the very hands of those the system is designed to protect. Under the current system, the OFLC is placed in the unenviable position of having to choose between allocating content a rating that is largely misunderstood by the community, or refusing classification entirely. The former option frequently results in minors being exposed to content with high levels of violence or sexual themes, while the latter carries with it serious financial implications for the software producers and distributors.

It should also be noted that while policy makers have shown little inclination to consider a change to the way games are classified in Australia, regulatory bodies themselves are responding positively to the challenge posed by interactive media. The fact that members of the Classification Review Board actually played *Manhunt* for an extended period points to a recognition that games are not experienced in the same way as films or books, and that interactivity itself requires a special set of media skills that can only be acquired over time. Prior to this, games had been classified primarily on the basis of videotaped excerpts of gameplay, reducing an interactive experience to a linear exhibition. However, even as regulators become more experienced with games as a form of entertainment, the rapid rate of technological advancement that characterizes the medium is sure to make games problematic for some time to come.

In this respect, it is interesting to look at the release of *Grand Theft*

Auto: Liberty City Stories (GTA:LCS), the first GTA title produced for Sony's new PlayStation Portable (PSP) platform. *GTA:LCS* is essentially a port of the original *GTA3*, with a different storyline and different characters, but same setting and basic mode of gameplay. Significantly, the game also allows the player to engage in exactly the same activities that were characterized as "sexualised violence" by the Classification Review Board just four years earlier. Despite this, the game has been released with an MA 15+ classification, and at the time of writing there appears to have been little controversy over that rating.

If the standards used to classify *GTA3* are applied to *GTA:LCS*, then one might assume that the portable title will eventually face a similar fate. Indeed, it is possible to argue that the PlayStation Portable title might even be considered *more* harmful than its PlayStation 2 counterpart because the form now allows for multiplayer play via the PSP's wireless connection. This means that players are now able to kill and maim digital representations of other players (as opposed to computer controlled characters), and commit these crimes in public.

This last point is especially significant, and is likely to complicate the classification debate even further. Up to this point, gaming has primarily been a private activity, conducted in players' homes or is specially designated gaming venues. The development of sophisticated hardware such at the PSP and Nintendo's DS means that players are now able to engage with potentially contentious game content in public spaces. PSP fan sites on the Internet already contain stories of players who have been asked to turn down the volume on their devices when playing in public spaces, not surprisingly given the frequency of coarse language in games like *GTA:LCS*. In fact, the ability to engage with game content in public may well work to consolidate the position of those opposing an "R" rating for games in Australia, allowing them to argue that its absence helps ensure that offensive content out of public spaces.

The fact that there has so far been little controversy over *GTA:LCS* can perhaps be attributed to the newness of the title; it is possible that the game has yet to appear on the radar of the groups that usually express concern over video game violence. Alternatively, it could also indicate awareness on the part of regulators that the content of games such as the Grand Theft Auto series might not be as harmful as was previously thought, at least to the adult audience for which it was intended. What is certain, however, is that as the gaming audience matures, developers will continue to produce content designed specifically for adults, and that this content will continue to pose problems for an Australian classification system unable to accommodate it.

Works Cited

Anderson, Craig A., and Catherine M. Ford. "Affect Of The Game Player: Short Term Effects Of Highly And Mildly Aggressive Video Games." *Personality and Social Psychology Bulletin* 12 (1986): 390–402.

Anderson, Craig A. "Effects Of Violent Movies And Trait Hostility On Hostile Feelings And Aggressive Thoughts." *Aggressive Behavior* 23 (1997): 161–178.

_____. "Video Games and Aggressive Behaviour," *Kid Stuff: Marketing Sex and Violence to America's Children.* Ed. Dianne Ravitch and Joseph P. Viteritti. Baltimore: Johns Hopkins UP, 2003.

Anderson, Craig A, and Karen E. Dill. "Video Games and Aggressive Thoughts, Feelings and Behaviors in the Laboratory and In Life." *Journal of Personality and Social Psychology* 78 (2000): 772–790.

Brand, Jeffrey. *Gameplay Australia 2005.* Gold Coast: Centre for New Media Research and Education, 2005.

Classification Review Board. "40th Meeting, 11 December 2001." *OFLC Website.* 2001. Office of Film And Literature Classification. 12 Mar. 2003 <http://www.oflc.gov.au/resource.html?resource=101&filename=101.pdf>.

_____. "Meeting Report, 20/28 September 2004." *OFLC Website.* 2004. Office of Film And Literature Classification. 10 Oct. 2005 <http://www.oflc.gov.au/resource.html?resource=358&filename=358.pdf>.

Commonwealth of Australia. *Classification (Publications, Films and Computer Games) Act 1995 (Act No. 7 As Amended).* 2002. Attorney General's Department. 18 Sep. 2003 <http://www.oflc.gov.au/resource.html?resource=177&filename=177.pdf>.

Ellingford, James. Personal interview. 16 Apr. 2003.

Gauntlett, David. "Ten Things Wrong with the Effects Model." *Newmediastudies.com.* 1999. 19 Sep. 2003 <*http://www.newmediastudies.com/effects1.htm*>.

Goldstein, Jeffrey. "Does Playing Violent Video Games Cause Aggressive Behavior?" *Playing by the Rules Conference Website.* 2001. U of Chicago. 20 Dec. 2005. <http://culturalpolicy.uchicago.edu/conf2001/papers/goldstein.html>.

Griffiths, Mark, and Imogen Dancaster. "The Effect of Type-A Personality on Physiological Arousal While Playing Computer Games." *Addictive Behaviours* 20 (1995): 543–548.

Heins, Marjorie, and Joan Bertin. "Brief *Amici Curiae* of Thirty-three Media Scholars in Support of Appellant's, and Supporting Reversal." *Free Expressions Policy Project.* 2002. United States Court of Appeals for the Eighth Circuit. 13 Jan 2005. <http://www.fepproject.org/courtbriefs/stlouis.pdf>.

IGN. "*Grand Theft Auto III* Refused Classification in Australia." *IGN Website.* 2001. 15 Apr. 2003 <http://ps2.ign.com/articles/100/100454p1.html?fromint=1&submit.x=48&submit.y=15>.

Interactive Digital Software Association. "Computer and Video Games are Here to Stay." *IDSA Website.* 2002. Interactive Digital Software Association. 16 May 2003 <http://www.idsa.com/5_22_2002.html>.

Koepp, Matthias J. et al. "Evidence for Straital Dopamine Release During a Video Game." *Nature.* 393. (1988): 266–268.

Lewis, Jordan. "Petition for the Creation of a R18+ Category in the Classification of Video Games in Australia." 2004.16 Oct 2004 <http://www.petitiononline.com/oflcr18/petition.html>.

Monnox, David. "*GTA3* to be Re-released Down Under." *Madgamers.net.* 2002. 11 Apr. 2003 <http://www.madgamers.net/news404.html>.

Office of Film and Literature Classification. "*Manhunt* Classified MA 15+ by Classification Board" *OFLC Website* 2003. Office of Film and Literature Classification. 10 Jan. 2005 <http://www.oflc.gov.au/resource.html?resource=279&filename=279.pdf>.

O'Hehir, Andrew. "The Myth Of Media Violence" *Salon.com.* 2005. Salon Media Group. 22 Dec 2005 <http://www.salon.com/books/feature/2005/03/17/media/index.html>.

Roberts, Michelle. "WA Minister Instigates National Ban On Violent Computer

Game." *West Australian Government Website*. 2004. 18 Jan. 2005 <http://www.medi-astatements.wa.gov.au/media/media.nsf/d3ea7ba6c70aeaae48256a7300318397/f01 287fa29e4380548256f1e00257ea6?OpenDocument>.

Ruddock, Phillip. "*Manhunt* Computer Game Referred For Review." Department of Federal Attorney General. 2004. 23 Dec. 2005 <http://www.oflc.gov.au/resource.html?resource=334&filename=334.pdf>.

Sefton-Green, Julian. *Digital Diversions: Youth Culture in the Age of Multimedia* London: UCL P, 1988.

Tamborini, Ron. et al. "Violent Virtual Video Games And Hostile Thoughts." *Journal of Broadcasting & Electronic Media* 48.3 (2004): 335–350.

Zillmann, Dolf and James B. Weaver. "Effects Of Prolonged Exposure To Gratuitous Media Violence On Provoked And Unprovoked Hostile Behavior." *Journal of Applied Social Psychology* 29 (1999): 145–165.

3. Virtual Gangstas, Coming to a Suburban House Near You:

Demonization, Commodification, and Policing Blackness

DAVID LEONARD

While video games grew in popularity for several years, the release of *Grand Theft Auto III (GTA3)* in 2001 propelled the industry to new heights, resulting in several copycat games, including the game sequels *Grand Theft Auto: Vice City (GTA:VC)* and *Grand Theft Auto: San Andreas (GTA:SA)*. While much has been made of the violent and sexual nature of this series, there has been little public debate or outcry regarding the racialized content of these games. Instead of condemning their promotion of stereotypes and the promotion of racialized state violence, which compared to the inclusion of sex and violence gamers have no power in determining levels of participation, the likes of Hilary Clinton and David Walsh have denounced the series as a moral pollutant necessitating governmental action. It is in this context that this chapter explores the societal reaction to both *Grand Theft Auto III* and *Grand Theft Auto: San Andreas*, in terms of both political discourses and those of gamers. By examining online discussion groups, fan commentary, and political speeches (including those from elected and unelected "leaders") this chapter seeks to generate thoughts about the racial context of these games, generating insight as to how race contributes to both the societal condemnation and widespread popularity of these games and the racialized bodies that inhabit these virtual ghetto spaces.

Focusing on the racial content of these discourses, this chapter additionally makes note of the ways in which new racism defines yet simultaneously emanates from this discursive field. While offering some discussion of the ways in which these games deploy longstanding racialized stereotypes, how they offer primarily white suburbanites the opportunity to experience America's dangerous ghettos, and how they sanction and legitimize state violence, our focus here lends itself to the reactions—outrage and pleasure—of both cultural pundits/politicians and gamers, of both those who decry these games as a dangerous threat to children and those who celebrate these offerings of virtual reality as transgressive and even potentially oppositional, in the end demonstrating the centrality of race and violence within both discursive fields.

Dr. Dre once stated that "People in the suburbs, they can't go to the ghetto, so they like to hear what's goin' on. Everyone wants to be down." bell hooks, in *Outlaw Culture,* complicates this idea, situating processes of commodification, fetish and the pimping of a corporate ghettocentric imagination, arguing that "the desire to be 'down' has promoted a conservative appropriation of specific aspects of underclass black life, who in reality is dehumanized via a process of commodification wherein no correlation is made between mainstream hedonistic consumerism and the reproduction of a social system that perpetuates and maintains an underclass" (152). Using such arguments of the basis of inquiry into the Grand Theft Auto series (most specifically *GTA:SA*), this chapter explores the ways in which the reaction, where race is explicitly absent yet central, legitimizes a conservative project that maintains a permanent underclass, whether in gamers' internet discussions about the games, political rhetoric condemning the message of the game, or the consumptive pleasure derived from a ghetto existence that rarely penetrates American consciousness.

Do You Know What Your Children Are Watching? Just Say No to Virtual Gangstas

The release of *GTA:SA* in fall 2004 not only promoted lengthy waitlists at Amazon.com, release parties throughout the nation, and ample online discussions, but an infrequent level of unity in Washington D.C. and in state capitals throughout the United States. During the subsequent six months, the calls for governmental intervention and legislative regulation over the content available within virtual gaming grew louder, especially after reports of the "hot coffee modification," which allowed players to simulate sex with naked women during *GTA:SA* play. In introducing the Family Entertainment Protection Act, Hillary Clinton (D-NY) called upon the government "to make sure their kids can't walk into a store and buy a video game that has graphic, violent, and pornographic content." Joseph Liebermann (D-CT) concurred, emphasizing the importance of protecting children from "a silent epidemic of media desensitification" and "for stealing the innocence of our children" (McCullagh; Loughrey; Sweeting), pointing to the dangers of violent and overly sexualized games:

> There is a growing body of evidence that points to a link between violent video games and aggressive behavior in children. We are not interested in censoring video games meant for adult entertainment but we do want to ensure that these video games are not purchased by minors. Our bill will help accomplish this by imposing on those retailers that sell M- rated games to minors [Loughrey].

The Clinton and Liebermann legislation, which would prohibit the sale of "mature" games to anyone under the age of eighteen; order the FCC to investigate "misleading" ratings and solicit complaints about video games; and require "an annual independent analysis of game ratings," along with their successful call for an investigation into Rockstar and Grand Theft Auto as a result of "Hot Coffee" controversy, demonstrates the level of interest and outrage emanating from political circles concerning portions of the virtual gaming industry. Ted Stevens (R-AK), during hearings concerning the "decency" of computer games and television, captured the level of panic-driven anger directed at *GTA:SA* and the entire industry, all of which centers the notion of protecting America's youth (read: white middle class) from these indecent and immoral games: "America lacks the kind of moral compass the country should have for our young people" (McClluagh). In his estimation and that of Clinton, Liebermann, and a host of others from both sides of the aisle, the government had to be that compass.

Such rhetoric and the calls for legislation are neither isolated nor particular to discourses emanating from Washington D.C. From speeches on state House floors, to ample press releases, the condemnation of video games has become commonplace in recent years, as evident by the ubiquitous condemnation of *GTA:SA*. Following its release, Representative Fred Morgan (Oklahoma), reflecting the nature of the discourse and the almost obsessive focus on video games as a cultural and moral pollutant, offered the following assessment of virtual gaming in a press release that called for legislation banning particular types of games within his state:

> If someone on the street offered to teach your children to decapitate their enemies, physically abuse women, and assassinate world leaders, you

would probably call the police. But when a video game manufacturer
providers the same "service," many parents are actually paying for their
children to get a tutorial in violence and depravity. And instead of calling
the police for help in many popular games your kids will be killing police.
[Morgan].

Such outrage, rhetoric, and panics have promoted efforts to regulate
video games in state after state, from Illinois and California to Michigan
and Pennsylvania. In Illinois, Governor Blagojevich (D-IL) led the first
and most successful effort to regulate virtual reality. In fact, Governor
Rod Blagojevich was the first public official to call for legislation that
would make it illegal for anyone under the age of eighteen to buy violent or sexually explicit games: "This is all about protecting our children
until they are old enough to protect themselves," the Governor stated
in an issued statement. "There's a reason why we don't let kids smoke
or drink alcohol or drive a car until they reach a certain age and level
of maturity" (Slevin A08).

The trend toward governmental regulation of video game content,
which has resulted in the courts overturning legislations that either
restrict or seek to censor content, reflects a panic driven by a racial logic
that fears the ghettocentric imagination available within contemporary
gaming. The panics concerning the effects of (ghettocentric) video
games on American (white middle-class) youth has not been limited to
political officials seeking reelection and news coverage during relatively
quiet times, but has found great resonance within church-based and otherwise conservative media organizations. The National Institute on
Media and the Family (NIMF), led by Dr. David Walsh, has emerged as
one of the most prominent critical voices directed at the video game
industry. Providing "resources," reviews, and other information regarding the "appropriateness" of particular games for children, while lobby-
ing politicians and game retailers to protect "children and teens" from
"killographic" and sexual content, NIMF embodies this ongoing culture
war. Others, like The Lion and Lamb Project and Mothers Against Video
Game Addiction and Violence (MAVAV), have been equally instrumental in successfully pushing the issue of the effects of video games within
American culture and in turn defining the nature of the discourse. For
example, MAVAV recently compared playing video games to alcohol and
drug abuse, working toward "educating parents" on "today's fastest and
increased threat and danger to our children's health and way of life."

What links together these various voices, as well as others (such as
those panic-driven debates regarding the effects of video games found
on numerous white nationalist websites) is not merely the reduction of
video games to a pollutant on American cultural values, the threat that

both sexually-explicit and violent games pose to youth, or the reconstitution of the state as institution that is supposed to protect children, but the types of games that cause outrage, induce panics, result in anxiety, and warrant governmental/communal intervention: those inside American ghettos and allowing players to "become gangstas." It was *GTA:SA*, not even *Grand Theft Auto III*, that lead to calls for legislation. This is not a coincident and reveals much about the nature of a discourse as it was a virtual world of street gangs, drive-by shootings, and strong-armed robberies that sent America's political, moral, and cultural elites into a tizzy. While reflective of a myriad of factors, it is not surprising that *GTA3*, with its celebration of an Italian mob family (see Leonard 2003) and racial tropes, never resulted in national debates and cries for governmental intervention.

In the end, it was the release of *50 Cent: Bulletproof, The Warriors, 187: Ride or Die, Narc,* and *True Crime: Streets of LA/NY,* as well as the proposed release of *25 to Life* and *Gang Wars,* and not *America's Army, Socom,* or any number of war games that encourage youth to kill, destroy and maim that prompted calls for protection. It is not truly about violence, or even the affects of violent on youth, but their exposure to particular types of violence, with violence committed by gangsters and criminals, particularly those of color, who also seem to represent a disproportionate number of these characters, against the state identified as a significant threat against the moral and cultural fabric of the nation. Violence committed by the state, whether from a virtual military or police force, which tend to be overwhelmingly white within virtual reality, is certainly not a threat or dangerous to America's youth; in fact, it seems as if the discourse constructs these type of games as offering a desirable message concerning safety, security and the state, as needed to control the savages who inhabit the Third World or America's inner cities. While ignoring the racial aspects of this process, Clive Thompson describes the outrage directed toward video games as being based in the celebration of state violence as opposed to individual violence or criminality as the basis of which games receive praise and which elicit cultural panics:

> Nine times out of 10, when you're blowing people's chests open with hollow-point bullets, you aren't playing as a terrorist or criminal. No, you're playing as a cop, a soldier or a special-forces agent—a member of society's forces of law and order.... Yet anti-gaming critics didn't really explode with indignation until *Grand Theft Auto III* came along.... Why weren't these detractors equally up in arms about, say, the Rainbow Six series? Because games lay bare the conservative logic that governs brutal acts. Violence—even horrible, war-crimes-level stuff—is perfectly fine as long as you commit it under the aegis of the state. If you're fighting

creepy Arabs and urban criminals, go ahead—dual-wield those Uzis, equip
your frag grenades and let fly. Nobody will get much upset [Thompson].

Although Thompson offers a powerful assessment of the current discourse concerning video games, he fails to consider the racial implications here, with a vast majority of current outrage being directed toward
ghetto or hip-hop (those defined by blackness) games. The Family Media
Guide top 10 most violent games for 2005 includes six games which all
offer gang narratives concerning inner city crime. The supposed lack of
values in "those communities" reflects the focus on protecting children
from ghetto violence in ways beyond formal segregation. In this scenario,
inner-city kids are already lost due to their daily exposure to violence
and a "culture of poverty." This discourse ultimately reifies common-
sense understandings of blackness as a source of moral indecency and
cultural decay. To understand the efforts of Clinton, Lieberman or Walsh
is to move beyond a focus on generational splits, geographic battles, or
mere cultural/value differences. More importantly, as evidenced by varied reactions to the various installments of GTA series, the publicity
afforded to the "hot coffee modification" controversy, or the questions,
if not panics, afforded to the release of a wave of ghettocentric video
games, demonstrates the racial nature of panics, that public displays of
blackness, that the presumed opportunity to "become" a black thug or
visit America's ghettos, fulfill longstanding fears of black sexuality, physicality, and violence, contributing to a particularly powerful panic centering on the affects of virtual blackness on white suburban youth. The
series of moral panics that constructed these virtual ghettocentric spec-
tacles as transgressive, as violations of community standards, rather than
commodities that not only sought to capitalize on the publicity resulting from such panics, reflects a longstanding white supremacist fears
about black masculinity, sexuality, and violence.

Whether manifesting in a backlash against hip-hop, sports or television, culture is historically and ideologically specific, such panics reflect
longstanding practices of fearing black and brown bodies. Herman Gray
persuasively argues: "The discourses of regulation and the moral panics
that they helped to mobilize worked for a time in the 1980s to consolidate a neoconservative hegemonic bloc. This bloc routinely used media
images of black men and women, the poor and immigrants to represent
social crisis" (24–25). In his estimation, hegemonic images, whether
those emanating from popular culture or the political pulpit "became
the basis for a barrage of public policies and legislation intended to
shore up this hegemonic position and to calm and manage the moral
panics construction around race in general and blackness in particular"

(24–25). Others have argued similarly on the intersections of fear, race, moral panics, and calls for state intervention. The signifiers of black violence and markers of black hypersexuality ubiquitously enter into public discourses as sources of consumption and scorn, as "corrupting and pathological, whether on screen or through welfare debates" (Gray 135). Within the American imagination, "what is forbidden in American culture often seems to be projected outward onto the outsider or scapegoat," notes Joy James. "Blackness has come to represent sex and violence in the national psyche. Although they gain notoriety as the most infamous perpetrators of unrestrained criminality, African Americans are given little resignation in media, crime reports or social crusades as being victims" (127).

The ongoing questions and debates regarding the effects of *GTA:SA* on youth (read: white suburban males) and the larger questions regarding the effects of a ghettocentric imagination on America's cultural values and morals not only signify a generational battle, culture war, or even moral panic, but the longstanding visions of race and gender within the American cultural landscape. Herman Gray encapsulates the racial logic that informs moral panics, revealing the powerful ways which popular culture mobilizes and consolidates racialized fear in maintaining white supremacy:

> So often media narratives presume and then fix in representation the purported natural affinity between black criminality and threats to the nation. By fixing the blame, legitimating the propriety of related moral panics, these representations (and the assumptions on which they are based) help form the discursive logic through which policy proscriptions for restoring order—more jails—are fashioned [25].

To him, "the production of media representations of blackness (along with those of sexuality and immigration) as threatening the natural fabric and policy proscriptions for reimagining and consolidating a traditional vision of the American nation" defines contemporary representations of blackness (Gray 25). According to this racist logic, the values and morals offered through playing *GTA:SA*, or any numbers of games pose a threat to the national fabric, just as those who inhabit those real-life communities pose an equal danger. In each case policing and surveillance are needed to protect families who reside outside of both South Central and San Andreas from the physical and cultural dangers facilitated by potential contact with blackness.

Notwithstanding the conservative and reactionary presumption that sees the GTA series as offering players the opportunity to kill, rape, rob or form a gang challenges the dominant cultural landscape, these games work in concert with dominant discourses and cultural expectations. Yet, such logic is not exclusive to the haters or those who seek to regulate certain types of games, as those who celebrate GTA tend to offer similar understandings of race, difference, and Othered bodies and spaces. In their estimation, these games provide those outside of the imagined ghetto an opportunity to enjoy the controlled moral decay found within these games. The commodification and celebration—enjoyment—of these games, and their visions of blackness, is an all too common facet of the virtual gaming complex (players, designers, critics, government regulators, cultural watchdogs, etc...), which mirrors many aspects found in the panics and condemnation so prevalent over the last two years.

Celebration

Amid the widespread panicking and calls for legislation to protect America's (white middle class) youth from the violence and hyper sexuality (blackness) supplied within virtual reality, there has been a sustained voice of defense, if not celebration, of the Grand Theft Auto series, particularly *GTA:SA*, and other ghettocentirc games. If judging by sales and profit margins, it is fair to say that in both message and content, the Grand Theft Auto series has been immensely popular. By 2005, the GTA series had amassed sale numbers surpassing 44 million units. Additionally, each of the installments proved critically worthy, receiving ample awards from within the industry. In 2005, *GTA:SA* received five awards at the Golden Joystick awards, which included Play Station 2 Game of the Year. Yet, the greatest counter discourse and opposition to the efforts of Hillary Clinton and Jack Walsh has manifested on the Internet, where gamers have advocated for their right to kill, maim, fuck, or behave as any good (virtual) thug might do if given the opportunity.

From gamer forums to Amazon.com, the Internet is saturated with not just efforts to defend the GTA series amid this culture war, but denunciations of the enemies of GTA, video game culture, and a virtual reality uninhabitable to a wealthy elitist older generation. While focusing on the oversensitivity of politicians and organizations like MAVAV, and the generation gap reflective of older generations not understanding a youth culture that is progressive and transcendent, several themes emerge within these online chatrooms: first off, it is just entertainment. Denying the social, political, ideological, racial, or cultural significance of the GTA series or any number of virtual gaming, exasperated gamers scoff at the alarmist rhetoric of its opposition, describing *GTA:SA* as "harmless entertainment" and a "virtual play" space or "fantasyland" that poses no harm to society or its members. Similarly, a second prominent defense of *GTA:SA* has been to focus on the level of pleasure garnered in becoming a virtual gangsta. On Amazon.com, Frank Ponce, speaking in gleeful terms, could not contain his excitement from the possibility of becoming a gangster: "Like all the other 'Grand Theft Auto' games, this is going to be great. Only this is the ultimate game.... Playing a gangsta this time is going to be tight."

While recognizing the potential harm that comes from these games (promoting violence, demeaning women, teaching kids immorality and reinforcing stereotypes), gamer after gamer celebrated the pleasure and excitement generated from playing inside both Liberty City and San Andreas. In their estimation, their pleasure and the enjoyment of these games superseded any questions about their effect on society. Likewise, most gamers dismissed claims about the potential harm of playing this game, emphasizing over and over again that the GTA series was intended for adults. Acknowledging the potential harm on kids—white middle class kids—a vast majority of gamers called upon parents, rather than a censoring government to protect America's impressionable minds.

Moreover, much of the discourse wondered about the universality of harm on all youth—in other words, would GTA affect all youth identically? Questioning the logic that bemoans the effects of playing in San Andreas on all children, much of the online discussion focused on its potential harm on certain youth, those without parental involvement, those who already live in violent communities, those who lack morals and values, and those already likely to commit crime (read: black and poor). At this level, the culture war exists as a battle between one segment determined to protect white middle-class suburban youth from the pollutants and moral turpitude available in San Andreas or those "lessons" offered within a world dominant by hip-hop, and those who find pleasure in this world, yet simultaneously seek to protect *their* children from the cultural values offered within GTA and the dangers that define contemporary life. While these discourses seem to agree on a number of fronts—that there should be some method of shielding children from the messages of these games—the method of protection is often a bone of contention. This presumed battle, between those who think the state should be held responsible and those who take the family to task nonetheless seek the same goal of policing the imagery consumed by impressionable youth. As reflective of a new racist discourse that in spite of the increasing visibility of people of color, especially with the cultural marketplace, the efforts to police and protect these bodies and those signifiers of blackness from impressionable white youth, who because of the increase visibility, are under siege embodies the realities of new racism.

Fourth and probably most revealing, much online discussion focused on the realism offered within these games. In other words, the criticism offered by Clinton, Lieberman, Walsh, or from MAVAV is unwarranted and baseless in that *GTA:SA* and *True Crime* merely attempt to capture the reality of ghetto life within contemporary America. On Amazon.com Orlando describes the game in the following terms: "The violence is real and it happens everyday, so this game cannot be seen as violent but for its realism in gang life. You see it from a perspective of a former gang banger trying to straighten his life until he is sucked back in…. This is the type of thing that happens when you grow up in a life like this." "A Gamer" concurs, focusing on the realism of the game not merely as a point of celebration, but as a response to those racist "haters."

> This game is gonna be sweet, no doubt about it. But to the racist saying that it is a disappointment [because] the character is black, please shut up. Why you think Vincetti was Italian? Because it's cool to be Italian? NO! Because the game parallels a gangster's lifestyle. Now wouldn't it be a bore if he had a Minnesotan accent?! Could you serious imagine a game about urban strife during the early 1990s in LA and based on movies like *Boyz n the Hood* with a white guy. Seriously. Your racism blinds your whole concept of character and setting. Please, keep your whole white victimhood to yourself.

On Rotten Tomatoes website, "David the Black Heart," agreed, noting the realism as the reason why *GTA:SA* surpassed even the previous installments of GTA: "Using the 80s was much more of a novelty than a real setting so that they could please fans of *Miami Vice*. SA's use of the 90s feels infinitely more authentic and real and the story is great because it explores a lot of what street life is like. To me, ghettos and gangs are real whilst mafia themes aren't." While others focused on playing a gangsta as "innovative" and a "tight" change of pace, "A Gamer" focused on the realism of the game as to challenge those who did not want to be a black gangsta and those who question the manner of representation. In other words, don't hate the game, hate the realism that it portrays; don't denounce this virtual reality, but the reality it reflects; don't call for legislation to outlaw ghettocentric games, work to undo the existence of ghetto inside America. Whereas some chatters wondered if the realism offered in the game resulted in an unfortunate celebration of the worst available within society (its "sewer" and "criminal elements"), Orlando and others not only dismissed critiques by citing the game's realistic portrayals of the ghetto, but noted the transformative possibilities in the GTA series. Calling it educational and full of profound life lessons, Orlando clearly saw a power in learning about the ghetto from the safety of his home. While lacking time and space to fully discuss this disturbing reconstitution of *GTA:SA* as an oppositional and informative glimpse into an authentic ghetto experience, it must be noted that GTA erases much of what happens daily within America's ghettos, from mothers and fathers working and sons and daughters playing and going to school to families eating dinner and activist organizing against the construction of jails or other potentially dangerous structures. To claim realism is to accept the idea that America's ghetto is nothing more than war zones inhabited by lawless gangstas in need of policing, surveillance, and state control, whether through putting more cops on the street, or outlawing virtual play within ghetto spaces.

Lastly, there seems throughout these online discussions to be an effort amongst chatters, and even my students and certain academic gaming circles to celebrate GTA as a safe vehicle to address larger problems. Soraya Murray, for example, in her provocative, yet at times troubling celebration of virtual gaming, describes GTA in the following way: "For me, these depictions of urban spaces can serve as neutral zones to which to manifest more pervasive" and more "real lived social situations" (97). Erasing power differentials and the ubiquity of state violence, Murray, like much of the discourse, sees a transformative and even oppositional quality within GTA: "Liberty City, Vice City, the streets of the staggeringly expansive state of San Andreas—these are all boundaries zones in which it becomes possible to experiment safely with extremely disorienting aspects of modern life" (97–98). Similarly, a review on Game-Brains celebrates *GTA:SA* as a "politically engaged" piece of art that "*San Andreas* presents a scathing critique of American consumer culture, the horrible social inequalities that it perpetuates, and the damage it causes to the rest of the world" ("Modding Community Gets Angry"). Like the chatter who dismissed questions about violence by suggesting the possibility of using GTA to thwart violence ("Detroit leads the U.S. in murder, rape, armed robbery. Most people in Detroit can't afford a PS2 and GTA. Detroit led the U.S. in murder, rape, armed robbery, and etc. long before video games. My idea ... give people in Detroit a PS2 to give them something to do") or Brandon, who describes *GTA:SA* as a "Fantastical virtual playground" and "a way out of the suburbs" (Vargas), the efforts to celebrate the GTA series and *GTA:SA* particularly in the face of criticism legitimizes dominant understandings of race, place, and state. This "way out of the suburbs" is not mere escapism, as the play of the privileged speaks to the normalization of institutional violence towards the less privileged in U.S. society. The reduction of violence within marginalized communities to individual choices devoid of societal influence provides two key functions in the context of GTA: it justifies unquestioning consumption of racist imagery, and justifies violent state policing of America's "morally (whiteness) deficient."

State Violence and a Race-Based Critique

Amid the widespread debates about the GTA series, and particularly *GTA:SA*, as to its effects on children, and the impact of playing highly sexualized and violent games, little has been made of the racial content, particularly how these games reinforce dominant understandings of America's ghettos, blackness, and state control. As with the discussion, these games reduce America's ghettos and the bodies of color who inhabit these locales to spaces of danger and decay that necessitate state surveillance and regulation. Although the panics and celebration routinely come from outside of urban communities of color, a sustained engagement from within communities of color and other anti-racist advocates is necessary given the ways in which these games legitimize dominant racial discourses and practices. A defining characteristic of *Grand Theft Auto: San Andreas* is the ability to commit home invasion robberies, on top of the usual murders, pimping, car theft and other missions. Carl Johnson—the player-controlled character—along with your crew can sneak into "innocent people's" homes in search of goods and cash to steal. At some points in the game, home invasions allow you to sneak up on sleeping families, holding them at bay with a shotgun or another weapon of your choice. During one game playing session, Carl breaks into a house, only to find an unsuspecting white couple. As the white male resident attempts to protect his blonde wife by challenging Carl to a fight, he states: "you probably can't read." As with the rest of the game, this stand off, with Carl murdering these two individuals, further solidifies hegemonic visions of the ghetto as a war zone inhabited by black gangstas that not only prey on black residents, but those white families living outside its virtual ghetto center.

Another important element of *GTA:SA* is how this game disseminates dominant ideologies and common sense ideas of race toward the sanctioning of state violence. Beyond playing on hegemonic visions of people of color and criminality, *GTA:SA* equally deploys reactionary visions of communities of color through its narrative and virtual representations. For example, as you drive throughout and between the game's various cities, the radio not only blasts a spectrum of jams, all of which further reflects the commodification of an imagined urban black aesthetic, but a series of reactionary public service announcements, which embody a virtual moral panic and contribute to those efforts outside of this virtual urban space. Paired with the deployment of racialized images of criminality (even black cops are corrupt), dysfunctionality and danger, these radio spots highlight the game's reactionary political orientation, playing on hegemonic myths of race, class and nation. "Notice food lines are getting too long. Wonder why? 19 million illegal aliens are in this country. Most are in San Andreas." The violence and mayhem that define this virtual reality reflect the number of illegal aliens that view America as a place of handouts. Obviously playing on white supremacist mythology of immigration and welfare, such representations justify increased spending on the war against immigrants—decreasing the social welfare budget while increasing the power of the state to police borders would be productive in solving this problem. In another instance, the game reflects on the state of poverty and welfare inside this virtual America. "Those of you, who are poor, should just stop whining. Enjoy it and sit back to do what you do best: watch TV." In a third moment, a talk radio show further articulates the racist orientation of the game and its effort to link representation and state violence. Amid a talk show debate concerning immigration into San Andreas, one contributor noted how Asian immigrants were flooding the area with drugs while those from South America brought nothing since "South America has less culture than a toilet bowl." In each instance, the game gives voices to white supremacist ideologies legitimized by the game's narrative and racialized representation, sanctioning the current course of state violence. *GTA:SA* is not simply teaching kids to be violent, but eliciting consent for the ways the state enacts violence on communities of color.

While unable to provide a complete analysis of the ways in which the GTA series aid white supremacist discourses and practices, each of which has elided the dominant discourse, I think it is important to make mention of a key narrative element that further illustrates its sanctioning, if not promotion of state violence, that has a particular effect on communities of color. Whether participating in an urban colonial project of taking territory, or participating in random acts of virtual violence, a core element of *GTA:SA* is the murdering of people of color. While this premise is a defining character of this genre of games, *GTA:SA* elucidates the role (or lack thereof) of the state in protecting and serving communities of color. Throughout the game, the police ignore the murder of other "gang members," often intervening only in moments where violence is directed at the "innocent." In other words, Carl can, at times, kill rival gang members in front (or close to) police without consequences. Killing an innocent citizen brings the police swiftly and with the full force of the law. Furthermore, as these individuals lie in the street in virtual wait for medical attention, the paramedics rarely arrive. The murder of the innocent in the game frequently leads to not only a quick ambulance response, but also the resuscitation of these characters. *GTA:SA*, thus, concretizes hegemonic ideologies regarding criminality and the state's role in only protecting the "innocent." In reveals the nature of new racism, which celebrates the visibility and commodifiable opportunities available to people of color, even as those outside the cultural landscape and the representations within popular culture as subjected to regulation and demonization.

New Racism

While ideologies of colorblindness emanate from a spectrum of state institutions, ranging from the media to the academy, popular culture represents a crucial site in the deployment of frames of colorblindness given the ready ease of global dissemination and the increased visibility of celebrities of color (Collins; Andrews and Jackson). It has become a space worthy of celebration, whereupon American discourses pay tribute to progress and possibilities, thanking popular culture for what various individuals have described as the "browning of America," a "racing of American culture" or an "explicit darkening, blackening and coloring of American culture, at least in terms of operation of its dominant institutions of cultural production and legitimation" (Gray 18). In other words, popular culture does not merely embody a changed or colorblind moment for America, but is simultaneously facilitating greater advancements toward a more equitable racial politics given that popular culture breaks down barriers whether through artists or shared adoration experienced by fans. It facilitates a destruction of racial boundaries, whether with white and black youth sharing a love of hip-hop, various communities learning about one another through television and films, or the virtual travels that come through video games. Serving as evidence for racial progress given the popularity of celebrities of color, or the visibility of Othered cultural practices or aesthetics, and a vehicle that allows for greater contact toward a new racial politics, the presumption of colorblindness obfuscates the persistent of symbolic and everyday violence that defines our current racial moment. Charles Barkley, in his recent conversation-based book, *Who's Afraid of a Large Black Man*, reflects this discursive field, not only finding ways to celebrate the colorblind and diverse realities of contemporary popular culture that demonstrate immense racial progress, but the transformative possibilities. "You had a generation, the one before mine, who are now in their forties, who are in positions of power and influence in their companies in the music industries," writes Barkley. "Now you have a brother in a movie like XXX, you know what I'm saying. Just because rap has kind of churned the soil. The kid who might have been a total racist without rap is like, 'Yo, I like this, I like this. I like everything that has to do with rap culture. I like Spike. I like Jordan. I like Jay-Z. You know it's not so hard to accept.'" (131). Reflecting a colorblind discourse, Barkley links progress to ascendance of people of color into dominant institutions and the visibility of celebrities of color. In his estimation, the popularity of hip-hop or black cinematic productions is evidence of a new racial politics. Ice Cube follows suit during his interview with Charles Barkley, surmising this celebratory vision of popular culture, one that does not account for the complexity of race and racism within contemporary America:

> I think three things transcend race: music, entertainment, and athletics.... Race truly goes out of consciousness too, in sport.... It's pretty much the same in the entertainment industry. In a certain instance you could care less who it is because you saw something and you loved it.... I think there are things that, on a day-to-day basis, transcend race and put us all on the same plane, you know? But to me, it's also natural for people to root for their own kind to succeed, no matter who it is [Barkley 132].

While immensely problematic on many counts, Ice Cube captures the widespread sentiment regarding race within contemporary America and hegemonic understandings of race as an individual act or taste. Likewise, it obscures the continuations of white supremacist discourses and practices in post-civil rights America, all of which are further displaced from the national consciousness through celebrations of visibility and the ubiquity of moral panics fixated with sex and violence.

The ascension of the civil rights movements during the 1950s and 1960s resulted in an end to the formal enactment of the color line. Through protest, struggles inside the courts and in the streets, and "ceaseless agitation" the civil rights movement was successful in forcing the state to formally outlaw Jim Crow segregation. The 1964 Civil Rights Act, the 1965 Voting Rights Act, and the numerous Supreme Court cases that preceded and followed these landmark cases, all of which came as the result of widespread protest did not, however, eliminate racism or racial inequality. "The problem of the twenty-first century seems to be the absence of a color line," notes Patricia Hill Collins. "Formal legal discrimination has been outlawed yet contemporary social practices produce virtually identical racial hierarchies as those observed by Du Bois" (32). Whether talking about rates of educational attainment, rates of incarceration, wealth and income disparities, infant mortality rates, AIDS or sickle cell infection rates, residential segregation or any other measure of political, residential, economic, social or cultural inequality, people of color remain clustered at the bottom of America's political, economic, and social hierarchies.

The persistence of inequality is not merely the result of vestiges of the formalized color line and slavery, or the persistence of ideas of race, dominant ideologies, and social practices, all of which define racism (and facilitate similar racialized outcomes, but also new forms of racism (ideologies, practices and discourse) that contribute to contemporary racial organization. As Collins describes this exact historical moment, new racism "reflects a situation of permanence and change" (33). In other words, as the outcomes and realities of inequality mirror those of 1896, 1919, 1968, the realities of racial formation, institutional organization, and contemporary racial politics embody a new form of racism. The persistence of "new racism" is dependent on the dissemination of supportive imagery, and post-civil rights, colorblind offerings within virtual reality of other sources of entertainment are now more important than ever, as the fervent need to consume, and thus believe, that "we have overcome" is probably stronger at this post-civil rights moment than it has been since the late 1960s. The symbolic violence that is offered within games like *GTA:SA* or *True Crime: NY* is emblematic of such representation. Violence that justifies, naturalizes and rationalizes persistent inequality, while simultaneously shifting public discourse away from racism and toward morals and values—the condemnation of hip-hop or thugs (i.e. blackness) is thus not a racial phenomenon but one about behavior; it is the sin and not the sinner.

Yet, as evident in the ongoing debate regarding GTA, the various lines of debate emanate from a similar place that does not question the ways in which these games perpetuate violence through distorting, dehumanizing, and reifying dominant understandings of race and racism. Each accepts the virtual inscriptions of the ghetto, or these game's vision of hip-hop or blackness, one celebrating their ghettocentric imagination as evidence for their own racial enlightenment ("we like black people—even the thugs and gangsters—so we can't be racist"), the other condemning a community and its values because of its violence, criminality, acceptance of drugs, or hyper sexuality. This "racism without racists"—positing deficiencies and differences as cultural and race as incidental—is a defining quality of new racism, constituted through the discourse surrounding GTA in particular, and ghettocentric video games in general.

One of the more salient elements of new racism, especially as it relates to popular culture and political discourse, is the constancy of signs of dysfunction among communities of color that require societal control and regulation. While neither the demonization of black bodies, nor calls for societal regulation are new, the scale of the discourse of representation of dysfunctionality, the extent of commodification, and the establishment of clear class-based boundaries has rendered these old-style ideologies in its new form. Rhonda Williams describes this moment of old and new racism as living at the crossroads, where the celebration of racial progress and the visibility of black public figures does not match the persistence of violence, inequality, and representations of dysfunctionality. "Today's African American college students have come of age in a political culture that regularly recycles two signs of black dysfunction: anti-social black (male) criminality and (female) sexuality are the behavioral manifestations of contemporary black cultural chaos. From "scholarly and journalist treatises," to popular music and cinema, representations and debates regarding the black "underclass anchor contemporary race talk, and speak the language that distinguishes the aberrant underclass from the striving middle class" (Williams 141). Throughout the discussion of varied reactions to GTA, and some textual analysis, this chapter ultimately concludes that both the game itself and the various receptions replicate such practices reducing blackness to a sign of criminality, hypersexuality, and cultural/moral chaos, to which some call for regulation/state intervention while others celebrate in "their world," enjoying the opportunity to play in a world defined by criminality, dysfunctionality, and cultural chaos.

Conclusion

In both the demonization and celebration of the virtual reality offered through the GTA series, the horror and praise resulting from suburban bodies entering the otherwise impenetrable (segregated) world of gangstas, thugs, hip-hop, and ghettos, and the surrounding discourse of reception, dominant understandings of race, hegemonic rationalization (explanations) of contemporary social inequality, and the advisable methods (policies) needed to address current issues become visible. In other words, the GTA series and the myriad of reactions each concretize common sense understandings of blackness and the ghetto as a spectacle in need of state control and surveillance, each centering and naturalizing narratives and representations of violence and sexual deviancy, at once finding pleasure here with others paralyzed by fear. "Constructions of deviant sexuality emerge as a primary location for the production of these race and class subjectivities," writes Micki McElya in *Our Monica Ourselves: The Clinton Affair and the National Inter-*

est. "Policy debates and public perceptions on welfare and impoverished Americans have focused relentlessly on the black urban poor—blaming nonnormative family structures, sexual promiscuity, and aid-induced laziness as the root cause of poverty and mobilizing of welfare queens, teen mothers, and sexually predatory young men to sustain the dismantling of the welfare state" (159). The representations and images available within *GTA:LCS, GTA:VC*, and most transparently within *GTA:SA*, the dialogue and narrative deployed within these games, and the subsequent public discourse and eventual racialized culture war defined by both panic around and fetishization of ghetto violence and hyper sexuality function as "naturalizing narratives of deviant sexuality and aberrant family structures" toward the legitimacy of persistent inequality, ongoing white privilege, the destruction of social welfare programs, and the erection of stronger walls of segregation and more powerful arms of state violence.

The discourse concerning *GTA3*, and especially in the wake of the release of *GTA:SA*, in both celebrations and within those efforts to denounce these games for the good of America's children ultimately reify dominant understandings of blackness and a hegemonic ghettocentric imagination. Whereas its fans cite pleasure and authenticity in the game's display of violence, deviant sexuality and other signifiers of a gangsta's way of life, its critics cite these same aesthetics, behaviors, and morals as the cause for alarm and the basis of their calls for state intervention. Moreover, the positioning of this discourse as one regarding the moral or cultural harm of ghettocentric games (and not war games) elides crucial questions regarding white supremacy, state violence, and new racism. As Lauren Berlant laments in her discussion of cultural citizenship and the conservative focus on sex and intimacy, their use of "divisive rhetoric" as the basis of their seizing power since the election of Ronald Reagan, and the ubiquity of sexualized culture wars ultimately obscures and erases public debates and questions regarding justice, equality, and state violence within contemporary America.

> It is my view that critical engagement with what ought to constitute the social privileges and obligations of citizenship must be reorganized around these questions—of national capitalism, metropolitan and rural poverty, environmental disintegration, racist thinking, and ordinary concrete practices and other banalities of national evil [8–9].

The widespread debate between gamers (players, designers, industry supporters, academics) and the "haters" (politicians, media critics, conservative cultural groups, and the religious right) have successfully erased the racist, patriarchal, heteronormative, and xenophobic representational and textual utterances of the entire series. From its reification of blackness as the ontological sign of decay and moral indecency to its demonization of Latino immigrants as economic parasites, the manner in which these games uncritically give life and voice to "concrete practice and other banalities of national evil," is elided from the discourse. Likewise, the dialectics between the virtual and the real, whether in discourse (culture of poverty, the racialization of communities of color) and practice (police brutality; the war on drugs) is further obscured by the discursive focus on sex, violence, and the efforts to protect the purity and innocence of (some) children.

Notwithstanding the rhetoric of protecting children from harmful representations of black men, or the virtual erasure of women of color, none of these officials have publicly denounced or called for regulation of racist or racialized games. These same legislative bodies have not elucidated plans to insulate "our children" from white supremacist narratives promulgated by the video game industry. None have questioned the racial content of games like *Grand Theft Auto: San Andreas*. There is no discourse concerning the dissemination of racial stereotypes or the affirmation of the racist status quo. Outrage remains in a discourse of children, its focus being violence and sexual content, rather than the effects/significance of these games in society, especially as spaces of racial meaning and state violence. The nature of *Grand Theft Auto* reflects this fact, as does the silence of politicians, cultural commentators and antiracist proponents; make clear about war against youth.

While the motivations of profit and appealing to a marketplace driven by the allure of hip-hop and black cultural styles with white consumers drives the continued production of games like *GTA:SA* or *Gang Wars*, its gaming dimensions and its surrounding discourse of reception (celebration and condemnation) must be understood within a racial context. "The black other occupies a complex site, a place where fears, desires, and repressed dreams are lodged," argues Norman Denzin (7). More than fears and repressed dreams, the black body and those racialized spaces exist in virtual reality and the national imagination as "a site of spectacle, its blackness" existing as "a potential measure of evil, and menace," necessitating containment and control. The representation of blackness or inner-city communities through a hegemonic ghettocentric imagination, the celebrations of adults becoming gangstas, and the fears caused by the appearance of hypersexual and violent ghetto games follows longstanding white supremacist logic that "focuses, organizes, and translates blackness into commodifiable representations and desires that [can] be packaged and marketed across the landscape of American popular culture" or otherwise confines it outside the dominant racial order

(Gray, "Watching" 165). In other words, black bodies will continue to be marketed and commodified by a global video game industry just as those same bodies will be subjected to the rules and logic that emanate from white supremacy.

Moreover, the similarity in frames and discursive logic that emanate from all circles (haters and players alike) reveals that its providing players the chance to don the costume (hair, muscles, tattoos, gear) of a true "gangsta" or visiting America's most violent spaces does not represent a transgression to traditional (white supremacist, hetero-normative, patriarchal) values that is either worthy of condemnation or celebration, illustrating how corporate commodification reifies dominant ideologies and racial/gender/sexual logics, all while the game industry cashes in on their ghettocentric representations, politicians and other public figures cash in on the controversy and moral panics, and gamers continue to cash in on their whiteness.

As politicians focus on video game violence and the moral offerings within gaming culture, thereby eluding the racial and ideological dimensions of these games and ignoring broader societal problems, and its defenders obscure similar dimensions and their connections to virtual reality, it is important to remember that the GTA series, *GTA:SA* particularly, and a ghettocentric virtual reality matters because racism kills— the celebrations and demonizations of blackness jointly facilitate the hegemony of new racism, which in the end maintains color lines and white privileges, whether manifesting in the perpetuation of the prison industrial complex or systemic poverty that reared its head in wake of Hurricane Katrina. It matters because social justice—the ability of all people to live their lives free of oppressions based on race, class, gender, sexuality, and ideology—is a goal that U.S. society has long forgone for profit at any cost. It has never been "just a game." It has always been lives, livelihoods, injustice, and a desire for much, much more.

Works Cited

Barkley, Charles, and Michael Wilbon. *Who's Afraid of a Large Black Man?* New York: Penguin, 2005.

Berlant, Lauren. *The Queen of America Goes to Washington City: Essays on Sex and Citizenship.* Durham: Duke UP, 1997.

Collins, Patricia Hill. *Black Sexual Politics: African Americans, Gender and the New Racism.* New York: Routledge, 2004.

Denzin, Norman. *Reading Race: Hollywood and the Cinema of Racial Violence.* Thousand Oaks: Sage, 2002.

Gray, Herman. *Cultural Moves: African Americans and the Politics of Representation.* Berkeley: U of California P, 2005.

_____. *Watching Race: Television and the Struggle for Blackness.* Minneapolis: U of Minnesota P, 1995.

Hooks, Bell. *Outlaw Culture: Resisting Representation.* New York: Routledge, 1994.

James, Joy. *Shadowboxing: Representations of Black Feminist Politics.* New York: St. Martin's, 1999.

Kellner, Douglas. *Media Culture: Cultural Studies, Identity, and Politics Between the Modern and the Postmodern.* New York: Routledge, 1995.

Leonard, David. "'Live in Your World, Play in Ours': Race, Video Games, and Consuming the Other." *Simile* 3.4 (Nov. 2003). 15 Dec. 2005. <http://www.utpjournals.com/jour.ihtml?lp=simile/issue12/leonardfulltext.html>.

Loughrey, Paul. "Family Entertainment Protection Act." *Game Daily Biz* 11 Nov. 2005. 15 Dec. 2005 <http://gamesindustry.biz/news.php?aid=13330>.

McCullagh, Declan. "Senators Target 'Graphic' Video Games." *ZDNet News* 29 Nov. 2005. 15 Dec. 2005 <http://news.com.com/Senators+target+graphic+video+games/2100-1043_3-5975913.html>.

McElya, Micki. "Trashing the Presidency: Race, Class and the Clinton/Lewinsky Affair." *Our Monica Ourselves: The Clinton Affair and the National Interest.* Ed. Lauren Berlant and Lisa Dugan. New York: New York UP, 2001: 156–174.

"Modding Community Gets Angry." 26 July 2005. 15 Dec. 2005 <http://www.kotaku.com/gaming/san-andreas/index.php>.

Morgan, Fred. "Video Games Offer Tutorials in Violence." 5 Dec. 2005. 15 Dec. 2005 <http://www.muskogeephoenix.com/apps/pbcs.dll/article?AID=/20051205/OPINION/51204012/1014>.

Murray, Soraya. "High Art/Low Life: The Art of Playing Grand Theft Auto." *Performing Arts Journal* 80 (2005): 91–98.

Slevin, Peter. "A Push to Restrict Sales of Video Games Illinois Governor Seeks to Prevent Minors From Purchasing 'Adult Material.'" *Washington Post* 16 Dec. 2005: A08.

Sweeting, Paul. "Bill Targets Video Game Retailers." *Video Business* 1 Dec. 2005. 15 Dec. 2005 <http://www.videobusiness.com/article/CA6288381.html>.

Thompson, Clive. "The Bad Lieutenant." *Wired* 23 Nov. 2005. 15 Dec. 2005 <http://www.wired.com/news/culture/games/0,69626-0.html>.

Vargas, Jose Antonio. "Gamers Intersection." *Washington Post* 27 Sept. 2005: C01.

Williams, Rhonda. "Living at the Crossroads: Explorations in Race, Nationality, Sexuality, and Gender." *The House that Race Built.* Ed. Wahneema Lubiano. New York: Vintage, 1998: 136–156.

4. Play-Fighting:

Understanding Violence in *Grand Theft Auto III*

TANNER HIGGIN

> Popular culture, commodified and stereotyped as it often is, is not at all, as we sometimes think of it, the arena where we find who we really are, the truth of our experience. It is an arena that is *profoundly* mythic. It is a theater of popular desires, a theater of popular fantasies. It is where we discover and play with the identifications of ourselves, where we are imagined, where we are represented, not only to the audiences out there who do not get the message, but to ourselves for the first time.
>
> —*Stuart Hall*

Bridging the Violent Gap

I don't know any violent criminals, but I know plenty of people who enjoy playing Grand Theft Auto (GTA) games. Given the prevailing climate of discussion surrounding the latest iteration entitled *Grand Theft Auto: San Andreas (GTA:SA)* many would assume this to be practically impossible. Recent games in the GTA series have often been utilized as the primary examples of a trend of excessively illicit and deviant content saturating the medium. In conjunction, many now fear that this content will manifest itself in the player's behavior. These claims were newly galvanized by the unlocking of embedded code within the PC version of *GTA:SA*, a controversy that has been referred to as the "Hot

Coffee" scandal. "Hot Coffee" was the name of a hidden mini-game within the PC version of *GTA:SA* that was ostensibly not intended to be played at release, but was unlocked by players allowing them to participate in explicit sex acts with the characters of the game. Fallout from the discussion over the scandal has resulted in the Entertainment Software Ratings Board's (ESRB) unprecedented revoking of the game's mature rating, proposed Congressional legislation,[1] and increased media attention and public awareness. While "Hot Coffee" involved exclusively sexual content, the debate has been fueled by a host of research studies on the effects of video game content, specifically violence, on the players. Results have been inconclusive and have failed in establishing any direct causal links between violent behavior in video games and violent behavior in real life. However, some of the studies have located connections between video games and increased levels of aggression. These studies have been both behavioral and physiological in nature[2] and have provided the necessary research background with which to pursue action against violent video games. Significantly, due to their noted methodological issues the overall trends are far less convincing than they appear to be.[3] As John Sherry confirms in his meta-analysis, "There is a small effect of video game playing on aggression, and the effect is smaller than the effect of violent television on aggression" (427). Further complicating matters, Dmitri Williams and Marko Skoric's recent longitudinal study "Internet Fantasy Violence: A Test of Aggression in an Online Game" found no significant relationship between gameplay and aggressive behavior. The varied landscape of research illustrates the complicated and highly mediated process of media effects. Lacking direct causal links, the discussion about video game violence would benefit from more long-term studies and a sensible understanding of the variety of factors that result in acts of violence. Legislative action would undermine and devalue the importance of this research and is already in the process of manufacturing a negative cultural climate that forces some to ask why exactly it is they know so many players of Grand Theft Auto games and so few criminals.

As James Paul Gee and many other educational games scholars now argue, the video game is more than a playful diversion, it is a tool within which incredibly intricate and highly effective processes of learning get exercised. These conclusions have an obvious lineage rooted within the social learning theory wielded by media effects researchers to explain how the consumption of media can influence behavior. When someone plays a Grand Theft Auto game they are learning something, but how and what they are learning is still, for the most part, elusive. Given the significant attention devoted to the study of gaming and violence, in conjunction with the known expert educational capabilities of games, the diving rates of crime reveal a disconnect between what is being hypothesized and researched and what is being observed. If the proliferation of violent video games is contemporaneous with a drastic decline in violent crime, then why not study those connections too? Regardless of whether players experience more, less, or indifferent amounts of aggression during or after playing, the fact remains that the actual *violent expression* of this behavior is significantly reduced outside of the game world in almost all cases. In fact, according to the United States Department of Justice, violent crime rates have been steadily declining as games sales (including those of all the games in the GTA series) have been experiencing enormous growth.[4] Historically speaking, video games are in the midst of a recurring cycle of paranoia and misunderstanding of media effects that new technologies have consistently undergone (Wartella and Reeves). These other debates have evolved and are less focused with discovering direct causal links between violent media and behavior and more concerned with the dynamic and highly individualized experience of media consumption.

The profound nature of the violent experience of GTA is not in its ability to cause aggression, rather its that a player can be immersed and willfully participate in a criminal world and then step outside of it with limited expression of violence. Even though rates of youth violence are the lowest on record, many researchers are continuing to struggle to find ways in which games such as those in the GTA series incite violence or work to create connections between school shootings and gaming. Meanwhile, the enormous empty gaps between virtual consumption and real production of violent spectacle in GTA games remain unexplored and demanding to be explained. Doing so via an analysis of the mechanisms of learning within the games are beyond the scope of this essay. Instead, the focus will be on what it means to play-fight. To this end, this essay will look at *Grand Theft Auto III (GTA3)*, *Grand Theft Auto: Vice City (GTA:VC)*, and *Grand Theft Auto: San Andreas* as performative spaces wherein the player stages a fantasy that satirizes and de-mythologizes the outside world. By participating in this performance the player undergoes a becoming, facilitated by the player-avatar assemblage, which re-sensitizes her to the violent structures of the world in order to better understand and navigate them.

School Space and Game Space

One of the most damaging omissions in the current research about violence in video games is the lack of consideration of cultural context.

As I have already mentioned, there has been a persistent decrease in youth crime congruent with violent video games, which appears to be consistently ignored or cast as irrelevant. More cultural trends and perspectives that contextualize this discussion can be revealed in how other texts address this issue. Unfortunately, controversy over violence in video games has become so culturally embedded post–Columbine that few have made the choice to actually narrate it. One can assume that the topic's political divisiveness and its saturation in the media have discouraged many artists from providing a perspective that may be offensive or corrupted by over-mediation of a particular image or images. Gus Van Sant's 2003 film *Elephant* is a product of this anxiety over the Columbine shooting and the media coverage that mythologized it. Consequently, critics have recognized that rather than offer solutions for the senselessness of violence, Van Sant retreats into the safety of a voyeuristic perspective that "offers explanations" yet "isn't overly interested in them" (Garry III). While this is a valid reading, a closer analysis brings into relief the film's exposure of the very real and damaging problems of social hierarchy in youth experience. Furthermore, the function and nature of the space in recent GTA games correlates to *Elephant* and addresses and simulates the antagonism of the hierarchical school space. Therefore, GTA is not just channeling its own urban environment but a host of other spaces, providing a dynamic environment of social navigation and education wherein a fantasy of freedom can be enacted.

In *Elephant*, the camera drifts from person to person and place to place to imply the disinterestedness that critics have identified. However, it also refers to a distant innocence or an invisible student presence that is ignored yet ever-present. The mundane and drifting peacefulness of this perspective is perverted halfway into the film when the student killers, Eric and Alex, are first revealed walking briskly into the school with their weaponry hanging ominously off of them. With the invisible presence finally disclosed as that of the killers, the camera's methodical roaming no longer suggests innocence but anxiety over innocence lost and the anticipation of a bloody climax. The students are now refocused under the lens and criticized as potential fuses for this inexorable violence.

Elephant alludes to almost all of the media conjured causes for the Columbine incident. Eric and Alex watch a TV program about Nazi Germany, they order guns online, kiss in the shower, and, of course, play violent video games. The video game playing, as in all scenes dealing with the potential causes for violence, is given passing attention. Eric plays a simple first person shooter while Alex plays Beethoven's "Für Elise" on the piano nearby. Eric shows no aggression or pleasure as he plays the game which itself is rather boring and tame. The juxtaposition of the banality of the game and beautiful intensity of the music surreptitiously parodies the vilification of video games as deviant low culture. Significantly, the only time we see either of the boys being emotionally affected is in two crucial scenes involving Alex that occur after his introduction as one of the killers. These scenes, overlooked by critics as not indicating motivation, demarcate the school environment itself as the sole instigator. In the first of the two scenes, Alex is pelted with spitballs by another student during a science class. Afterwards, he enters the cafeteria and is visibly flustered, a notable deviation from his and Eric's emotionless demeanor throughout the film. The noise level increases and collapses around him as a passing student bumps into him. This collision delivers the final blow to the implications of the camera's airy meandering. The viewer is transported into the claustrophobic pits of Alex's life and offers a comparison to the free and open spaces of possibility and comfort that the drifting camera signified. The school space, manufactured by the floating perspective, is now exposed as a space dominated by the upper castes of high school society. The third person perspective, from this point forward, connotes a navigation of dangerous space rather than a safe journey.

Van Sant's confession that he "played *Tomb Raider* until he was obsessed with it" (Peary) also informs the use of this style. The characters in the film appear like video game characters, stalking the corridors and trying to find their way out and beat the game. The school is transformed into the video game space of corridors and stalking foes. However, the connections between school and video game are not intentionally obvious to the viewer until an actual mapping of game space onto school space. Just prior to Eric and Alex's stalking of the corridors they sit down to discuss their plan. This discussion is punctuated with images from the impending rampage. At one point the camera suddenly shifts positions from third to first person, the gun taking up the signature bottom space of the frame, firing a shot in direct reference to the first person shooter genre of video game that Eric had been playing. This shocking, singular jolt of perspective forces the viewer into recognizing the school space as a game space. The third person perspective maintained throughout the film is re-signified and reminds the viewer that this is not something new, but that the school has always been this way but limited only to the tortured existence of the invisible presence. Prior to beginning their rampage, Alex reminds Eric that their plan should give them many opportunities to shoot jocks but to "have fun" while doing it. Their fun, and thus the fun of the game, is in a disturbed emptying of the school of obstacles and systems of hierarchy, turning the claustrophobic space into a free and easily navigable space.

Turf Wars

As Gonzalo Frasca has noted, amongst the gamer community the one word most often used to describe *Grand Theft Auto III* when it was released was "freedom" (2003). According to Frasca, this response is generated by a few brilliant design innovations, one of which is its lack of forced linear progression. This is encouraged through a sparse narrative and an almost complete omission of dialogue. As he concludes, "the main pleasure lies in the simulation of crimes and not in achieving a Hollywood ending" (2003). The general concept of urban crime simulation underwent some revision in later versions of the game, most notably with an increasingly plot driven storyline, more dialogue, and a boost in goal possibilities; however, the general concept has stayed the same. Each new edition of the game has been sold, in part, on its promise of explorative possibility and spatial freedom. *GTA:SA* boasts having three separate cities (Los Santos, San Fierro, and Las Venturas) each larger than the totality of Vice City. This affords the player a massive space littered with criminal possibility in the forms of combustible vehicles, reactive and emotive people, and gun stores with which to simulate a fantasy life of debauchery. That is not to say this is all the world has to offer. Beginning with *GTA:VC* and continued within *GTA:SA* are a host of additional features and elements of play borrowed from the roleplaying game genre such as customizable clothing, hair styles, and tattoos as well as the ability to alter one's physicality through working out or overeating. Player housing options and businesses are also available.

As the series evolves, the games offer ample opportunity to refuse participation in criminal simulation by expanding the space and filling it with other choices. A player can easily spend hours engaging in nonviolent mini-games or traveling the vast expanses of the game world without ever firing a gun or killing a person. To compensate for the game's surrendering of nonviolent player agency to a narrative propelled by violence, *Grand Theft Auto: San Andreas'* main character CJ combats neighborhood drug dealers throughout the game and is rewarded with money upon killing random dealers on the street. This is in direct opposition to Tommy Vercetti of *GTA:VC's* direct involvement in the drug trade and its operation and is just a small example of the greater change in morality *GTA:SA* represents. However, these changes do not eclipse the propensity of a player within the simulation to act out violently.

Supporters of the games often make the point that GTA is not forcefully violent and that the player can easily play the game without ever participating in violence.[5] This argument, while mostly true, misses the more significant commentary that the games offer society, as represented in *Elephant,* via their antagonistically violent space. The game space is not only populated with objects that equate to *potential* criminal acts, but they move and interact with the player in such a way to make it *unavoidable.* If we accept the notion that GTA is primarily about simulating an environment and navigating a game space, then the populating people, objects, and vehicles within this space operate as both interactive set pieces and obstacles to navigation. These are the threats that, in Eric and Alex's case, must be emptied. This becomes apparent when one hops into the front seat of a sports car and cruises around any one of the cities. The other cars and people both function as the immersive elements of the simulated environment and as mechanisms of play by offering challenging objects which one must maneuver around. However, as any player quickly realizes, the world is populated just enough to allow free navigation but force collisions and explosions at rather frequent intervals. The player is enticed with the possibilities of freedom and then confronted with the consequences of exercising it. A constant conflict arises between participating in the liberating exploration of the game's spaces and the need to destroy its contents simply to get around.

Spatial antagonism is compounded by the presence of malicious rival gang members, the jocks of GTA, in all three recent games. As the player progresses through the narrative and mini-games, they gather enemies and form alliances. Their allies protect them on the streets whereas their enemies will attack them without warning. *GTA:SA* elevates the importance and functionality of this feature making it its own mini-game in which Los Santos is divided up into pieces of gang "turf" that can be fought for, owned, and then defended against subsequent counterattacks. To reclaim the turf the player must enter the space and provoke the rival gang. The turf under contention is then emptied of bystanders and the player must eliminate several groups of rivals to claim it as her own. If the player desires to travel throughout the cities unimpeded then they need to repeat this conflict within every piece of turf in the game until it is completely emptied of rivals. Consequently, this also boosts their "Respect Meter" a viewable measurement of the credibility garnering violence, destruction, and resulting influence one has over their surroundings.

While none of these in-game encounters occur in schools, the connections to the central conflict of *Elephant* are fairly blatant. GTA, particularly *GTA:SA*, positions the character's masculinity so that it is, as Derek Burrill states, "constantly at odds with its surroundings, eternally under attack, always threatened" (2006). This incessant demanding of masculine performance is a model of the often upheld social hierarchies of society that Eric and Alex are caught in. To gain control and usurp their perceived captors, they must eliminate the obstacles to their unimpeded navigation of the school space. They do so in an uber-masculine and vicious display, emerging from margins of the third person perspective and asserting themselves in the first person, extending ownership over the school by turning it into a game to be won, a turf to be claimed.

Getting the Joke

GTA provides a space for the player to act out and stage a performance of this type of violence in situations which reflect, distort, and exaggerate those of real life yet are contained within the safety of the virtual sphere. Beginning with Brenda Laurel's influential *Computers as Theatre,* a growing number of scholars have been examining the ways in which gaming can involve a theatrical or cinematic performance. As it has been recognized, gaming is "not only a primary space of pleasure for the cultures (and cultures) but a space where performance is more and more a part of the discourse" (Burrill). Thus it is imperative to understand how this mass scale theater of violence interfaces with real world extensions of violence both as an enabling and inhibiting mechanism. Often lost in the consideration of GTA's translation of the real world into virtual performance is the satirical critique of society that it engages in. When regarded as a tool to satirize culture, the violence of GTA suddenly seems less dangerous to individuals in society and more dangerous to the mythologies of society.

Grand Theft Auto III, Grand Theft Auto: Vice City, and Grand Theft Auto: San Andreas each represent a pop culture memory of a specific decade and locale (90s New York, 80s Miami, and 90s L.A. respectively), but with the blemishes not only present but emphasized. To this end the game immerses the player in a carnival of caricature surrounding her with urban, suburban, and rural and ethnic stereotypes as well as a commercially saturated environment of decadence and superficiality. As a result no person on the street has questionable identity. Just as the player constantly has to perform masculinity, people on the street perform roles according to popular myth and stereotype. For example, Asians are suit-wearing triads, Italians are mobsters, and the people in the backwoods of San Andreas are skinny, slack jawed yokels. Each game is certainly multifarious, but homogenized by its staunch adherence to stereotype. Each group, whether delineated ethnically, socially, or economically has its own turf, identified by architecture, style of vehicles on the road, and people on the street. Traversing the game space one gets the impression of a land of diversity yet great gaps and fissures. The uniting mechanism between all of these groups is their involvement in crime and violence. In the same way that Eric and Alex shatter and literally destroy the obstacles and divisions of their high school, the player in GTA assumes the role of a character, whether Claude of *GTA3*, Tommy Vercetti of *GTA:VC*, or CJ of *GTA:SA*, trying to make his way to the top. As established above, it becomes quickly apparent that the only way the environment will let you survive is if you adapt its violence for your own ends. Rather than encouraging a fantasy of boundless and senseless violence, GTA immerses the player in a world that provokes her into using violence to survive and thrive, critiquing the capitalist system of hard work and self promotion at all costs, parodying it and exposing the implied wickedness of the process that often defines success. This is representative of the way GTA encourages a politicization of myth.

Barthes has recognized that "Myth does not deny things, on the contrary, its function is to talk about them; simply it purifies them, it makes them innocent, it gives them a natural and eternal justification, it gives them a clarity which is not that of an explanation but that of a statement of fact" (143). The intention of myth is to pack a message into a structure of form and meaning that obscures the political determinism of the message. Myth manufacturers the opinion that the 80s were an era of acceptable decadence, yuppie emersion, and national pride while the 90s were an era of economic prosperity, forgetful of the economic and social costs that harbor criminals such as Tommy Vercetti and CJ within the system. Myth is also the superficial posturing of Nazi paraphernalia, mail order weapons, heavy metal music, and video games that obstruct and distract from the reality of a life of ridicule. GTA exposes the lenses of hegemonic positivity and racial stratification that have warped popular conception and allows for the introduction of silenced margins into the discourse. It also provides a space to reenact, in a fantasy world, both a version of the past that is satiric and cathartic for the player and an alternate simulated present in which to clear out real world obstacles.

The problem, as with any form of satire, is that the audience will not get the joke or that players will feel the need to continue the joke outside of virtual space and into real space. This is a healthy concern, as the satire of the game relies on players to understand the difference between the message and the delivery method. For example, the games require the player to recognize the facetiousness of the proliferation of Ammunation stores and advertisements in cities rampant with crime. This message gets obscured as the player is awarded with status, money, and respect with each successive robbery and assassination. *GTA3* and *GTA:VC* have the player performing a role that is selfish and motivated solely by greed, immersing the character in the life of both a thug and up-and-coming drug lord respectively. In these cases, the satirical nature of the story is meant to reconcile the occupation of the player-character. *GTA:SA* injects some semblance of a moral logic into the storyline through CJ's more moral inclinations. CJ is a gang member but his life is rationalized as a man fighting for family and community, a role played out in the many missions that focus on ousting drug dealers from his neighborhood and city. This narrative turn represents a way in which GTA's producers and designers have reacted to the concerns about a public "not getting the joke" and thus making the games into their own myth of dumb violence. *GTA:SA* extracts the 90s gangsta mythos, fuses the player with this Other, and stages a performance of violence to force a reevaluation of identity and mythic understanding. Burrill correctly notes how this "choreographing" of performance in *GTA:SA* summons "the twin processes of anxiety and desire" catching the player "in the crosshairs between the narrative justification for CJ's behavior ... and the virtual excitement of the thug life" (2006). Placing the character in the position of performing the violence of society's margin is cathartic but more importantly it is experiential. Feeling the anxiety of the precarious situation of living in a 90s L.A. neighborhood and needing to survive, and the desire to submit to senseless violence due to an antagonistic circumstance aids the player in not only getting the joke, but realizing that the larger societal joke is on them. GTA forces a reflection on the societal sources of violence and facilitates identification with one's own contemporary frustrating battles of anxiety and desire.

Third Person

GTA is symptomatic of the historical erasure of the mythmaking process; it is reactionary politicized speech meant to satirize through the reformation of identity and participation in the metaphoric destruction of societal obstacles. It is the mirrored fantasy space in which silenced voices are annunciated and performed. But even if *GTA:SA* and other games offer a situation that is illustrative and symbolic of real world situations, such as those of Eric and Alex in *Elephant,* and critical of the structures that create such horrific events, the danger remains that such games may encourage real world violence through normalization or training. In "Representation, Enaction, and the Ethics of Simulation" Simon Penny proposes that simulation and its consequences be considered ethically. One of the most critical points in his cogent argument is as follows:

> When soldiers shoot at targets shaped like people, this trains them to shoot real people. When pilots work in flight simulators, the skills they

develop transfer to the real world. When children play "first person shooters," they develop skills of marksmanship. So we must accept that there is
something that qualitatively separates a work like the one discussed
above[6] from a static image or a misogynistic beating, or even a movie of
the same subject. That something is the potential to build behaviors that
can exist without or separate from and possibly contrary to, rational argument or ideology [80–81].

It is rather sobering to think of the highly effective ways in which interactive technologies such as video games, ostensibly indistinguishable
from those on the mass market, are being used to train soldiers to fight
wars. Penny's main concern is that the violent behaviors, having been
cultivated over hours and hours of repetitive practice in games such as
Quake, will be disconnected from the instantiating medium and irra-
tionally exercised outside of it. Rather than relating it to a form of moral
desensitization, he views it more like a virtual extension of instinct by
stating "We must assume that these 'learned responses' can also transfer to the real world, if triggered" (82). As already established, it is one
of the goals of this essay to examine ways in which GTA does not cause
violence but absorbs and dissipates it. Even though GTA may allow the
player to perform a satire, it is still possible that this performance may
also be training the player to act violently elsewhere.

The answer to this problem is found in Penny's comparison of actors
in theater to users of interactive media in regards to their capacity to
install behaviors that might be exercised in the real world. In a response
to potential critics of his media-as-training hypothesis who would contend there is no difference between a stage actor and an interactive
media user, Penny asserts that interactive media is different from theater because theater is not truly interactive. It is "reflexive and double"
in that "it is a world open on one side to the audience, who are not in
that world, but are keen to engage in the illusions that they are." Whereas
the user or player of interactive media is meant to be immersed in an
illusion, the actor is tasked with manufacturing one for the audience.
An actor "looks reflexively at the artifice" while someone in a simulation
is "encouraged to believe there is no 'outside'" (81). Penny rightfully
believes that this intention and structural necessity for simulation or virtual reality to conceal any seams between the virtual and real space
requires ethical consideration. Critical to the appeal of a virtual simulation is its ability to conceal seams or signs that force reflexivity or a recognition that the virtual space is a model. For military training simulators
to be successful the virtual action must be indistinguishable from the real,
convincing the user that simulated actions can transmit into real world
practice. Implied in this seamless environment is a slippage of behaviors

between realms. However, this model does not apply to the seamed environment of GTA.

Unlike Penny's model, GTA consciously establishes barriers between the virtual space and real space to facilitate its critical discourse with the outside world. As established above, GTA enters into a satiric dialogue with the decade and region it is set in and to accomplish this it introduces immersive elements meant to maintain an illusion necessary for play but also remove the player routinely from that illusion for comic effect. One of the best examples would be the use of the in-vehicle radio stations in *GTA:VC* that contain licensed popular music such as Loverboy "Working for the Weekend" or Gary Numan's "Cars" that one might have heard in 80s Miami but packaged with commercials for fake products that often parody other possible sources of violence, like the "Exploder Survival Knife" or "BJ Smith's Fit for Football." The exaggerated signs of GTA depend on a system of signification across the virtual/real seam and recognition that this network is taking place. Nowhere is this more apparent than in *GTA:SA* with its over-saturation of fast food chains with familiar names such as "Cluckin' Bell" and "Burger Shot." The player is forced to eat to maintain the health of their character, yet the only options available are these chains which then cause CJ to gain weight that must be worked off at the gym or by running around or biking in order to maintain optimal stamina and punching power. These features introduce immersive gameplay elements that are common in other titles like *The Sims* but in such a way as to enter into critical dialogue with the decadence of a "Fast Food Nation."

The interface is an important component of the simulation and one of the physical barriers that must be assimilated. Penny claims that games such as *Quake* train players in a form of marksmanship and encourage a tactical logic of survival that involves treating approaching strangers like enemies. Although the gestures of the game, accomplished through the traditional QWERTY keyboard and mouse interface, are not in themselves violent or much like the weapons they control, the digital battlefield is continually blurring the distinction between the joystick, keyboard, and military devices of destruction. In conjunction, the development of realistic physics engines as seen in Valve Software's *Half-Life 2* consistently work toward the very realistic goal of indistinguishable modeling of real world physics. GTA, however, has a rather awkward control scheme due to its reliance on the third person perspective—the most significant seam of all. This does not result in the intense, ultra-realistic, and immersive battles of most first person shooters, but rather highly violent and explosive yet extremely clumsy encounters that are both participated in and witnessed. Consequently, this allows for a necessary amount of mayhem without the impression of being in a dangerous environment or cultivating skills or behaviors that can be seamlessly transitioned into the real world. When playing GTA the player is not spectating nor acting nor interacting. There is no term that describes the unique positionality of the avatar and the dynamic way in which it amalgamates all three activities. The analyses of this essay have been attempting to understand this process and to expose the mechanics involved in the performance I termed play-fighting in my title. Crucial to play-fighting is the avatar and its role as the central processing unit of signification— the most important seam between the real and virtual that performs violence so the player doesn't have to. Thus, the conclusion will deal with the non-violent results of play-fighting and how they are achieved through the avatar's performance.

The Theater and Its Avatar

Bob Rehak's "Playing at Being: Psychoanalysis and the Avatar" forms the theoretical basis for the understanding of the avatar as play-fighter. Rehak's primary assertion is that the video game avatar "merges spectatorship and participation in ways that fundamentally transform both activities" (103) effectively blurring the distinction between actor and interactor as discussed above. This stymies the transmission of violent behavior from the virtual to the real by "enabl[ing] players to think through questions of agency and existence, exploring in fantasy form aspects of their own materiality" (123). Involved in this cognitive process in GTA is the acquisition of freedom through the destruction of obstacles, the politicization and exposure of myth, and the satirical critique of society. Through the avatarial performance of violence in GTA, the player is confronted with an exaggerated yet deeply resonant world that affords her an understanding of the sources of violence and allows her to destroy them. I used Eric and Alex in *Elephant* to frame the motivations for this discussion as examples of the situations in which GTA provides an alternative. It is important to acknowledge that the game they play was not similar to GTA but avatar-less; an environment already emptied and with nothing to offer, devoid of the very mechanisms which might avert such a tragedy. The game, as portrayed in the film, was ancillary and contextual, it was neither modeled on the school nor inciting the violence of the school. It only represents a void, an empty space that could be filled with an alternative mode of expression. Given that, as Rehak states, "[the avatar's] correspondence to embodied reality consists of a mapping not of *appearance* but *of control*," (107) the out of control situation in *Elephant,* through the performance of the avatar, would have allowed for a redistribution of control and a potential virtual catharsis for Eric and Alex.

Play-fighting is not so much a new concept as is it is a revision of a problematic one. The performative, revelatory, and culturally critical nature of the gameplay within GTA not only resembles the learning proposed within Antonin Artaud's *The Theater and Its Double* but also solves some of its primary complications. The most famous discussions within this work are Artaud's concepts of the "Theater of the Plague" and "The Theater of Cruelty." The former is his comparison of his ideal theater to a plague, in that it "bring[s] forth, the exteriorization of a depth of latent cruelty by means of which all the perverse possibilities of the mind, whether of an individual or a people, are localized" (30). The latter sets forth a loose framework that can be deployed to realize this goal. Initiating and then haunting Artaud's theories have always been the issues of representation and communication. In his preface, Artaud explains that he sees culture as confused and unable to understand its "hunger" and generating this confusion is "a rupture between things and words, between things and ideas and signs that are their representation" (7). Resulting in this breakdown of signification and understanding is a civilized man "whose faculty of deriving thoughts from acts, instead of identifying acts with thoughts, is developed to an absurdity" (8). Action is only interpreted after the fact rather than being a unity of signification— a meaningful act. Eric and Alex's rampage in *Elephant* is representative of this blind, meaningless action, which begs for interpretation after the fact with little result. GTA, in comparison, through its satirical criticism and performative space, fills violence with a meaning that can then be absorbed by the player. Significantly, Artaud links the absence of a mode of expression for the driving hunger within us all to "the unprecedented number of crimes whose perverse gratuitousness is explained only by our powerlessness to take complete possession of life" (9). Artaud's visionary theater was meant to repossess life and to satiate hunger and reveal a collective taste for crime, erotic obsessions, savagery, and other suppressed yet ultimately driving characteristics that were only finding expression in the criminal world.[7] These theories seem to illuminate the inexplicable drops in crime congruent with GTA's success.

The model that was meant to fulfill Artaud's concept and which seems to predict many of the functions of GTA is the Theater of Cruelty. While often misinterpreted as a reduction to violent spectacle, Artaud was careful to clarify that a Theater of Cruelty would only be "bloody when necessary but not systematically so" (122). His violence and cruelty, much like that of GTA, was not based on gore but on aggressively confronting passivity and horror and creating a metaphysical experience that transcended traditional theater by communicating through "the visual language of objects, movements, attitudes, and gestures" which would form a "language in space" (90). It was intended to be a deeply moving experience revealing the purity of signs and immersing the audience in a revelatory moment that would expose their suppressed tendencies and cause a reflection which would inform future action. However, Artaud's spatial language was dependent on expression beyond the capabilities of traditional language and representation, or as he says, "half-way between gesture and thought" (89).[8] Ultimately, due to the theater's reliance on the representational structure of actors and a stage, this was not possible.

The avatar, however, networks between the cruel experience of GTA and the player, facilitating Artaud's immersive spatial language and providing the tools with which to manufacture such signification. Play-fighting summons a spectral being which temporarily unifies the self and Other in ways the theater cannot. The space of GTA, filled with exaggeration and explosions of color and sound, fulfills Artaud's desire to turn the theater into a system of hieroglyphs (90). Immersed in this position of both self and Other within the carnage of hieroglyphs, the play-fighter's anxiety, desire, and cultural baggage are expressed in the grand orchestration of violent gesture throughout the space. However, these tendencies need only to be revealed and once expressed the player can separate from the Other and leave the game space and the incendiary mechanism of the Other behind. This death-drive or tendency to return to an earlier state is embodied in the player's irresistible urge to place the avatar in dangerous situations that often lead to its demise. The destruction of the player's puppet serves the symbolic function of freeing oneself from the outside influences that both encourage and condemn violence. CJ's violence, for example, while necessitated by his social situation in the narrative, is also condemned by the very society that is, in part, responsible for his circumstance. Through CJ's destruction and the eventual separation of player and avatar, the connections that produce violence are not only revealed but symbolically destroyed.

Becoming

Play-fighting, in its spatial networking and dynamic alteration of identity via the violent destruction of the Other, is a process of becoming. Understanding the nuances and significant ways in which GTA exposes exterior and interior sources of violence through performance, satire, and the politicizing myth and then facilitates the destruction of these obstacles explains the obvious gaps between consumption and production of violence in video games. The becoming is the structure of assemblage that allows this exploration of identity. Play-fighters in the world of GTA are not learning violent behaviors and becoming desensitized. As Eugene Thacker has proposed, the play-fighter is "developing new modes of navigating real world spaces, through the lens of simulation technologies...." This is not so much desensitization as "a resensitizing to the dematerialized and totally malleable world of simulation" (Penny 74–75). This malleable world of simulation, however, does not inherently create a criminal. Rather it provides a fantasy space of hypersignification that can enter into discourse with the outside world and simulate the exposure of latent tendency and the destruction of the sources of these tendencies. The play-fighter as avatar enters into an assemblage that does indeed become-criminal, but the destruction of the Other and violent break from the game severs the cables that compose this assemblage and leaves it[9] and the circumstances that produced it behind. The player walks away from GTA having performed violence rather than rehearsed it, leaving her to navigate the antagonistic spaces with a greater sensitivity to the structures and sources (both interior and exterior) of violent tendency.

Notes

1. On November 29, 2005, "motivated" by the "illicit sexual content" found within *San Andreas*, Senators Hilary Rodham Clinton and Joe Lieberman announced their proposal of the Family Entertainment Protection Act. This act would prohibit retailers from selling or renting video games rated "Mature" or "Adults Only" to minors. Additionally, it subjects retailers to federal audits to ensure compliance and calls for an annual review of the ratings system.

2. For an example of a recent behavioral study see C.A. Anderson and K.E. Dill, "Video Games and Aggressive Thoughts, Feelings, and Behavior in the Laboratory and Life," *Journal of Personality and Social Psychology* 78 (2000): 772–790. For an example of a recent physiological study see René Weber, Klaus Mathiak, and Ute Ritterfield, "Does Playing Violent Video Games Induce Aggression? Empirical Evidence of a Functional Magnetic Resonance Imaging Study," *Media Psychology*, 2006.

3. Henry Jenkins states that many scientific studies linking games and aggression "are based on the work of researchers who represent one relatively narrow school of research, 'media effects.' This research includes some 300 studies of media violence. But most of those studies are inconclusive and many have been criticized on methodological grounds. In these studies, media images are removed from any narrative context. Subjects are asked to engage with content that they would not normally consume and may not understand. Finally, the laboratory context is radically different from the environments where games would normally be played. Most studies found a correlation, not a causal relationship, which means the research could simply show that aggressive people like aggressive entertainment."

4. For more information about the Bureau of Justice statistics on crime rates see <http://www.ojp.usdoj.gov/bjs/welcome.html>. I am also indebted to the *Game Revo-*

lution article "The Truth About Violent Youth and Video Games" <http://gr.bolt. com/oldsite/articles/violence/violence.htm> for bringing many of these statistics to my attention.

5. This is because the GTA games are considered *paidia* or forms of play that possess structure and rules, but not to the extent there are winners and losers. Frasca adapted this term from Roger Callois and used it to illustrate that in GTA one can potentially kill prostitutes but it is not a goal required for advancement in the game. As he states in his essay "Simulation versus Narrative" very clearly, "Rhetorically, a game where you may kill sexworkers is very different from a game where you must kill them in order to win" (232).

6. Penny is referencing an interactive installation he viewed entitled *Kan Xuan* by Alexander Brandt. It consisted of a projection of an Asian woman on a crumpled piece of cloth. The user could stomp on her image and cause her pain, eventually making her fade away and then return for more. Penny saw this as an example of "the potential of electronic representations to encourage or reinforce behaviors in the real world, in this case racist and/or misogynist behaviors" (80).

7. See Artaud, *The Theater and Its Double*. 92.

8. Derrida has famously interpreted Artaud's vision as follows: "The stage, certainly, *will no longer represent*, since it will not operate as an addition, as the sensory illustration of a text already written, thought, or lived outside the stage, which the stage would then only repeat but whose fabric it would not constitute. The stage will no longer operate as the repetition of *present*, will no longer re-present a present...." (45)

Works Cited

Artaud, Antonin. *The Theater and Its Double*. New York: Grove, 1958.
Barthes, Roland. *Mythologies*. New York: Hill and Wang, 2000.
Burrill, Derek. "Check Out My Moves: Choreography in Virtual Space." *Social Semiotics* (2006).
Derrida, Jacques. "The Theater of Cruelty and the Closure of Representation." *Mimesis, Masochism, & Mime: The Politics of Theatricality in Contemporary French Thought.* Ed. Timothy Murray. Ann Arbor: U of Michigan P, 2000. 40–62.
Elephant. Dir. Gus Van Sant. HBO Films, 2003.
Frasca, Gonzalo. "Sim Sin City: Some Thoughts About *Grand Theft Auto III*." *Game Studies* 3.1 (2003). <http://www.gamestudies.org/0302/frasca/>.
Garry III, John P. "*Elephant*: An Ordinary High School Movie. Except That It's Not." *Jumpcut: A Review of Contemporary Media.* 47 (2005). <http://www.ejumpcut.org/currentissue/elephant/index.html>.
Grand Theft Auto III. New York: Rockstar, 2001.
Grand Theft Auto: San Andreas. New York: Rockstar, 2004.
Grand Theft Auto: Vice City. New York: Rockstar, 2002.
Hall, Stuart. "What Is This 'Black' in Black Popular Culture?" *Black Popular Culture*. Ed. Gina Dent. New York: New P, 1998. 21–33.
Jenkins, Henry. "Reality Bytes: Eight Myths about Video Games Debunked." *PBS: The Video Game Revolution*. <http://www.pbs.org/kcts/videogamerevolution/impact/myths.html>.
Peary, Gerald. "Interview with Gus Van Sant." *Geraldpeary.com.* <http://www.geraldpeary.com/interviews/stuv/van-sant-elephant.html>.
Penny, Simon. "Representation, Enaction, and the Ethics of Simulation." *First Person: New Media as Story, Performance, and Game*. Ed. Noah Wardrip-Fruin and Pat Harrigan. Cambridge: MIT P, 2004. 73–84.
Rehak, Bob. "Playing at Being: Psychoanalysis and the Avatar." *The Video Game Theory Reader*. Ed. Mark J.P. Wolf and Bernard Perron. New York: Routledge, 2003. 102–127.
"Senators Clinton, Lieberman Announce Federal Legislation to Protect Children

from Inappropriate Video Games." *Senator Hillary Rodham Clinton.* 29 Nov. 2005. <http://clinton.senate.gov/news/statements/details.cfm?id=249368&&>.

Sherry, John L. "The Effects of Violent Video Games on Aggression: A Meta-Analysis." *Human Communication Research* 27.3 (2001): 409–431.

Wartella, Ellen, and Byron Reeves. "Historical Trends in Research on Children and the Media: 1900–1960." *Journal of Communication* 35.2 (1985): 118–133.

Williams, Dmitri, and Marko Skoric. "Internet Fantasy Violence: A Test of Aggression in an Online Game." *Communication Monographs* 22.2 (2005): 217–233.

5. The Subversive Carnival of Grand Theft Auto: San Andreas

DAVID ANNANDALE

One of the defining characteristics of the Grand Theft Auto (GTA) series is the sheer size of each game. Size, here, is understood to mean the scope of the narrative, the geographical area over which the player roams, and the range of activities in which the player can engage. Each new console or PC entry in the series has been a bigger game than the one before, reaching a climax (for now) in *Grand Theft Auto: San Andreas (GTA:SA)*. The storyline is epic, recounting the struggle of Carl Johnson (CJ) to avenge the murder of his mother, purge his community of hard drugs, and consolidate the rule of the Grove Street Families on the streets of Los Santos. Not content with the bustling cities of *Grand Theft Auto III (GTA3)* and *Grand Theft Auto: Vice City, Grand Theft Auto: San Andreas (GTA:SA)* has CJ's quest sweep across an entire state, incorporating three major cities (Los Santos, San Fierro and Las Venturas, standing in, respectively, for Los Angeles, San Francisco and Las Vegas) and the rural regions between (farmland, desert and small town). It then caps everything off with full-on urban riots in Los Santos, a deliberate echo of the LA upheavals of 1992 (the era in which the game takes place). As for the activities that the player, in the form of CJ, gets up to, these include assassinations, arson, armed robbery, surveillance, military campaigns with remote-control model airplanes, evidence planting, freeing illegal immigrants from container ships, gang warfare and urban street racing, to name only a few of the requirements of the main, story-driving missions.

Numerous and varied as these missions are, it is the optional, incidental activities that create the illusion that San Andreas is a living, breathing world. At the player's discretion, and over and above an enormous miscellany of criminal activities, CJ can do such things as race bicycles, perform stunts, collect oysters while swimming, take pictures, work out at the gym, shop for clothes, hairstyles and tattoos, restore his energy and health by eating at different fast-food franchises, or gorge himself into obesity at the same establishments. Or he can simply drive around, channel-surfing through eleven radio stations (twelve if one counts the one made up of music installed on the hard drive by the player).

It is tempting, given the degree to which this world is fleshed out, to consider *GTA:SA* in the light of Jean Baudrillard's concepts of the hyperreal and the simulacrum. However, my interest here is in the game's immensity as a deliberate form of excess, and in the overtly satirical nature of every aspect of its imagined world. *GTA:SA* transforms huge swatches of American culture and society into ridiculous caricatures. From radio ads that are recognizable in form and style but subversively honest in content, to a vision of corruption that extends to all reaches of society, creating a world of inverted moral and ethical values, the game is a digital incarnation of Mikhail Bakhtin's concept of the carnivalesque. Like the works of Rabelais that Bakhtin celebrates, *GTA:SA* is so excessive in its size as to be encyclopedic. But to go further, its free-roaming form and the extraordinary contingency of its background events make it carnivalesque to an even greater degree than the carnivalized literature that Bakhtin celebrates, suggesting that the video game may be an art form particularly well suited to the embodiment of these energies. Further still, the hysterical reaction of political and other authorities to the game suggests a terror that this carnival exceeds its boundaries, that its subversion is real, and will drag the world outside the game into carnivalesque chaos.

Bakhtin describes four "carnivalistic categories" of activity. The first is "free and familiar contact among people" (*Problems* 123). All the usual barriers between different levels of social hierarchy are collapsed. This first category of activity thus leads to the second: "a new mode of inter-relationship between individuals" (123). Not only do people normally segregated from each other come into contact, but the manner in which they do is also purged of the restraints and expectations normally associated with their respective social classes. Carnival then goes beyond interpersonal connections:

> Linked with familiarization is a third category of the carnival sense of the world: *carnivalistic mésalliances.* A free and familiar attitude spreads over

everything: over all values, thoughts, phenomena, and things.... Carnival brings together, unifies, weds, and combines the sacred with the profane, the lofty with the low, the great with the insignificant, the wise with the stupid.

Connected with this is yet a fourth carnivalistic category, *profanation*: carnivalistic blasphemies, a whole system of carnivalistic debasings and bringings down to earth, carnivalistic obscenities linked with the reproductive power of the earth and the body, carnivalistic parodies on sacred texts and sayings, etc. [123, emphasis Bakhtin's].

Bakhtin here is talking about the medieval street festivals, but he might as well be describing daily existence in San Andreas.

San Andreas: A World of Mésalliances

A new player's first experience of being out on the streets of San Andreas can be both disorienting and intimidating. One finds their avatar, CJ, in the midst of a city as big as it is foreign, and it is also densely populated. Pedestrians stroll in all directions, offering up a stream of non-sequitur observations to CJ, to themselves, and to each other. When two pedestrians meet, bizarre casual conversations ensue. For example, after preliminary greetings, I heard the following exchange on the streets of San Fierro: "Ever touched fake breasts?" asks a lisping male. "I agree," replies the woman he is speaking to. "It's the best." Background events such as this have no bearing on the success or failure of the player's game, but they encapsulate the carnivalesque spirit of *GTA:SA*. The contact between the pedestrians is utterly free and familiar: they have but to meet head-on to engage in banter. The character models are distinct types and ages, with social hierarchies coded into their visual appearances, but, in keeping with carnival's elimination of these divisions, the middle-aged businessman is just as likely to ask the club girl if she has tried juggling with knives as he is the African Nationalist.

As the cited dialogue shows, the conversations are frequently very earthy and profane, but they are also good cases of *mésalliances*. Because each character sticks to his/her own particular obsessions, the conversations take on a surreal quality. The fact that the pedestrians greet one another and wish each other goodbye codes their interaction as an actual dialogue, and their tones of voice suggest that each is listening and responding to what the other is saying. But the content of the exchange is almost always a yoking together with violence of utterly unrelated topics. The fusion is invariably comical, as the player is made to see connections where none, outside of carnival, would exist. Thus, when the shirt-sleeved mystic asks the high-society woman if she can feel the spirits, and she tells him to try it naked, the player is invited to view the interchange not as utter nonsense, but as a somewhat opaque window onto erotico-metaphysics. Bakhtin's free and familiar contact between not just people but *everything* is thus taken to its fullest extension. The events taking place on the streets also have the randomness necessary to maintain the carnival's unpredictability. Orderly conversation can give way to mayhem without a moment's notice. Thus, I saw the society woman, after talking to the mystic, assault a police officer, which led to shots being fired and the nearby pedestrians running and screaming in blind panic.

Immersion in the Carnival of San Andreas

Given how lively the world that surrounds CJ is, one might be forgiven for wanting simply to have him walk around and watch.[1] However, Bakhtin reminds us that "carnival does not know footlights, in the sense that it does not acknowledge any distinction between actors and spectators.... Carnival is not a spectacle seen by the people; they live in it, and everyone participates because its very idea embraces all the people. While carnival lasts, there is no other life outside it" (*Rabelais* 7). Participation works at two levels here, one involving CJ, and the other the actual player. To begin with the first level, the extent of the carnivalization of the game's world is signaled by the fact that CJ is simultaneously important and unnecessary. He is, certainly, the narrative's protagonist, and some fairly large-scale events in the world happen because of him. One might well crown him the carnival king, a figure about which more is said below. But the vast majority of the population of San Andreas, even during the main story missions, regard him (when they notice him at all) as just another face in the crowd, to be admired or fought with only as the contingency arises.

CJ is obviously not a spectator; he participates in the carnival, but the carnival goes on around him regardless of his own actions. Sirens and gunshots, for instance, do not necessarily mean that the police are after CJ; they will often be in hot pursuit of, or engaged in fierce combat with, other computer-controlled characters, as if CJ's story were but one of many such concurrent tales of the naked city. To take a particularly concrete example, in the "555 We Tip" mission, CJ disguises himself as a car park valet, and waits for the District Attorney's car (in which he will plant drugs) to arrive. The player is shown the D.A.'s vehicle leaving an office building, and a minute or so can pass before the car arrives at the hotel. The implication is that the car is in transit. This illusion could be fostered by simply having the car appear on-screen after a given delay. This in itself would not add to the sense of carnival. However, I was forced to repeat this mission several times, and on one occasion, the car arrived badly damaged and missing its passenger door. In other words, it bore all the signs of its trip having been a highly eventful one. The carnival thus carries on far beyond what constitutes the player's horizon at any given moment. Similarly, on those occasions when planes mysteriously fall out of the sky to burst into flames on the street or against buildings, the player is left with the sense of playing in just one small corner of a vast game.

As for the second level of participation, and at the risk of belaboring the obvious, it is worth emphasizing the fact that one is a player, not a spectator. While in the game there is, as with any carnivalesque display, plenty to be observed, the engagement of the player is unlike that with any other narrative art form. A novel or a film will play out in the same way every time it is read or watched. The reader or viewer's interpretation of the narrative can alter, but the actual events depicted do not. In the case of a game such as *GTA:SA*, while the broader narrative arc is unalterable, the details of the arc are not. Depending on the player's choices, events take place in different orders or never occur at all, and the precise way in which each mission is completed is never the same twice.[2] For all the carnivalization of literature, the reader must still experience the carnival at a remove, and though a sufficiently active engagement with the text can arguably involve the reader in carnival strategies, that move is already well underway with a game (and is, in fact, the source of the principle social anxieties surrounding the game). For Bakhtin, from the end of the seventeenth century, the actual carnival disappears from European life, and with it goes the unmediated experience. The language of carnival, he writes, "cannot be translated in any full or adequate way into a verbal language, and much less into a language of abstract concepts, but it is amenable to a certain transposition into a language of artistic images that has something in common with its concretely sensuous nature; that is, it can be transposed into the language of literature" (*Problems* 122).

I would contend that the medium of the video game in general, and *GTA:SA* in particular, is as fully capable of carnivalization as is literature, but in some respects it goes further. Dean McWilliams argues that

> elements of [Bakhtin's] analysis of the novel can be applied, with even greater force, to film narrative. Film ... is not so much a new art as an elaborate fusion of existing arts: theater, photography, prose narrative, and music are among the many resources mobilized by electronic tech-

nology to create film narratives. In effecting this unique new fusion, the cinema combines and reconfigures the many genres and subgenres of the arts it absorbs. Film, then, might be termed the ultimate carnival of the arts and of the modes of discourse they encompass [247].

All of the above is also true of the contemporary video game. In fact, creative talent increasingly moves back and forth between the forms. Thus, composer Danny Elfman provides the music for *Fable*; J.T. Petty, the writer/director of *Soft for Digging* and *Mimic Sentinel*, is the writer of the *Splinter Cell* games; and *GTA:SA* lists Samuel L. Jackson, Chris Penn, Peter Fonda and James Woods among its voice actors.

A frequently stated goal for games is for them to become "interactive movies." While it is true that the cut scenes in many games are very cinematic, the drive to ape the other form, to be "movies plus" if you will, strikes me as potentially limiting. This is misguided medium envy, in the same sense that, at the time that cinema was still a young art form struggling for respectability, theorists such as Eisenstein drew comparisons between films and the novel. Calling games "interactive movies" is as much a shackling move as calling movies "visual novels." To the characteristics games share with films (a commonality made possible by the fact that both are audio-visual media with full motion), one must add a length associated with novels[3] and, of course, the impact that the player has on the narrative. It is this direct involvement that restores some of the unmediated carnival experience to the player.

Carnival Laughter and Minority Alliances

I have mentioned the humor of the street conversations. Here, let me be emphatic: *GTA:SA* is very, very funny, sometimes joyously, on other occasions in a very dark register. This range is characteristic of carnivalistic laughter, which is, Bakhtin, says, directed

> toward a shift of authorities and truths, a shift of world orders. Laughter embraces both poles of change, it deals with the very process of change, with *crisis* itself. Combined in the act of carnival laughter are death and rebirth, negation ... and affirmation.... This is a profoundly universal laughter, a laughter that contains a whole outlook on the world. Such is the specific quality of ambivalent carnival laughter [*Problems* 127].

The humor of *GTA:SA* can be purely situational: CJ is flabbergasted when he learns that Chinese gang leader Wu Zi Mu ("Woozie") is blind. How can this be possible, CJ wants to know, since he and Woozie just had a cross-country car race? "He's very lucky," is the reply. Woozie's refusal to let his blindness be a handicap becomes an ongoing source of humor, sometimes at CJ's expense—Woozie thrashes him at video games—and sometimes at Woozie's own—he does not carry a cane, and will run at full tilt with one arm outstretched, in one case slamming into a wall. This latter case does not feel like a descent into Helen Keller jokes, however. Poised, self-assured, supremely competent and loyal, Woozie is one of the most likeable characters in the game. His and CJ's friendship springs not out of necessity (though they do wind up working together hand in glove) but out of mutual respect. CJ helps Woozie in his battles with the Vietnamese gangs not because of ties of family and neighborhood, as is the case when CJ works with the ultimately treacherous Big Smoke and Ryder (missions that CJ is often reluctant to be dragged into in the first place), or because he is being forced to (as with the Officer Tenpenny and Mike Toreno missions), but because he *wants* to. The humor involving Woozie is almost always the laughter between friends. This is affirmative laughter, suggesting the possibility that things can be better than they are.

The friendship with Woozie is also part of the extension of carnival's free and familiar contact among people. Beyond the comical street carnival, this contact is also the locus of the game's more optimistic elements, and is a crucial element of the carnivalistic renewal. Though much of the game's conflict is rooted in racial tension, it is in the breaking down of racial barriers that the possibility of a better future is seen, and this is no small part of CJ's journey. Upon his arrival in Los Santos at the beginning of the game, he is instantly drawn back into the racial insularity of the Grove Street Families. One of the initial points of contention involves his sister, Kendl. Older brother Sweet is furious that her boyfriend, Cesar Vialpando, is Hispanic. CJ is initially deeply suspicious of Cesar, too, but his willingness to give Cesar a chance proves to be crucial. Grove Street disintegrates as Big Smoke and Ryder turn out to be traitors, and the dogmatic Sweet winds up in jail, but he and CJ survive thanks to Cesar's warning. Through Cesar, CJ cobbles together a multicultural alliance. The members of this group can be excluded from the mainstream power structure due to their race (Cesar, Woozie), but some of CJ's allies are Caucasians marginalized due to beliefs and lifestyle (conspiracy theorist The Truth) or physical weakness and interests (the nerdy model-builder Zero).

Gender marginalization plays a much smaller role, but is still addressed. Kendl, it must be said, is very much a background character, resurfacing now and then to pour cold water over some of the more lunatic excesses of the male characters, she does not do much beyond facilitate the alliance between CJ and Cesar. There is a vast number of strippers and prostitutes, and most of the other female characters are not much more than romantic interests (at best) for our hero, making it abundantly clear that this is not a game world designed with female players in mind, to put it mildly. Nonetheless, Cesar's cousin, Catalina, who provides most of the missions in the Badlands section of the game, is worth noticing. First seen fighting off two men in a bar, Catalina compensates for her double marginalization (of gender and of race) with hyperbolic aggressiveness, transforming herself into a very explicitly *femme castatrice*. She is the dominant force in the relationship with CJ (quite literally, in one instance, as she drags him screaming into a sexual encounter involving pulleys and chains). Catalina's violent assertion of self means that CJ reacts toward her with wariness, if not outright terror, and though theirs is still a real alliance, untarnished by betrayal, she leaves him at the end of the Badlands missions for the protagonist of *Grand Theft Auto III* (a male who, significantly, is mute).

Carnival, again, is ambivalent, and the color-blindness of CJ's alliance is a trait also shared, to a degree, by his enemies. His nemesis, Officer Frank Tenpenny, is African-American, and he has a Caucasian toady in his partner, Eddie Pulaski. Far from being marginal, however, Tenpenny has completely inserted himself into the corrupt power structure, making it his own in order to achieve absolute power over the marginalized of San Andreas. He has thus become the worst of the oppressors, and can only be defeated by carnival at its most intense and destructive: the riots at the climax of the game.

Carnival with a Purpose: Parody and Social Commentary

The humor of the game, then, is often very sharply edged. For all the lunacy of the improbable events and larger-than-life characters, the game is grounded in a very recognizable reality of poverty, corruption, and violent race relations. *Grand Theft Auto: San Andreas'* primary comedic weapon in addressing these issues is parody. Bakhtin writes:

> to the carnivalized genres, [parody] is ... organically inherent.... Parodying is the creation of a *decrowning double*; it is that same 'world turned inside out'.... In carnival, parodying was employed very widely, in diverse forms and degrees: various images (for example, carnival pairs of various sorts) parodied one another variously and from various points of view; it was like an entire system of crooked mirrors, elongating, diminishing, distorting in various directions and to various degrees [*Problems* 127].

Perhaps the most insistent parody of the game, and one of its best examples of the decrowning double, is the radio stations. Given how much time the player spends in one vehicle or another, the stations provide the audio accompaniment for the lion's share of the game. They have three primary functions. Firstly, they provide a soundtrack for the action, a soundtrack the player can determine by changing stations, but one that is also suggested either by the luck of the draw, depending on what happens to be playing in a given carjacked vehicle, or by having certain stations associated with certain characters (so the permanently stoned, aging hippy The Truth has the radio in his van, the "Mothership," tuned to the classic rock of KDST). Secondly, they help establish the historical era of the game (Radio X, the alternative rock station, programs the likes of L7, Rage Against the Machine and Soundgarden). Thirdly, and most strikingly, they engage in very pointed social satire.

This satire is accomplished through parody. In "Modern Parody and Bakhtin," Linda Hutcheon defines parody as "a form of imitation ... characterized by ironic inversion, not always at the expense of the parodied text" (88–9). Certainly, these phony radio stations are very good imitations. The DJs sound very authentic (and in fact some of the voice actors are actual DJs), but this authenticity is in the service of caricature, given that the convincing voices are spouting outrageous dialogue. DJ Sage of Radio X, for example, is the personification of Generation X apathy and resentment of the Baby Boomers ("Good morning, San Andreas. The Baby Boom is officially over. You are all irrelevant. Now die."). Meanwhile, talk radio WCTR's slogan is "We talk, you listen," and its newscasts are preceded by "We distort, you can't retort." The dialogue is outrageous because of its brutal honesty: these are radio stations that are up-front about the manipulative techniques used by the real thing. Here the target of the parody is the parodied text itself.

The situation is rather more complex when it comes to the ads that play on all the radio stations (and that are even incorporated in between songs of the player-defined track). Consider this jingle for the Cluckin' Bell fast food franchise:

> TWO WOMEN SING:
> Cockle-doodle-doo, we're a huge corporation
> Cockle-doodle-doo, and we can't be stopped
> All of you protesters can go to hell
> It's time for Cluckin' Bell
> From the factory farmer to your plate
> A chicken's life is a sorry state
> Pumped full of chemicals, what the hell
> —(a chicken sings the next line)—
> They even make my breasts swell!
> Filled full of hormones so they get fat

> At least we no longer slip in a rat
> I love chicken with a shitty smell
> And that's why I love Cluckin' Bell
> MAN: Cluckin' Bell! Suffering never tasted so good!
> ["Radio Commercials Script"].

Though the parodied form is the commercial jingle, and it does suffer the same kind of distortion and inversion as the DJ patter, the primary target is battery farming and other fast food practices. The same is true of the other commercials. Over and over again, the same kind of perverse honesty is apparent, with the narrators of the ads cheerfully presenting the appalling as if it were an unqualified good. The laughter here is bitter, and among the most pointed in the game. The commercials are grotesque exaggerations. But the picture of society that they paint is not. This parody lifts up the socio-cultural rock and invites the player to see what squirms beneath. This is Bakhtin's "system of crooked mirrors." Distorted though the reflections may be, they are still depicting a recognizable reality, one that, to go further, *demands* recognition. The form the distortion takes is an indication of the social ill that needs addressing, or the tyranny that needs to be brought down.

Parody, Hutcheon points out, can be conservative, its inversions implying a norm that it ultimately supports. But this is less likely to be the case when, as Bakhtin describes, carnival laughter spares no one. A case in point is "The Wild Traveler," one of the programs on WCTR. Here, the British-accented and refined James Pedeaston is locked in combat with his callers. He represents cosmopolitanism and sophistication, and he extols the glory of travel. His callers are worst-case scenarios of American provincialism, spewing venom at anyone who would want to see the outside world. Pedeaston calls these people philistines, and the player is invited to agree with his judgment, so disagreeable and xenophobic are these callers. One might see the game lining up with an elitist, upper-class view of the middle-class as blinkered troglodytes. But then Pedeaston (whose name uncomfortably echoes "pederast") reveals himself to be a predatory sexual tourist, shamelessly exploiting a Sri Lankan youth for his own pleasures. He is also the very picture of the navel-gazing intellectual:

PEDEASTON: Where are you?
CALLER: I'm on a cliff.
PEDEASTON: How romantic.
CALLER: I want to jump.
PEDEASTON: I know what you mean. Jump into the unknown.... Where are you? Kenya?
CALLER: Verdant Bluffs.

PEDEASTON: Loathsome place. I'd jump too if I were you.
CALLER: I want to go to Hell.
PEDEASTON: Me too. Buy a refrigerator magnet when you get there. On
with the show!
Any callers?
["Radio Commercials Script"]

Pedeaston is so caught up in his own musings that he at first fails to realize that the caller is suicidal. When the information does penetrate, he doesn't care. The caller is beneath notice, his cry for help unable to pierce the host's self-absorption. Pedeaston therefore represents no more an acceptable norm than do his opponents.

The overall effect of the radio stations, then, is the creation of a sustained satirical environment. There are occasions, notably during the Badlands chapter, where the player has little choice but to drive vast distances between missions, and with a decrease in urgency of the action, the radio parodies claim more attention, driving home the idea of a society desperately in need of renewal. The carnival laughter here has a greater edge because this society is only *apparently* the real world turned upside down. The satirical point is that the exaggeration is not really that extreme. The inversion is that in San Andreas, these flaws are flaunted and celebrated. Les Benzies, president of the Edinburgh-based developer Rockstar North, describes his team as "fascinated observers of the American condition" (Price 40) and goes on to detail the extent of the research into the cities and the culture that was done to shape the game. This desire to "completely capture the feel of the West Coast 15 years ago" (40) highlights the importance of adding verisimilitude to the carnival world. The targets that are to be brought down are thus brought into sharper focus. The line between the game world and the real world, meanwhile, is blurred. The parodies, again, work as crooked mirrors. The laughter may be generated by the behavior of the game world, but the actual target of the laughter is in the real world.

Furthermore, these targets extend far beyond the boundaries of *GTA:SA* itself. With an entire state to play with, the game has most aspects of American society readily at hand to satirize. But in the character of Mike Toreno, the game looks to wider, geo-political travesties, and shows corruption (and worse) infecting all branches of government. At first appearing to be a powerful drug dealer, Toreno turns out to be a government agent. The agency he works for is unnamed. His fight is ostensibly against communism (which might infect the Midwest and thus people would wind up "sharing instead of buying stuff"), but his activities are exclusively criminal: dealing drugs and engaging in lethal conflict with other federal agencies. Toreno is a bureaucrat who fights turf wars with heavy artillery, as demonstrated in the following exchange:

> TORENO: Listen Carl, we've got a problem. Some traitors from another department think they can help the overseas situation by financing militaristic dictators in exchange for arms contracts.
> CJ: Hey, ain't that exactly what you do?
> TORENO: Well, kinda, but we get to pick our dictators, degenerates that *we* can control. We try to stay the hell away from these guys with *principles*, 'cause that just muddies the waters.... Okay, so, of course these *idiots* have stolen a consignment of land mines, and they plan to offload them in the Middle East, cause a little ruckus, and everyone goes crazy and have a lot of prob ... I mean ... Carl. Do you like maiming people? I'm curious.

As Toreno starts explaining the implications of the land mine deal, he speaks faster and faster until he becomes virtually unintelligible. He is merely going through the motions of justifying his actions, and has no real interest in what will actually happen in the Middle East, as he becomes very vague about the consequences, and then interrupts himself. He then returns to what really interests him: violence without fear of retribution. This, then, is the laughter of *GTA:SA* at its most bitter. The world's problems are a sandbox for the likes of Toreno to play in. CJ and civilians overseas are so much collateral damage in Toreno's battles with his colleagues, battles that are as petty and meaningless as Zero's remote-control model warfare.

GTA:SA and the Outside World: The Threat and Promise of Unending Carnival

Carnival laughter, Bakhtin emphasizes, "is universal in scope; it is directed at all and everyone, including the carnival's participants" (*Rabelais* 12). CJ and, by extension, the player are as likely to be laughed at as any of the other characters. CJ is very much the straight man to Catalina's explosive personality and The Truth's opaque ravings (he also begins to feel extremely unwell and light-headed when he and The Truth must set fire to an enormous marijuana grow-op). When the player fails, and CJ "dies" or is arrested, the words "WASTED" or "BUSTED" appear in a rather unsubtle mockery of one's feeble attempts. Insult is added to injury in cases of missions that are failed in the company of other characters: "You're a waste of good balls," Catalina helpfully informs us.[4] The laughter directed at CJ and the player is, however, of a different order than that targeting the rest of the gaming world. "The primary carnivalistic act," Bakhtin writes, "is the *mock crowning and subsequent decrowning of the carnival king*" (*Problems* 124). The carnival king, though a participant of the festival, is nonetheless singled out, much as CJ gathers importance in (without, again, ever being necessary to the functioning of) the world of *GTA:SA*. After all, the title of the first Badlands episode, when CJ is forced out of Los Santos by Tenpenny and Pulaski, is "King in Exile." When he is "WASTED" or "BUSTED," he and the player are decrowned, and so the challenge for the player is to keep the crown on CJ's head for as long as possible. No death is ever permanent, however. This is as it should be: "Under this ritual act of decrowning a king lies the very core of the carnival sense of the world—*the pathos of shifts and changes, of death and renewal. Carnival is the festival of all-annihilating and all-renewing time*" (*Problems* 124). Unlike most other games, when CJ's health drops to zero, he isn't really dead. He is taken to hospital, and re-emerges on the streets, lighter of wallet and stripped of his weapons (which are the staff of authority in this world). Much the same happens post-arrest. So CJ is constantly brought down and raised up again. The ultimate in annihilation—the riots—can lead to the ultimate in CJ's renewal, and since the game itself can be played indefinitely beyond the conclusion of the story missions, CJ is never permanently decrowned. The carnival is forever, and so is its king's reign.

The eruption of the riots in an already carnivalesque setting is particularly significant when considering the objections that have been raised to the idea that Bakhtin's carnival has any real subversive or liberatory qualities. Most frequently, the point has been made that carnival is temporary, and its subversion is sanctioned. Citing Bakhtin's own words, Linda Hutcheon points out that he describes "'temporary' 'suspension' and not permanent destruction of prevailing norms" (99), norms whose existence is emphasized by their very inversion. Umberto Eco also emphasizes the authorized (and thus defanged) nature of carnival. He argues that when "an unexpected and nonauthorized carnivalization suddenly occurs in 'real' everyday life, it is interpreted as revolution (campus confrontations, ghetto riots, blackouts, sometimes true 'historical' revolutions). But even revolutions produce a restoration of their own" (7). Nothing, he states, can remain carnivalesque forever.

What then, of the carnival in *GTA:SA*? The riots erupt out of a sense of legitimate grievance (the dropping of the charges against the hated Tenpenny), but they are not a liberatory carnival in which CJ and his friends rejoice. They are a threat to be contained, where possible. They nevertheless provide the context in which the tyranny of Tenpenny will finally be ended. If the riots are carnival at its most uncontrolled, then it should be no surprise that carnival's ambivalence is also at an extreme. The riots are dangerous, but they are also the cleansing fire that leads to renewal.

Outside the narrative of the game, the same questions regarding carnival, its temporary and authorized nature, persist. The nature of gaming implies a temporary activity—the player enters the carnival, wreaks merry havoc for a period of time, and then shuts the game off, returning to the real world. The same, of course, can be said for any art form— no audience engages with any medium permanently. Furthermore, as Robert Stam observes, "the political limitations of real-life carnivals are not necessarily those of carnivalesque strategies in art" (96). In fact, Bakhtin argues that "it is only in literature that popular festive forms can achieve the 'self-awareness' necessary for effective protest" (Wills 86). Carnivalized art, to repeat, is not the carnival itself, but the translation of its tactics and characteristics into a new form, but with the same goals. Among these goals: "the highest earthly authority were put to shame and ridiculed to force them to *renew themselves*" (*Problems* 126–7). One is loathe to grant too much power to any art form, let alone one specific work, but it is interesting, at this point, to reconsider the controversy surrounding *GTA:SA*.

I will not revisit the brouhaha in detail (the very existence of this book is testament to the game's high visibility, due in no small part to that controversy). Briefly, then, the recurring fear, among critics of the game, is that what happens in the game might not stay in the game. The "Hot Coffee" furor reached a lunatic climax of sorts with Senator Hilary Clinton calling for a federal investigation into the game (and here one cannot help but think of carnival's goal of making the highest earthly authorities appear ridiculous). Clinton's comments are typical of the anxieties surrounding the game: "In [a] speech to media experts and child advocates, [Clinton] singled out *Grand Theft Auto* as particularly harmful, saying it 'has so many demeaning messages about women and so encourages violent imagination and activities and it scares parents.... They're playing a game that encourages them to have sex with prostitutes and then murder them. You know, that's kind of hard to digest'" (*USA Today*). I will not dwell on the specifics of the "Think of the Children" nature of the argument, other than to remark that, distorted description of the game aside, *Grand Theft Auto: San Andreas'* narrative voice is no more aimed at children than is *Reservoir Dogs*. The interesting aspect of the worry over the corrupting influence of games today is that it rehearses the same anxieties as did the movies, and before them the novel, and before that the theater. The perennial fear that art will lead to unregulated behavior suggests that Bakhtin's carnival, in its artistic form, is perhaps *not* so temporary after all.

I am not arguing that the game necessarily does alter behavior, anymore than any other work of art must. But its parody is very pointed, not simply engaging in mockery for its own sake. Oddly enough, *GTA:SA* does, like any satire, take certain moral positions (it is quite ferociously anti-drug, and one of the few characters CJ takes a special satisfaction in killing is Jizzy, whom he condemns for being a pimp and a pusher). What is important here is the *perception* that the game is dangerous. Thanks to this perception, the question of whether or not a game intended for older players actually modifies behavior becomes irrelevant. The game is marked as the sort of nonauthorized carnival Eco describes. The denunciations from on high ironically grant the game the very powers the hegemonic forces fear. Playing the game therefore becomes an act of unauthorized rebellion. Carnivalization, in this way, gains the potential to break out of its traditional limits, as the player meets the game halfway. The player is engaging in an act of carnival simply by deciding to play. The result, I contend, is carnivalized art in its purest, most effective form: play with a purpose.

Notes

1. This is precisely what the creators of one example of machinima have done. Machinima is cinema made using video game footage. The most popular example is the Red vs. Blue humorous shorts set in the *Halo* universe. "My Trip to Liberty City" has the protagonist appear, not as a gangster, but as a Canadian tourist visiting the sights of *GTA3*.

2. There is not even any need to complete any of the storyline at all. One player I observed avoided the missions entirely. Instead, she was content to carjack one vehicle after another and drive around at random, creating ever increasing chaos with her passage.

3. Given, as one review puts it, that in *San Andreas* there are enough "activities to keep you busy for over 200 hours" (Hsu 114), the novel length comparison might need to be reconsidered, unless the novel one is thinking of is *Remembrance of Things Past.*

4. *GTA:SA* is not the only game to carnivalize the player's "deaths." *The Bard's Tale* is a game-long parody of *Dungeons & Dragons*-style role-playing, and includes a narrator who delightedly chortles "That really makes my day" when the ill-mannered and venal protagonist succumbs to his enemies.

Works Cited

Bakhtin, Mikhail. *Problems of Dostoevsky's Poetics.* Trans. Caryl Emerson. Minneapolis: U of Minnesota P, 1984.
_____. *Rabelais and His World.* Trans. Hélène Iswolsky. Bloomington: Indiana UP, 1984.
Bogenn, Tim and Rick Barba. *Grand Theft Auto: San Andreas Official Strategy Guide.* Indianapolis: Pearson, 2005.
"Clinton Seeks Grand Theft Auto Probe." *USA Today* 14 July 2005 <http://www.usatoday.com/news/washington/2005-07-14-clinton-game_x.htm>.
Eco, Umberto. "The Frames of Comic 'Freedom.'" *Carnival!* Ed. Thomas A. Sebeok. Berlin: Mouton, 1984. 1–9.
Grand Theft Auto: San Andreas. Rockstar, 2005.
"*GTA:SA* Radio Commercials Script."< http://db.gamefaqs.com/computer/doswin/file/grand_theft_auto_sa_commercial.txt>.

Hsu, Dan. Rev. of *Grand Theft Auto: San Andreas. Electronic Gaming Monthly* 194: 114.

Hutcheon, Linda. "Modern Parody and Bakhtin." *Rethinking Bakhtin: Extensions and Challenges.* Ed. Gary Saul Morson and Caryl Emerson. Evanston: Northwestern UP, 1989. 87–103.

McWilliams, Dean. "Bakhtin in Brooklyn: Language in Spike Lee's *Do the Right Thing.*" *Carnivalizing Difference: Bakhtin and the Other.* Ed. Peter I. Barta et al. London: Routledge, 2001. 247–261.

Price, Tom. "*Grand Theft Auto: San Andreas*: The Prodigal Gangster Returns." *Official Xbox Magazine* 45: 36–44.

Stam, Robert. *Subversive Pleasures: Bakhtin, Cultural Criticism, and Film.* Baltimore: Johns Hopkins UP, 1989.

Wills, Clair. "Upsetting the Public: Carnival, Hysteria and Women's Texts." *Bakhtin and Cultural Theory.* 2nd ed. Ed. Ken Hirschkop and David Shepherd. Manchester: Manchester UP, 2001. 85–108.

6. Grand Theft Video:

Running and Gunning for the U.S. Empire

Dennis Redmond

Comedy, as a famous saying goes, is a loaded gun—pointing it in the wrong direction can be fatal. What stamps Rockstar's Grand Theft Auto series as a landmark in the videogame culture, however, is its devastatingly accurate sense of humor. While other games outshone *Grand Theft Auto III (GTA3)* and its successors *Grand Theft Auto: Vice City (GTA:VC)* and *Grand Theft Auto: San Andreas (GTA:SA)* in areas such as control systems or visual effects, none could match the series' intoxicating blend of open-ended game-play, outrageous action sequences, and uproarious satire. In an epoch of nightmarish political regression, Rockstar gave the world the comic relief it desperately needed, by staging a prison-break from the jail-house of the U.S. Empire.

This is a remarkable achievement, considering the game industry's chronic inability to develop a funnybone. Game companies are notorious for churning out legions of formulaic shooters, soporific driving simulations, hackneyed role-playing games and lead-footed crime thrillers. Yet, recent Grand Theft Auto games somehow fuse the intensity of the shooter, the kinetic energy of the racing game, the immersive questing of the role-playing game, and the cat-and-mouse suspense of the gangster tale into a new kind of urban action game. The result deserves the name "grand theft video," due to its capacity to parody, pastiche and subvert vast swathes of the mainstream media culture.

The key to Rockstar's success was its willingness to shine a spotlight on the dank underbelly of the U.S. Empire. One of the most astonishing realities of U.S. society during the late 20th century has been the mass incarceration of its own citizens. Currently, more than 5 million Americans are in jail, prison or on parole in the self-proclaimed land of the free. This is a population larger than the entire prison population of the rest of the planet. By contrast, the fundamental narrative premise of the Grand Theft Auto series is the almost unlimited freedom of the game-world—which includes the freedom to escape from the Empire's jails, over and over again. The result is one of the great mass media burns on that Empire ever created, a pungent social satire refreshingly free of heavy-handed bombast or hairshirt moralizing.

This is not to say that the series is above criticism. For all of its achievements, it also has some glaring weaknesses. These include occasionally clunky controls, repetitive mission levels, meandering storylines and a complete lack of credible female characters. Still, it's worth asking why Rockstar succeeded so brilliantly, precisely where so many other game companies failed. Part of the credit belongs to the game designers at DMA, a quirky game studio based in Scotland. DMA's first two versions of the game, *Grand Theft Auto* (1997) and *Grand Theft Auto 2* (1999), pioneered many of the interactive elements of the Grand Theft Auto series, but experienced limited success due to their 2D interface. *Grand Theft Auto III* was the first true 3D version of the game, and its runaway success in 2000 led Rockstar to buy DMA outright in 2001. More often than not, the sale of a game company signals the death-knell of its creative life. Rockstar is to be commended for bucking the trend, and investing the post-production resources necessary to flesh out the promise of DMA's original scenario.

Perhaps Rockstar's biggest coup was delivering just the right game, at just the right time, to just the right audience. For most of the 1990s, the only games capable of rendering large-scale 3D worlds required expensive personal computers. As a result, the most innovative 3D games were developed for the personal computer market—most famously, id Software's *Doom* (1993) and *Quake* (1995–1997) games, as well as Valve's magnificent *Half Life* (1998). All this changed, thanks to the arrival of the PlayStation 2, X-box and Gamecube consoles in 2000–2001. Suddenly, for a fraction of the cost of a high-end computer, millions of consumers could play 3D games equal to or superior to anything the personal computer could offer.

Rockstar seized this window of opportunity to do three things that no game firm had done before. First, its designers expanded the concept of playable game-worlds pioneered by Nintendo's classic Mario and Zelda franchises, and honed to perfection by Valve's *Half Life* and Hideo Kojima's *Metal Gear* franchise. The virtual cities of the Grand Theft Auto series pulsate with real-time traffic, realistic weather effects, and impromptu conversations with passersby. While large open areas made most other games slow and tedious, Rockstar cleverly built vehicle movement into its game-world, creating a virtual space large enough to be drivable, but detailed enough to be walkable.

Second, Rockstar filled its game-worlds with citations from a dazzling array of other mass media, ranging from the Hong Kong martial arts thriller to the world music industry. For example, *GTA3* parodies the Mafia epic and the action buddy film, *GTA:VC* borrows from the soundtrack and set-design of the *Miami Vice* TV series and the cocaine gangster movie, while *GTA:SA* pastiches the early 1990s gangbanger film and early 1990s hip hop. Third, Rockstar took the open source software revolution to heart by privileging public over proprietary game-space. Surprising as it sounds, *GTA3*'s game-worlds contain not a single iota of real-world advertising. All of the vehicles, ads, and corporate icons featured in the game are parodies or fabrications. Even the one seeming exception, namely Rockstar's own logo, turns out to prove the rule: the logo signals nearby bonus items to players.

Individually, each of these changes marked a significant advance. Collectively, they sparked a revolution in gaming. Simply, most videogames depict static worlds, through which players have to move. But *GTA3* presented a world that moves along with its players. This sounds simple, but creating such a world is fiendishly difficult.

The reason is that showing a world is very different from making it playable. Surprisingly few of the tools and techniques developed by filmmakers and video artists work well in videogames, mostly because games are driven by player interaction rather than image or sound selection. Game designers have learned to compensate by limiting the on-screen action to a single memorable building or structure. The wondrous opening sequence of Hideo Kojima's *Metal Gear Solid 2* (2001), for example, showcases Snake against the silvery girders of New York's George Washington bridge, while the explosive finale of *Max Payne* takes place inside the glass-and-steel vault of the fictional Aesir corporate tower.

Rockstar's solution to this problem was ingenious. Rather than trying to duplicate a real city with millions of cars and individuals, its game designers reduced the problem to manageable size in two ways. First, they divided a single city into recognizable neighborhoods, often based on real-world urban districts. For example, Liberty City features a New York–style Chinatown, a Little Italy, and various lower-class, middle-class and upper-class neighborhoods. Similarly, Vice City has Miami's Cuban and Haitian neighborhoods, and resort and beach districts, while *GTA:SA* offers San Francisco's hills and Golden Gate bridge, Los Angeles' Watts Towers and freeways, and Las Vegas' casinos and desert landscape.

Second, Rockstar's designers linked these neighborhoods with dense networks of roads, pathways and transport systems. Because the game software could not realistically depict the images of more than a handful of cars and trucks, let alone the tens of thousands of people in urban crowds, *GTA3* compensated by filling in these networks with layers of sound. Where other games have eyes, *GTA3* and later games have ears. Fenders snap, engines roar, horns honk, trains clack, passersby shout, helicopters chop, and tires screech, sometimes all at once. These sound-layers are accompanied by sound-cues, ranging from footsteps and car horns to travel noise and weather effects, which help to orient players in the game-world. These games also employ silence to good effect, particularly on stealth missions. This is especially remarkable, considering that sound-design has been the perennial Achilles heel of the videogame culture. For decades, game designers have focused more on graphical effects than on auditory ones. The honorable exception has been Shigeru Miyamoto, who has always managed to balance Nintendo's stylish in-game visuals with some of the most memorable sound-tracks in videogame history. It's also worth noting that all of the truly great videogames of the early 2000s, ranging from Remedy's *Max Payne* to Capcom's *Devil May Cry*, have followed in Miyamoto's footsteps, by making their sound-tracks an integral part of their game-worlds.

In essence, Rockstar's designers retrofitted the visuals of American place with the acoustics of multinational space. The result was an unprecedented fusion of game-play freedom with real-time intensity. As a player, you can go anywhere you please, any time you like. You can drive, steer, and pilot hundreds of vehicles (a miniature on-screen map helps you navigate the city). You can listen to any sound-track you wish, on several in-game radio stations. Passersby react to your presence, friends will aid you and enemies will chase you, and so forth.

It's important to stress that while Rockstar's game-world is extraordinarily immersive, this is not because it is even remotely realistic. Paradoxically, it succeeds precisely because it is so utterly *unrealistic.* For example, there are no traffic jams, streets are far wider than in real life, cars routinely slam into each other and fall to pieces, and above all, you are given the completely unrealistic (but astonishingly exhilarating) freedom to fail. There are usually several ways of completing a mission or assignment, and players are given plenty of opportunities to acquire specific skills such as flying a plane or learning to swim. If you don't complete a mission, there's no penalty—just reequip and try again. Even your character's occasional demise in a fiery car-wreck signals nothing more onerous than a trip to the emergency room. You reappear outside the game-world's hospital, a little lighter in the wallet but hopefully wiser for wear. There is no "game over" in *GTA3* and later games, there is just gaming. This openness also applies to your player-character's actions. It is true that you can play the role of the villain, and assault and rob innocent civilians. But you pay a price. The police will chase you, forcing you to either bribe them or pay money to disguise your vehicle. It's much easier to earn money legitimately as a taxi driver, courier, firefighter or medic. The fundamental lesson of the game is that small-time crime doesn't pay, only hard work and meticulously-planned heists against the real criminals—the ones which infest penthouses and corporate boardrooms—do.

One of the greatest achievements of the Grand Theft Auto series is its unflinching satire of two of the most noxious political ideologies of those boardrooms, namely market fundamentalism (also known as neoliberalism) and its dim-witted provincial cousin, petro-fundamentalism.[1] Money, in Rockstar's far-from-satirical game-world, can buy just about anything—guns, police protection, and occasionally entire governments. The only thing money cannot buy is the loyalty of the in-game radio stations. These stations are truly one of the high points of the Grand Theft Auto games, mixing live skits, talk radio parodies, and bogus advertisements with a slew of top tier musical hits from the 1980s and 1990s. The result is an unprecedented burn on the U.S. consumer culture, a mediatic Molotov cocktail that torches everything from get-rich-quick hucksters to sleazy neoconservative politicians. Much of the credit for *GTA3's* sound-track goes to Craig Conner and Stuart Ross, who created and mixed many of the tracks. Particularly impressive is reggae station K-JAH, which samples a highly underrated 1981 album, *Scientist Rids the World of the Evil Curse of the Vampires,* mixed by legendary producer Henry "Junjo" Laws. The hip-hop station, Game Radio FM, features hip-hop artists such as Royce Da 5'9" (the Detroit rap artist who co-wrote the superb "Bad Meets Evil" track on Eminem's *Slim Shady LP*). In a nod to the 1980s gangster movies, the Flashback 95.6 station plays songs featured on Brian DePalma's *Scarface.* Meanwhile, the Chatterbox FM station features one uproarious sketch after another, co-written by real life U.S. radio star Lazlow Jones and Rockstar's own Dan Houser.

Grand Theft Auto reaches its pinnacle in *GTA:VC,* which plays off its sparkling sound-track against every 1980s visual cliché in the book, from pastel clothing to the *Miami Vice* TV show. The play-list is astounding, covering hits as diverse as Nena's "99 Luftballons" and the Buggles' "Video Killed the Radio Star" to Michael Jackson's "Billie Jean." Station V-rock features classic heavy metal by Ozzie Osbourne and David

Lee Roth, Motley Crue and others, while the Wildstyle station showcases the earliest hip hop tracks of Afrika Bambaataa, Grandmaster Flash and Run DMC. There is also an R&B station and a Latin music station, featuring classics by Tito Puente and others.

The talk radio sequences are truly priceless. Station KCHAT features side-splitting interviews with a fictional heavy metal band, Love Fist (several in-game missions involve getting this band into—and out of—trouble). Meanwhile, VCPR (Vice City Public Radio) offers a hilariously snide send-up of National Public Radio. One of the funniest sketches is an interview with a corrupt and sleazy Far Right politician named Alex Shrub (voiced by Chris Lucas), a patent reference to a certain real-life Southern political dynasty we could all name. *GTA:VC* is Grand Theft Auto at its smartest, savviest and most politically astute. Unfortunately, this also marks the point when the franchise begins to go into decline. This is surprising, considering that the next installment of the series, *GTA:SA*, has some of the most extensive environments and the most varied missions to date. There are now three cities to explore instead of just one, and large outdoor areas to swim, climb and fly through. *GTA:SA* also broke new ground by introducing the first African American player-character of the series, Carl Johnson (CJ) (superbly voiced by Young Maylay). In fact, the game has one of the most multicultural roster of characters, music and environments ever assembled in a videogame. K-JAH makes a welcome return, and there are early 1990s techno, dance and Latin music stations, brimming with dazzling hip hop tracks from Big Daddy Kane, Public Enemy, Cypress Hill, Ice Cube and Kid Frost. Even the radio sketches by Lazlow Jones and Dan Houser are as mordantly funny as ever.

Yet, despite moments of gravity-defying zaniness, *Grand Theft Auto: San Andreas* has a number of gnawing structural limitations. Prime among these is Grand Theft Auto's stereotypical male characters, as well as its tendency to privilege specific aspects of American place over the narrative possibilities of multinational space. This was less of an issue in *GTA3*, due to the low profile of Claude Speed, the game's player-character, and the endless variety of missions. In *GTA:VC*, Ray Liotta's fine voice-acting and the game's inexhaustible storehouse of 1980s media quotations paper over this contradiction. In *GTA:SA*, however, the simmering tension between American place and multinational space erupts with the irresistible force of the 1991 Los Angeles uprising, the key event cited by the conclusion of the game. CJ, the main character of *GTA:SA*, is an ex-gangbanger trying to clean up his life and his drug-riddled neighborhood. He is forced to take on the Establishment, however, after being framed by crooked cops. The main storyline follows CJ's running battle with Tenpenny (voiced by Samuel Jackson), a corrupt African American cop implicated in the murder of CJ's mother. Eventually CJ acquires friends and allies from outside his community, ranging from Mexican-American Cesar to Chinese-American Woozie (Wu Zi Mu), as well as sympathetic white allies such as Mike Toreno. This is very much in keeping with the corporate multiculturalism of the late 1990s, namely the ideology of a family-friendly, ethnically diverse capitalism that glosses over the monstrous realities of U.S. racism with slick multicultural marketing.

One of *Grand Theft Auto: San Andreas'* great achievements is to peel off the layers of this marketing, revealing the cauldron of violence beneath. By the same token, perhaps its greatest limitation is its inability to depict the true source of that violence, namely the U.S. Empire. We noted previously that five million U.S. citizens are in jail, in prison or on parole. This outrageous number has an even more outrageous corollary: 44% of all inmates are African American. A report by Human Rights Watch calculated that one out of every ten African American men between the ages of 20 to 29 is incarcerated in the United States. The primary reason, notes the report, is racial disparities in the sentencing of drug offenders—a polite way of saying, carceral racism.[2]

The social roots of this racism can be traced back to the political triumph of neoliberalism in the late 1970s, which smashed trade unions, razed the U.S. industrial base, and enriched the few at the expense of the many. While the rich flourished as never before, real hourly wages for the vast majority of Americans either stagnated or fell.[3] In retrospect, the prison boom has been a diabolically effective way of scapegoating the victims of neoliberalism. Instead of taxing the rich or funding education for all, the government's resources are increasingly limited to jailing the poor and funding obscene colonial wars.

The fundamental narrative dilemma facing *GTA:SA* is that CJ's quest for personal redemption cannot serve as a template of collective resistance to neoliberalism. To be sure, there are moments that hint at such a possibility. The "Reuniting the Families" episode of the game depicts a Black Panther–style neighborhood uprising, crushed by brutal repression and internal betrayal. One could also point to CJ's belated rescue of Madd Dogg (voiced by legendary rap artist Ice-T), or CJ's mission to help Cesar reclaim control of the Latino neighborhood, as examples of multicultural solidarity. But these tantalizing possibilities are never fleshed out with actual game-play. One could easily imagine missions where the street gangs unite to fight Los Santos' power-elites, or where CJ becomes the ally of the social movements of Central and Latin America.

That said it would be unfair to dismiss CJ as Bojangles with a shotgun. He is simply the latest iteration of the depoliticized, mainstream late 20th century African American media star, in the lineage from Richard Roundtree's eponymous Shaft in the 1970s to Mr. T in the 1980s, and finally to Laurence Fishburne's Morpheus in the *Matrix* trilogy.

It doesn't have to be this way. Videogames ranging from *Max Payne* to *Devil May Cry* have found creative ways to outflank and defuse the noxious racism, sexism and other malignant identity-politics that permeate the mass media, usually by means of a subversive geopolitics.[4] For example, Rockstar's game designers could have accessed the rich archives of independent African American film. Given the early 1990s setting of *GTA:SA*, this could include everything from Melvin Van Peebles' *Sweet Sweetback's Baad Asssss Song* (1971) and Sidney Poitier's revisionist Western, *Buck and the Preacher* (1972), all the way to Charles Burnett's *To Sleep with Anger* (1990) and Julie Dash's *Daughters of the Dust* (1991).

In fairness to Rockstar, some of the most interesting incidental characters do hint at independent and non–U.S. media genres. Catalina is a nod in the direction of the Zapata film, The Truth alludes to the countercultural film and paranoid thriller, Zero refers to the hacker movies, while sight-challenged Woozie is the Chinese-American version of Zatoichi, the legendary blind Japanese swordmaster who stars in countless Japanese films (including a superb contemporary remake by Takeshi Kitano). Perhaps the closest *GTA:SA* comes to its own self-critique is the figure of Mike Toreno, the sleazy national security agent. Toreno is the rough equivalent of Bill Clinton, someone who understands the language and mentality of the streets, while faithfully serving neoliberalism. Some of the best and most revealing dialogue in *GTA:SA* takes place at the beginning of the "Stowaway" mission:

> *CJ is at the airfield. Three cars and a plane arrive at the airstrip.*
> TORENO: "Listen, Carl. We've got a problem. Some traitors from another department think they can help the 'overseas situation' by financing militaristic dictators in exchange for arms contacts."
> CJ: "Hey, ain't that exactly what you do?"
> TORENO: "Well, kind of, but we get to pick our dictators. Degenerates that we can control. We try to stay the hell away from these guys with principles, because that just—muddies the waters."
> CJ: "Yeah, OK."
> TORENO: "OK, so of course these idiots have stolen a consignment of land mines and they plan to offload them in the Middle East, and cause a little ruckus...." *Rambling:* "And everybody goes crazy and has a lot of problems...." *Returns to point:* "Carl, do you like maiming people? Just curious...."
> CJ: *nonplussed:* "Maiming? Some people, shit...."
> TORENO: "Anyway, the point is—you and me, Carl, we're the same. Now yeah, it's a dirty job, but somebody's got to do it. But if you screw this up, it

causes a tinderbox situation all over Latin America and the Middle East. Now look, I spoke to the big man. You've got clearance to eliminate these fuckers. How's that?"

CJ: "Huh, man, kill Government agents?"

TORENO: *flippant:* "Kill, schmill. Come on ... don't look at it that way, will you? Think of it as pest control. It works for me."

Pest control, indeed! This ironic inversion of the social history of the U.S. Empire into natural history does briefly unmask the U.S. Government as the ultimate bug-eyed monster of science fiction lore. But that's as far as *GTA:SA* can take us. Behind the mask of the space alien and the self-promoting hype of Mike Toreno lurk the meathook realities of the big business interests who control big government, thanks to a political system that runs on literally billions of dollars of campaign expenditures.

Yet, if *GTA:SA* cannot tell us what comes after the U.S. Empire, it does at least offer invaluable clues as to where the videogame culture is headed. Two episodes, in particular, stand out as the shape of things to come. "Just Business" features a thrilling, seamless admixture of first-person and drive-by action, while "Reuniting The Families" fuses deft action sequences with a marvelous on-the-fly reference to Neil Manke's legendary *They Hunger* maps for the *Half Life* engine.[5] At their most frenetic, these sequences do anticipate a real world geopolitical conflict being waged with vehicles and on roads, and located inside urban spaces. This is the deadly urban warfare raging in Iraq, where a ragtag guerilla movement, armed with little more than improvised explosive devices, rocket-propelled grenades, and an indomitable will, is successfully pinning down the mightiest military machine in human history.

If the next generation of urban action videogames is ever to fulfill the glittering promise of the Grand Theft Auto series, they must reach beyond the smog-choked highways, overflowing prisons and monstrous colonial wars of the U.S. Empire. They must create multinational spaces with a truly post-American sense of place. To do so, they must be willing to confront their own micropolitical limitations. In a nutshell, the urban action game needs to grow. It must reach far beyond the bounds of the United States, and include more cities, more countries, more media, and even more transport systems than ever before. Ultimately, the urban action genre can remain true to itself only by daring to transcend itself.

Notes

1. For a more complete discussion of the relationship between neoliberalism and petro-fundamentalism, see my essay *S11: The Day the Empire Died* at <http://www.efn.org/~dredmond/S11.html>.

2. "The national war on drugs has perhaps been the primary factor behind the

extraordinary rates at which blacks are incarcerated. Drug offenses account for nearly two out of five of the blacks sent to state prison. More blacks are sent to state prison for drug offenses (38 percent) than for crimes of violence (27 percent). In contrast, drug offenders constitute 24 percent of whites admitted to prison and violent offenders constitute 27 percent. African-Americans are arrested, prosecuted, and imprisoned for drug offenses at far higher rates than whites. This racial disparity bears little relationship to racial differences in drug offending. For example, although the proportion of all drug users who are black is generally in the range of 13 to 15 percent, blacks constitute 36 percent of arrests for drug possession. Blacks constitute 63 percent of all drug offenders admitted to state prisons. In at least fifteen states, black men were sent to prison on drug charges at rates ranging from twenty to fifty-seven times those of white men." (Human Rights Watch)

3. For further details of the U.S. prison boom, see Angela Davis, *Are Prisons Obsolete?* New York: Seven Stories Press, 2003. For the best single analysis of the self-serving ideological fictions and cruel economic realities of U.S. neoliberalism, see Doug Henwood, *Wall Street*. New York: Verso, 1997. Finally, the Economic Policy Institute has irrefutable and voluminous evidence of the decline in United States real wages since 1973. See Lawrence Mishel, Jared Bernstein, and Sylvia Allegretto, *The State of Working America 2004–2005*. Ithaca: Cornell University Press, 2005.

4. Remedy's *Max Payne* (2001) cagily linked Payne's personal tragedy back to the agency of the villainous multinational corporation. This permitted Payne's running battles through the tenements, docks, factories, and office towers of the multinational marketplace to represent one of the most remarkable allegories of multinational class struggle ever created. (For a fuller explanation of *Max Payne*, see <http://www.efn.org/~dredmond/PP7.html>). There is a strikingly similar transformation of a subversive geopolitics into a radical micropolitics in Capcom's *Devil May Cry* trilogy, the premier occult-action franchise for the PlayStation 2. Dante, the protagonist of the series, is the quicksilver negation of the bemuscled American superhero. *Devil May Cry 3* goes so far as to map out the space of a progressive East Asian geopolitics, capable of fighting East Asia's state-guided and keiretsu capitalisms on their own turf. No such leap from quantity to quality occurs in the Grand Theft Auto series.

5. This is the moment when a cop briefly lands on the trunk of your vehicle, just as your gun jams. This alludes to a similar moment in Manke's horror fiction trilogy, when a zombified police officer slips and falls on the ground, and gets up. Fortunately, the player-character is saved at the last second by a helpful helicopter blade. For a fuller explanation of Neil Manke's contribution to the 3D videogame, see <http://www.efn.org/~dredmond/PP6.html>.

Works Cited

Buck and the Preacher. Dir. Sidney Poitier. Belafonte Enterprises, Columbia Pictures Corporation and E & R Productions Corp, 1972.
Daughters of the Dust. Dir. Julie Dash. American Playhouse, Geechee Girls, and WMG Film, 1991.
Davis, Angela. *Are Prisons Obsolete?* New York: Seven Stories Press, 2003.
Devil May Cry. Dir. Hideki Kamiya. Capcom, 2001.
Devil May Cry 2. Dir. Hideaki Itsuno. Capcom, 2003.
Devil May Cry 3. Dir. Hideaki Itsuno. Capcom, 2005.
Doom. id Software, 1993.
Economic Policy Institute. *The State of Working America 2004–2005*. Washington DC: EPI, 2005.
Grand Theft Auto. New York: BMG Interactive, 1997.
Grand Theft Auto 2. New York: Rockstar, 1999.
Grand Theft Auto III. New York: Rockstar, 2001.
Grand Theft Auto: San Andreas. New York: Rockstar, 2004.

Grand Theft Auto: Vice City. New York: Rockstar, 2002.
Half Life. Valve Software, 1998.
Henwood, Doug. *Wall Street.* New York: Verso, 1997.
Human Rights Watch. *Incarcerated America.* April 2003. 15 Jan. 2006 <http://www.hrw.org/backgrounder/usa/incarceration/>.
Max Payne. Remedy, 2001.
Metal Gear Solid 2: Sons of Liberty. Dir. Hideo Kojima. Konami, 2001.
Miami Vice. TV series. Michael Mann Productions and Universal TV, 1984–1989.
Quake. id Software, 1995.
Redmond, Dennis. "Satellite Uplink." *Slorg/Net.* 1 Sep. 2004. 15 Jan. 2006 <http://www.efn.org/~dredmond/PP6.html>.
_____. "S11: The Day the Empire Died." *Slorg/Net.* 15 Dec. 2001. 15 Jan. 2006 <http://www.efn.org/~dredmond/S11.html>.
Scarface. Dir. Brian DePalma. Universal Pictures, 1983.
Scientist Rids the World of the Evil Curse of the Vampires. (LP) Henry "Junjo" Laws, 1981.
Slim Shady LP. Eminem, 1999.
Sweet Sweetback's Baad Asssss Song. Dir. Melvin Van Peebles. Yeah, 1971.
They Hunger. Dir. Neil Manke. Black Widow Games, 2001.
To Sleep with Anger. Dir. Charles Burnett. SVS Films, 1990.

7. From Stompin' Mushrooms to Bustin' Heads:

Grand Theft Auto III as Paradigm Shift

Laurie N. Taylor

The release of *Grand Theft Auto III (GTA3)* marks a pivotal moment in the history of video games. Amid the milieu of a new console generation and a larger and older group of potential gamers, *GTA3* offered content and levels of complexity not seen in earlier games. In addition to an emergent gaming system that permitted multiple types of interaction, the innovative elements of *GTA3* included expansive gaming environments, an abundance of objects, and intense satire.[1] Effectively, the release of this game shifted academic analysis of games to gameplay (from the earlier focus on narrative or visuality), stimulated journalism on games, garnered more gamers and more diverse groups of gamers, and changed public perception. Of course, *GTA3* also brought controversy. Though arguments over video games and violence rage even more heatedly now, *GTA3* was the impetus for many of the current concerns because it was, at the time, a highly visible mature game in a medium that the public believed to be immature.[2] While none of these aspects are singularly exemplary, the combined effects of internal elements and reception made *GTA3* medium defining. When contextualized within the history of gaming, *GTA3* represents a profound change in the way we talk about and study games. This chapter studies the history of video games to show how *GTA3* marks a paradigm shift from earlier games. In doing so, I explore the importance of *GTA3* within the Grand Theft Auto series and for gaming as a whole.

Constructing Textuality and Controlling Reception: Gaming Paradigms

As Thomas Kuhn explains, paradigms are the "accepted model or pattern" under which particular schools of thought operate. Paradigms help us construct methods for approaching different topics and problems and they "insulate the community from those socially important problems that are not reducible to the puzzle form, because they cannot be stated in terms of the conceptual and instrumental tools the paradigm supplies" (23, 37).[3] For instance, modernism and postmodernism can be seen as paradigms by which texts are produced and received. Even software design operates on paradigms of usability and transparency; the usability paradigm attempts to make choices accessible and its operations invisible to the user. In software design this is sometimes likened as a "restaurant" metaphor where the goal is to have all choices readily apparent as though on a menu, without having to direct users to the process by which to access or read the menu.

Prior to *GTA3*, gaming paradigms were founded on the distinction between console and computer games. Because of differences in processing power, price, and market, console games were often seen to be for children—in part because of their placement for children—with computer games being for both adults and children. By being classed as games for children, most console games were stereotyped as having cartoony graphics and childish themes. Part of the general visual simplicity was due to the limited processing power, and part was due to the perception of simplicity based on the limited graphical representations. The paradigm also stipulated that games consisted of simple worlds, simple problems, and simple interactions. Though the technology did rapidly advance, because console games had begun in child-friendly games, new iterations of favorite game series often continued with either the cartoon-like or blocky graphics, which perpetuated these perceptions. Thus, the artistic style and ease of the gaming interface led to often reductive views of the games themselves, which were generally classed under one larger paradigm of child's toy or game. This insured that console games were a smaller and less consequential media form than film or television. Given the different perceptions of gaming as based on platform, computer games enjoyed a much broader scope. Computer games were seen as games for both children and adults, and include game genres such as simulators, advanced war games, multiplayer online games, and action-oriented first-person shooters. The general perception of computer games reflected these variants, with computer games often presented as educational toys, and work-related games, as well as more frivolously portrayed "hardcore" games.[4]

Even prior to *GTA3*, gaming was much more diverse than this paradigm represents; the paradigm itself served to obscure many aspects of gaming. For instance, the existing paradigm obscured the changing gaming audience demographic, the increases in game variety and type, and many of the innovations in terms of graphical quality and in terms of the system of relationships between the objects in games. Curiously, while Nintendo's Mario games continually expanded possibilities for game design and game play, Mario was often classed under the rubric of simple games. Moreover, games with mature and adult content—like *Fear Effect, Resident Evil,* and *Silent Hill*—as well as games with dynamic innovations in terms of game physics were treated as aberrations rather than as indicators of the increasing diversity in games.[5]

For a paradigm shift to occur, the prevailing paradigm had to be proven inadequate. Or, as Kuhn stated, it must be "inaugurated by a growing sense ... that institutions have ceased adequately to meet the problems posed by an environment that they have in part created" (92). While this can be stimulated by the accumulation of numerous exceptions that show exactly how the prior paradigm failed, it can also be launched by a major event or text. For gaming and game studies, *GTA3* operated with a variety of other less discrete factors to instigate the paradigm shift. Because the existing paradigm focused mainly on playful games for children or entertainment, more serious games like flight simulators, military stealth games, and ninja stealth games were treated under paradigms from other media, including simulation, virtual reality, and cinema. Where other games had stretched the boundaries of gaming paradigms, *GTA3* thwarted conventional gaming definitions to such a degree that the changes it included could not be viewed under the existing paradigm of friendly, simple, non-violent games. *GTA3* pushed gaming paradigms and the remediated paradigms from other media to the breaking point.

Indeed, *GTA3* not only created a new paradigm,[6] but it showcased the new paradigm in such a manner that traits before dismissed as insignificant variants were noticed[7] and acknowledged by gamers, game designers, the gaming media, game studies, and the general public. This shift was both absolutely necessary for gaming to continue to evolve and, in some ways, devastating for games because the shift brought added controversy over video games and violence.

Emergence: GTA3's New Paradigm

GTA3 was released for Sony's PlayStation 2 (PS2) on October 22, 2001. This was shortly before the release of Microsoft's Xbox and

Nintendo's GameCube and approximately a year after the release of the PS2.[8]. Though the graphic quality and the perception of graphic realism in games was noticeably improved on Sony's PlayStation 2 console, those improvements went largely unacknowledged outside of gaming media. Nor did these changes constitute a rethinking of games; in fact, by the time *GTA3* was released the initial awe of gamers at the improvement in graphic rendering on the PS2 had subsided. At the same time, because gaming had been perceived as a niche market, the general public's awareness of gaming continued unchanged from gaming's early days and then that awareness was shaken dramatically with the release of *GTA3*. In terms of presentation, *GTA3* was played through a three-dimensional trailing point of view and the activities of gameplay were immediately accessible for players and viewers. With extensive media coverage highlighting violent acts of gameplay in *GTA3*, many people in the general public moved from a basic familiarity with Atari or early Nintendo graphics to seeing fairly realistic violence in *GTA3*. The changes in graphics, from Mario jumping and squishing an evil mushroom, to *GTA3*'s unnamed hero beating bystanders to death with a bat, were heightened by *GTA3*'s frame world. As a consequence, the public attentiveness to graphics and gameplay stimulated an extensive re-evaluation of video games by legislators, parents, reporters, and academics.

Like *GTA3*, all of the Grand Theft Auto games exhibit beautifully rendered emergent game worlds and it is this combination of rendering and emergence that allowed for the incremental changes in the earlier games to culminate in *GTA3* as a paradigm shift. Emergence, according to Katie Salen and Eric Zimmerman, arises from the use of a simple rule set applied to a system with multiple objects and "can come about through complex programmed mechanisms that simulate adaptive agents and systems" (158–9). In game worlds, emergence occurs when multiple programmed objects have their own attributes and then interact within a system with limited rules. For instance, in *GTA3*, one of the missions is a car race. In most racing games, players would have to out-maneuver a vehicle to finish the race first. Like most racing games, *GTA3* allows cars to be damaged and destroyed. Unlike most racing games, *GTA3*'s limited rule set does not stipulate how that damage inherently affects the race, instead using the limited rules from damaged cars in general. Most racing games either do not allow cars to be extensively damaged or only allow cars to be damaged up to the point at which they are destroyed and the cars reset. Because of *GTA3*'s rule set, which applies to the entire game including the race, players can play the race in the tank and win the race by destroying all other vehicles and then slowly progressing through the racetrack.

Underlying the interactions between elements that create emergence are the multiple elements themselves. *GTA3*'s use of varied elements that each have intrinsic properties and affordances within the game world demonstrate one of the key aspects of new media, as defined by Lev Manovich, modularity. Modular game play elements that can interact allow for emergent behavior. Whereas earlier games often had complex worlds with dynamically interrelated objects and actions, those dynamics were only visible to the seasoned game player. New players could not transparently visualize or access the variety of actions and objects with which other games operated. *GTA3*'s game world was more dynamic than most because of the avenues for exploration—spatially[9] and in terms of various missions, weapons, and activities for game play—and because additional objects could be rendered on screen simultaneously. *GTA3*'s explicit modular structure in the separately delimited parts of town, and their relationships to particular groups illustrated emergence and modularity in a manner not as clearly seen in the majority of games before *GTA3*, again marking a paradigm shift by the explicit inclusion of these elements.

Where most games prior to *GTA3* restricted players to behaving in a moral manner, *GTA3* utilized its mature content in relation to the emergent gaming system such that players were encouraged to explore all of the game play possibilities. Games prior to *GTA3* required players to behave ethically, either by preventing players from attacking any of the good people or by punishing players for doing so. For instance, players could sometimes attack the residents of Hyrule in *The Legend of Zelda*. Generally the residents were immune to attacks and when they could be attacked they could not be injured yet could fight back. Thus, players attacking residents could not earn anything but could be punished for acting in an immoral manner. As with earlier games in the GTA series, *GTA3* presented the player-character as a criminal in an amoral world. Within the loosely realistic constraints of the rule set, player-characters could attack whoever or whatever they desired.

In addition to relying on an emergent game world, *GTA3* also functioned as a "sandbox" game. *GTA3*'s emergent system allowed for game play that could follow the core missions, thereby allowing the game narrative to progress in a fairly linear fashion; or players could play as though the game were a sandbox, where the players did not seek to advance the basic game narrative but instead sought to play certain segments of the game. Sandbox games are defined as games wherein players can play in an emergent fashion with multiple elements and multiple game types. Under this definition, *GTA3* qualifies as a sandbox style game—it, in fact, popularized the term—through its open-ended game play that does not require players to actively progress in the game to continue playing, through the openness of the game world which allows players a variety of choices in any given situation, and through its use of separate smaller missions available for players to play.

While emergence can occur in sandbox and other styles of games, *GTA3* combined both in a well-designed synthesis. This synthesis showcased the possibilities for expanding traditional game design by allowing players to play in a relatively linear fashion to advance the game, to choose to play in a completely nonlinear fashion and to not advance the game, or to play in a combination of linear and nonlinear fashions, progressing the game as they chose—often through completing missions after stealing police cars or ambulances or through attacking pedestrians to steal money. *GTA3* foregrounded differences in game play styles, with many newer gamers playing to not destroy objects in the game instead of wreaking destruction. In this, *GTA3* highlighted that gameplay is not a simplistic one to one interaction, but a sequence of choices, actions, and results in a manner that games had not.

Perhaps the most pivotal element allowing *GTA3* to signal a paradigm shift is the humor. While the expansive world and emergent gaming—particularly as coupled with a mature theme—had not previously been seen to such a degree in a mainstream game, the satirical social commentary was even more novel. Earlier games, notably point-and-click adventure games like *Grim Fandango*, include humor based on social commentary; however, adventure games do not typify the perception of gaming. Because popular action-based games are often stripped of social relevance and divorced from their potential political and social contexts, *GTA3*'s satirical examination of society presented a needed entry in gaming. *GTA3*'s satires were also important because of their myriad references. The satires did not target one particular group or event, instead acting as an inclusive social satire akin to other popular texts like *South Park*, with *GTA3* using satire to critique contemporary social structures like the criminal justice system (with one mission requiring the player to deliver an adequate supply of prostitutes to the Police Ball), relationships (with the notorious Maria who dangerously dates members of different gangs), contemporary music (with versions that mock popular music genres), and capitalistic society (with radio commercials parodying commercialism and radio itself). While the older Grand Theft Auto games also included this sort of satire—as did older adventure games—*GTA3* included these elements within its already radical form. Like satire, the positives of *GTA3*'s new paradigm came at a price.

In short, *GTA3* emerged at a point in gaming history where games had not yet matured as much as their players. Before the release of the

PS2 and *GTA3*, the average age of players had increased as younger gamers had grown up and as older players were increasingly drawn into gaming. The majority of games were ranked appropriately for the perceived gaming age group. For instance, the Interactive Digital Software Association's "State of the Industry Report 2000–2001" states that year over 70% of the games ranked by the ESRB were ranked "E" for everyone (10). Although "E" for everyone was the norm, it was changing with additional teen-rated games because of the popularity of teen-rated games; "Nineteen of the top twenty best selling games in 2000 were rated 'E' for everyone or 'T' for teen" (IDSA 12). As a mainstream game rated "M" for Mature[10], *GTA3* led to concern over video games and violence specifically because it heralded the new paradigm while people at first viewed it within the old paradigm.

Where the earlier Grand Theft Auto games had been revolutionary for their emphasis on amoral and immoral behavior, for their emphasis on violence, and for their open world settings, they had not been widely played. Moreover, they were released to smaller audiences and exhibited lower quality graphics, again minimizing their impact on gaming. By presenting gamers with a graphically detailed emergent game world and by highlighting that fact with the mature themes, *GTA3* could not easily be accommodated by earlier gaming paradigms. Though the earlier games in the series, as well as many other games, had exhibited mature content and emergent game play, *GTA3*—as the marker of a paradigm shift—was the first game that most people recognized as signaling the fact that video games could be mature and could present emergent worlds.

Games, the Media, and Academia

In delineating paradigms, Kuhn posits that paradigms are the "universally recognized scientific achievements that for a time provide model problems and solutions to a community of practitioners" (viii). While Kuhn is speaking of scientific paradigms, the same holds true for gaming. For gaming, the community of practitioners is made up of the game players, game designers, the gaming media, and academia. Gaming media prior to *GTA3* was generally more limited to technology and gaming magazines. With the release of the PS2 and *GTA3*, gaming achieved a critical mass and exploded into mainstream media. This included the 2002 beginning of the video game television network, "G4: Videogame TV," as well as the increasing mention and inclusion of video game news in mainstream television, newsprint, and other media. While video games and violence served as the basis for many discussions of video games, *GTA3* also showed that adults were interested in games and that games needed to be covered in the same manner that films and television are included in mainstream media. The mainstream media's inclusion of games, coupled with the increasing availability of focused media on gaming, further increased the presence of games in everyday life and in terms of the general public's knowledge about games. For gaming media and game development, *GTA3* signaled the rise of a new group of gamers—gamers who could be typical and atypical in their methods of game play—including casual and older gamers.

GTA3 also marked a paradigm shift in terms of the beginning of game studies as a field related, but not subsidiary, to hypertext and digital media studies. While earlier studies had addressed games—as with Marsha Kinder's *Playing with Power,* which studied games as part of children's culture, Janet Murray's *Hamlet on the Holodeck,* which framed games within virtual reality and fairy tale narratives, and Espen Aarseth's *Cybertext,* which framed games within new media more largely—game studies had not evolved into its own field. Coinciding with, and in part because of, the release of *GTA3,* game studies as a field focused on games as their own form—drawing from theories of narrative, film and other media, while emphasizing game play—was born.

The *Game Studies* journal heralded game studies as a field in July 2001, stating that "2001 can be seen as the Year One of *Computer Game Studies* as an emerging, viable, international, academic field" (Aarseth "Computer Game Studies, Year One"). During game studies' first year as a field, game studies itself grew with *GTA3* because *GTA3* illustrated that games were a major media force capable of parody and capable of critiquing culture even in their most popular form. While game studies existed in academia before *GTA3,* the paradigm shift brought in conjunction with *GTA3* immediately allowed game studies to expand. Further, one of the aspects of the new form of game studies is this expansion as shown through the integration of blogging in game studies discussion. Marking the importance of *GTA3* to game studies *Grand Text Auto,* one of the more famous game studies related blogs, even draws its name from *GTA3* and the paradigm change it signaled.

As game studies took to blogging to discuss games, *Water Cooler Games* also marked serious games as an important aspect of the new paradigm. With the arguments over video games and violence and with the new emphasis on game play, the new paradigm for game studies also implicitly included an interest in serious games for political commentary and for social change. *GTA3*'s use of the radio stations to parody and satirize current events, like the expansion of SUVs and the popularity of techno music, offered a popular reference for other serious games to show that serious topics and game play are not contradictory.

Conclusion: Clearing the Path for Other Paradigms

While *GTA3* marked the most recent paradigm shift for gaming, new paradigms continue to develop. In the same manner that the original Nintendo Entertainment System shifted gaming's emphasis from arcades into living rooms, the new networked handheld systems and gaming on multiple platforms like PDAs and cell phones promise new paradigms in relation to mobile gaming in much the same way that the Sony Walkman and more recent Apple iPod changed the face of portable music. Other developing paradigms are indicated by the sheer expansiveness of Massively Multiplayer Online Communities as well as the rise in machinima art, Alternative Reality Games, advergames and advertisements within games, and especially by the development of serious games as with political games and games for health. In addition to the changes for gaming that follow *GTA3*'s new paradigm is the changed relationship between gaming and culture in general. As Kuhn remarks, the perceptual and theoretical change that indicate a paradigm shift have repeatedly "transformed the scientific imagination in ways that we shall ultimately need to describe as a transformation of the world within which scientific work was done" (6). Because games began as and remain mass entertainment media, their transformation changes not only the world in which they exist, but also have implications for culture at large. As Eric Hayot suggests in "Freedom, Leverage, and Outlaws in Video Games," analyzing the freedom *GTA3* allows must be considered within a framework that includes both gaming and the world in which gaming resides (*Print Culture*). While *GTA3* has now been overshadowed by newer games—including new Grand Theft Auto games like *Grand Theft Auto: Vice City* and *Grand Theft Auto: San Andreas—GTA3*'s full impact on gaming and culture at large is still being determined. Recognizing *GTA3*'s new paradigm allows for a theory of game development and history that is tied to technical innovation, audience reception, media, game studies, and cultural and social concerns, showing that *GTA3*, like so many others, is more than just a game.

Notes

1. The use of satire in a game was not uncommon before *GTA3*-as text based games, graphical adventure games like *Grim Fandango*, and many other games show. However, the insertion of satire into an action game format allowed for an uncommon gaming experience that doubled as social critique.

2. Prior to *GTA3* video games for adults had been created, but they were released to less fanfare and to a smaller group of players; these included games such as *Custer's Revenge* and *Leisure Suit Larry*.

3. Kuhn describes normal scientific inquiry as puzzle solving, so that existing models would be used to solve known problems. His use of the word puzzle inadvertently highlights the parallel by which existing play and design models would be used for game design as well as for game play.

4. For more on the differences between console and computer games, see Laurie N. Taylor, "Console Wars: Console and Computer Cultures," Gaming Culture and Social Life, Eds. J. Patrick Williams, Sean Q. Hendricks, and W. Keith Winkler, Jefferson, NC: McFarland Press, 2006.

5. As I have argued elsewhere, while this division has minimized, it still exists and is still relevant to both how games are perceived and to the different gaming cultures as based on gaming platform ("Console Wars").

6. The first *Grand Theft Auto* exhibited many of the features that would be expanded upon in *GTA3*, including the ability to drive multiple cars with relatively realistic controls, an emphasis on small details like pedestrians and the beeping of cars, an emphasis on large exploratory spaces, and an emphasis on completing separate missions, all within a mature theme. *Grand Theft Auto: London 1969* and *GTA2* built upon the prior successes by enhancing the level of detail and involvement, as with enhancing the police's ability to chase the player. As John Unger, Porter Lee Troutman, Jr., and Victoria Hamilton note, while the earlier Grand Theft Auto games all exhibited many of the same elements, *GTA3* developed these elements to a greater degree ("Signs, Symbols, and Perceptions in *Grand Theft Auto: Vice City*" 91).

7. In discussing how new theories are introduced, Kuhn states that their "assimilation requires the reconstruction of prior theory and re-evaluation of prior fact" (7).

8. In North America, the PS2 came out on October 26, 2000; the Xbox came out on November 15, 2001; and the Nintendo GameCube came out on November 18, 2001. Because the PS2 was released so far in advance of the Xbox and GameCube, the PS2 dominated the console market, changing the market in the process.

9. See Zach Whalen's article on the Grand Theft Auto games and space in this collection.

10. Within its own history, GTA games have maintained similar player-age ratings. For content, according to the ESRB *Grand Theft Auto* is ranked Mature (17+) for "Animated Blood, Strong Language;" *GTA2* is ranked Teen (13+) for "Animated Violence, Strong Language, Suggestive Themes;" and *GTA3* is ranked Mature (17+) for "Blood, Strong Language, Violence" ("Game Ratings Search").

Works Cited

Aarseth, Espen J. *Cybertext: Perspectives on Ergodic Literature.* Baltimore: Johns Hopkins UP, 1997.

_____. "Computer Game Studies, Year One." *Game Studies: The International Journal of Computer Game Research* 1.1 (July 2001): <http://www.gamestudies.org/0101/editorial.html>.

Calvert, Clay. "Violence, Video Games, and a Voice of Reason: Judge Posner to the Defense of Kids' Culture and the First Amendment." *The San Diego Law Review 39*.1 (2002): 1–30.

Entertainment Software Review Board. "ESRB Game Ratings–Game Ratings and Descriptor Guide." Entertainment Software Review Board. 1 Oct. 2005 <http://www.esrb.org/esrbratings_guide.asp>.

GrandTextAuto. 2005. Mary Flanagan, Michael Mateas, Nick Montfort, et. al. 1 Nov. 2005 <http://grandtextauto.gatech.edu/>.

Grand Theft Auto. New York: Rockstar, 1997.

Grand Theft Auto III. New York: Rockstar, 2001.

Grand Theft Auto: London 1969. New York: Rockstar, 1999.
Grand Theft Auto: San Andreas. New York: Rockstar, 2004.
Grand Theft Auto: Vice City. New York: Rockstar, 2002.
Grim Fandango. San Francisco: LucasArts, 1998.
Hayot, Eric. "Freedom, Leverage, and Outlaws in Video Games." *Print Culture.* 31 Jan. 2005. 1 Nov. 2005 <http://www.printculture.com/item-50.html>.
IDSA. "State of the Industry Report 2000–2001." *International Digital Software Association.* 1 Feb. 2001. 1 Oct. 2005 <http://www.idsa.com/releases/SOTI2001.pdf>.
Kinder, Marsha. *Playing with Power in Movies, Television, and Video Games From Muppet Babies to Teenage Mutant Ninja Turtles.* Berkeley: U of California P, 1991.
Kuhn, Thomas. *The Structure of Scientific Revolutions.* Enlarged 2nd ed. Chicago: U of Chicago P, 1970.
Legend of Zelda. Redmond: Nintendo of America, 1998.
Legend of Zelda: The Minish Cap. Redmond: Nintendo of America, 2005.
Manovich, Lev. *The Language of New Media.* Cambridge: MIT P, 2001.
Norman, Donald A. *The Design of Everyday Things.* New York: Basic Books, 1988.
_____. *Emotional Design: Why We Love or Hate Everyday Things.* New York: Basic Books, 2004.
Ray, Sheri Graner. *Gender Inclusive Game Design: Expanding the Market.* Hingham: Charles River Media, 2004.
Salen, Katie and Eric Zimmerman. *Rules of Play: Game Design Fundamentals.* Cambridge: MIT P, 2004.
Taylor, Laurie N. "Console Wars: Console and Computer Cultures." *Gaming Culture and Social Life.* Ed. J. Patrick Williams, Sean Q. Hendricks, and W. Keith Winkler. Jefferson: McFarland, 2006.
The Sims. Redwood City: Electronic Arts, 2000.
Unger, John, Porter Lee Troutman, Jr., and Victoria "Tori" Hamilton. "Signs, Symbols, and Perceptions in *Grand Theft Auto: Vice City.*" *Digital Gameplay: Essays on the Nexus of Game and Gamer.* Ed. Nate Garrelts. Jefferson: McFarland, 2005. 91–109.
WaterCoolerGamers. Ian Bogost and Gonzalo Frasca. 2005. 1 Nov. 2005 <http://www.watercoolergames.org/>.
World of Warcraft. Blizzard, 2004.

8. Everyday Play:
Cruising for Leisure in San Andreas
TIMOTHY J. WELSH

The industry push to make video games more immersive has, for many producers, meant making games more true to life. Hyper-realistic graphics, sophisticated real-world physics, expansive, fully-interactive environments free from the segmentation of load screens and separated levels all serve as strategies for eliminating anything that reminds the audience that they are playing a game. This trend toward immersion through life imitation has also meant the inclusion of common, everyday activities. Spearheading this movement was *The Sims*, a game based completely on managing the daily activities of a virtual family. In the wake of its incredible success, games in almost every genre, from action games like *Metal Gear Solid 3* to sports games like *Madden 2006*, have granted players the option to immerse themselves in the day-to-day of the playable character. Rockstar's Grand Theft Auto (GTA) series has followed right along with this trend toward the everyday, incorporating more quotidian elements with each successive release. As the game has developed from little more than running, stealing, driving, and shooting in the first edition to include everything from getting haircuts to playing video games in *Grand Theft Auto: San Andreas* (*GTA:SA*), the franchise has also garnered increasing praise from video game theorists for granting players the freedom to define their own gaming experience. Their praise is mainly in reference to the open, undetermined quality of the game design, which makes none of the playable options any more necessary than the rest. I argue, however, that the game's quotidian elements do not merely expand the list of playable possibilities. Rather, the very everydayness of these practices plays an important role in the sensation of freedom produced by *GTA:SA*. Referencing the cycles of daily life without holding players to their regularity, *GTA:SA* generates the illusion that one has escaped everyday life and all the responsibilities and monotony it entails.

The unique freedom supposedly offered by video games has been a central, and often politicized, issue revolving around the question of who controls whom. From one perspective, when a player picks up a controller, he accepts a design, meaning system, and purpose not his own, hailed in the full Althusserian sense. This is particularly true of narrative-based, "progressive" games, as Jesper Juuls calls them, in which "the player has to perform a predefined set of actions to complete the game" (qtd. in Smith). The manufacturer's instruction booklet establishes the rules for behavior and the symbolic meaning (press X to jump) a player will employ to progress in a linear, teleological narrative, which grants players the permission only to move forward to some end-goal. Moreover, most titles include in-game directives or instructions on how to complete the game (go here, find the gun, kill that bad guy, etc), which, it could be said, predetermine game play and organize information in support of a dominant ideology. Several theorists, such as Julian Stallabras, have focused on these aspects of gaming to argue that gaming creates passive subjects, practiced in exchange relations, and trained for industrial labor. From this perspective the player is under the control of the dominant capitalist culture as it works through the medium of video games to reproduce tractable labor power.

In response to this critique, many theorists have promoted games with de-centered narratives, non-linear progression, and expansive, unrestricted possibilities for play. These "emergence" games, as Juuls calls them, are defined by "a small number of rules that combine and yield a large number of game variations" thereby preventing play from becoming predetermined (qtd. in Smith). Kevin Parker argues:

> [...] as games shift from pre-rendered animation and simple behavior to physical modeling and advanced artificial intelligence, players find that this new realism further relaxes limits and expands gameplay. It takes power from authors—to break rules, control pace, and manage plots—and gives to players a more coherent world of places, people, and things. The product is more toy than movie, more sandbox than story. Video games are evolving into a grand anti-authoritarian laboratory.

As game play is opened up to include a greater variety of activities by building games around rule structures like physics and artificial intelligence rather than teleological, directive narratives, games allow users to define their own goals and experience. In short, the player is in control. Furthermore, as Ted Freidman and others have noted, game designs, which literally describe the world of game play, are ideological. Therefore, in as much as playing a game is testing the limitations of a set of rules, video gaming is a kind of ideological critique (*Making Sense of Software*). In Parker's words, such a game actually sets players "against contrived limits and inconsistencies." This is one of the reasons *The Sims* has received so much praise. Not only is its design and execution revolutionary, but as the game's creator, Will Wright, has emphasized, the ideological world it generates, in which a character's social status is dependent on the things he has purchased, highlights the materialistic, dehumanizing aspects of market capitalism. The argument follows that this quality of open-ended, rule-based games not only allows players to escape authoritarian structures, but can also be a viable option for critique of and resistance to the ideological social systems that organize daily life in modern capitalism.

In regard to the freedom the game makes available for its players, *GTA:SA* certainly offers players a great deal of possible activities without restricting play to any particular path or goal. The game contains a definite narrative and teleological progression that the player cannot influence. The main character, Carl Johnson (CJ), returns from Liberty City to find his mother has been killed and begins his quest to take back the streets. These elements, however, do not determine game play, for players can pick up a mission when and where they want, skip or ignore others, build their avatar as they wish, set alternate or side goals, or completely ignore the narrative aspect altogether. Writing in reference to the same feature of earlier editions of Grand Theft Auto, both Parker and Frasca praised the game's open design for allowing players to engage or not engage the variety of activities as they see fit. The narrative is just another one of these optional activities. Furthermore, when a player accepts a mission, and thus submits to a section of the narrative, the rules that govern play do not really change. The ability to determine one's own play not only between missions but also *during* them is precisely the freedom Frasca found so remarkably successful as compared to most games he identified as suffering from what he calls "errand boy syndrome" (*Sim Sin City*). If the game directs me to drive to Sweet's house, I still drive the car in the same way as at any other time in the game. The rules governing the physics of car driving are not suspended, nor are any real limitation placed on what I can do. The directions, if I choose to accept them (and there is no reason why I have to), are simply another set of rules, and, as compared to the more non-progressive rules, like gravity, are the most expendable. The extent to which the freedom generated by game play opens a space for social critique, though certainly a topic deserving of critical attention, is one for another paper.

Instead, I will focus on the realization, practice, and effect of the freedom produced by *GTA:SA*, which I argue is bound up with its relationship to the everyday.

In the first versions of GTA, this freedom did not amount to much. Despite opening the playable world for gamers to determine their own game play experience, the reality of that experience was limited to a few essential practices: stealing, shooting, punching, driving, and running. So, although I can jack a car whenever I like, that is about all I can do. With such a limited range of activity, game play tends to get repetitious rather quickly, or, in a word, *predictable*. Think about *Pong*, one of the first video games ever developed. No linear narrative, no obligatory action, but with action restricted to moving the blocker bar, it is only a matter of time before a player blocks the ball back to the other side. While early versions of GTA certainly offered more ways to play than *Pong*, the point is clear: the limits of practice are the limits of freedom. Thus it is not merely a non-obligatory structure that grants freedom to players, but the type and variety of activities available as well. In that area, few games rival the breadth and variety of playable activities available in *GTA:SA*. The plethora of mini-games, side goals, creative missions, and interactive environments combine to extend to players the freedom not only from determined play, but also the freedom to determine play.

Much of the feeling of variety in *GTA:SA* comes from juxtaposing the extraordinary elements of crime and violence with the more mundane elements from everyday life. I can give CJ a break from his life of crime to work at a regular job like taxi driver, delivery boy, or quarry worker. Then I can have him kick back and enjoy leisure-time hobbies like pool, basketball, weightlifting, or even video games. Of course, the marketplace is open for business. At fast food chains like Burgershot and Cluckin' Bell I can satisfy CJ's hunger to keep him healthy and strong, or have him indulge to fatten him up. New outfits from Zip and other stores parodying popular clothiers, hairdos, or tattoos all elicit a bevy of responses from passing pedestrians. Should I keep him in the same styles long enough, however, CJ's sex appeal will diminish and strangers will start to comment on the strength of his body odor, thereby suggesting that I ought to engage CJ in the daily practice of changing clothes. Of course, there is no reason why I have to follow the suggestion. Perhaps it amuses me to have my avatar receive verbal abuse on the street or start something with these audacious passers-by. Their comments, like all the everyday elements of *GTA:SA*, reference the daily activities that make up modern life under capitalism; however, how I respond to these references is up to me. In short, I am free to participate in the everyday or not. But it is not simply by offering more and various options that the everyday elements open up a sense of freedom for players of *GTA:SA*. Henri Lefebvre argues, "The everyday, established and consolidated, remains the sole surviving common sense referent and point of reference" by which one can "decode the modern world" ("Everyday and Everydayness" 8). The everyday, for Lefebvre, is a "concept" that gives order to experience, providing "a denominator common to existing systems" ("Everyday and Everydayness" 9). It is, therefore, against the everyday that one defines work versus leisure, routine versus innovation, and necessity versus freedom. Thus, the regular day jobs like taxi driver stand in comparison to the non-everyday jobs like pimp, thereby defining the ordinary versus the extraordinary.

Against the backdrop of the everyday, from which video games supposedly transport those engaged in them, *GTA:SA* immerses its players in a world that resembles the monotonous daily life of modern capitalism, but releases them from its pervasive responsibilities, restrictions, and requirements. Lefebvre argues that the everyday is made up of two kinds of repetition: cyclical and linear. Cyclical repetition refers to natural cycles, "nights and days, seasons and harvests, activity and rest, hunger and satisfaction, desire and its fulfillment, life and death" ("Everyday and Everydayness" 10). Though days and nights pass in San Andreas as the sun rises and sets in relation to the game clock, and CJ goes through spurts of activity, when I run him around the city, and rest, when I save the game by putting him to bed in a safe house, none of the natural cycles referenced in the game make real demands on game play. CJ may get hungry, but it would take a long time for him to starve. Sleep comes at the whim of the player and not according to the biological demands of the body. In particularly long gaming sessions, players can keep CJ active for weeks of virtual time before saving the game and setting him down to sleep. In even more blatant opposition to the natural rhythms of daily life is CJ's exclusion from the cycles of life and death. Day turns to night suggesting the passing of time, but CJ does not age a single day. He is never born and he never dies. When CJ gets "WASTED" he simply re-spawns at the hospital. Even mutilated pedestrians are resuscitated by paramedics. The other type of everyday cycle Lefebvre identifies, linear repetition, plays just as inconsequential a role in determining game play. Linear repetition describes modern life in capitalism as the day-to-day exchange of work and consumption, the earning of wages and the subsequent spending of them. Many available jobs appear in *GTA:SA* and it is certainly possible to assign CJ to regular employment; but given, it seems absurd, not to mention difficult, to have him observe a nine-to-five schedule. Consumption fails to compel players as well. Commodities like food, clothing, car customizing options, weapons, are available for purchase, but a player can go through a whole session without ever buying anything. For the most part, any commodity one might want can be stolen or found. Therefore, neither type of everyday repetition has any determining effect on how one plays the game.

Because neither cyclical nor linear repetition organizes life in San Andreas, CJ is not subject to the rule of the modern everyday. Instead, these suggested repetitions serve as a background and point of contrast against which the non-everyday activities that make up the playing experience can be recognized as extraordinary. CJ is liberated from the day-to-day grind of work, consumption, and leisure that all those who engage his character are not. His freedom from everyday repetition is coupled with his freedom from the social systems erected on the everyday, "including the judicial, contractual, pedagogical, fiscal, and police systems" (Lefebvre 9). Thus, he can walk down the street with weapons blazing, never go to school or work, and kill police officers and pedestrians, all without serious repercussion. It is not, however, CJ's freedom that interests us as gaming critics, but rather that of the everyday human being holding the controller. As players come to see the actions of their avatar as their own and guide CJ through San Andreas in defiance of natural cycles, modern capitalism, and the systems built on both, there is the sense that they too have escaped the requirements of the ordinary to perform the extraordinary. Though the game resembles the average, quotidian world of cyclical and linear repetition, day turns to night as shoppers and workers populate the fictional city, players need not observe the everyday, the rule of time or of the marketplace. They act within an everyday world, but they are beyond its grasp. Thus, with each extraordinary performance, each resistance to the responsibilities, requirements, and repercussions of daily life, they reassert that modern life has no hold on in the virtual world, that in San Andreas they are free.

But the everyday is not so easily escaped. In his review of *Grand Theft Auto III* (*GTA3*), Frasca recounts a conversation with a friend in which the two determine that the gaming experience should not resemble work:

> "I started getting this feeling of being in a bad job." Ouch! I knew exactly what he was talking about because at the time I was growing tired of *The Sims* for the exact same reason. We all eventually lose interest in a certain game, but you know there is something wrong when it swiftly brings back your worst summer job nightmares [Frasca].

Gaming is supposed to be something one does for fun, a leisure activity. It makes sense, then, that if playing feels like work, then the game is failing to transport players out of the boredom of the daily grind. But, as Lefebvre argues, even the most successful and entertaining leisure activity does not transcend the everyday. Leisure time is just as much a part of the everyday as work; it is merely *perceived* to be different, for it "*appears* as the non-everyday in the everyday" (*Critique of Everyday Life* 233, my italics). Work is alienating and unsatisfying and so the laborer occasionally needs a break, time away from his job to compensate for this discontentedness. Given this relation, leisure cannot be "separated from work," as the latter creates the need for the former; "We work to earn our leisure, and leisure has only one meaning: to get away from work. A vicious cycle" (234). In other words, it is the very function and definition of leisure to feel like a break from the obligations of the everyday, like a time of freedom, "free time" to indulge oneself as one pleases. Perhaps this is why the "freedom" *GTA:SA* offers is such an admired and sought-after quality in video games. As players look to escape the everyday, they turn to video games to find the "liberation and pleasure" that they do not find in the cyclical and linear repetitions of modern life (229).

Lefebvre specified that "the constitutive elements of leisure are more likely to be images and films" because they "are (or at least appear to be) as far away from *real life* as possible" (229). I argue that video games fulfill this role even more completely and are therefore the new "leisure machines," for they immerse players in virtual worlds "entirely outside of the everyday realm, and so purely artificial that it borders on the ideal" (229). In order for the break to be recognized, however, the new worlds must have an anchor in the real everyday. As Lefebvre writes, "how can this purely artificiality [this alternate, virtual world] be created without permanent reference to ordinary life, without the constantly renewed contrast that will embody this reference?" (229). The virtual world must make reference to the *real* world in order to be experienced as contrasting with it, as other than it. This becomes evident in the gaming industry trend to imitate, but not too closely, real life. The graphics and movements must be realistic, the action must be believable, but players must be able to do things in the game they cannot in their lived everyday. The real world must appear, but only to such an extant that it marks the virtual world as extraordinary.

Such is the case with the everyday in games like *GTA:SA*. Elements like eating, dating, working, etc, reference the everyday and thereby set up a contrast to the non-everyday elements like murder, theft, prostitution, etc, constituting the virtual San Andreas. Violence is thus imposed on the everyday, embellishing the day-to-day, making it fantastic and less banal. The brutal and gruesome are the entertaining, attractive, the fun parts of the game; just as Lefebvre says, leisure "makes the ugly beautiful, the empty full, the sordid elevated—and the hideous 'fascinating'" (230). But, as always with leisure, there are no consequences, no responsibilities, no liability. This is all just make believe and, which allows it to be both liberating and pleasurable. In sum, *GTA:SA* fulfills its function as a leisure time activity by giving the feeling of a complete break by entering players into a violently attractive fantasy devoid of "new worries, obligations, or necessities" (229).

To illustrate the nature of the sordid but fascinating escape to this other world, Lefebvre discusses the prevalence of nude and partially nude images in film, television, and advertising. He argues that "displays of sexuality and nudity break with everyday life," and thereby provide a brief but abrupt disruption of routine. The sexuality depicted, however, "is depressing, this eroticism is weary and wearying, mechanical. There is nothing really sensual in this unbridled sexuality, and that is probably its most profound characteristic" (230). This description could not be more apt to describe the depiction of sex in *GTA:SA*. A cut scene freezes the camera angle on a car or house; the frame bounces in erratic staccato rhythm with artificial moaning sounds as laudatory text runs along the bottom of the screen narrating the event. The "Hot Coffee" patch makes sexual encounters in the game much more explicit but not any more sensual. Reduced to the stilted rock of the "joystick," sex is quite literally mechanized. The result of the abrupt breaks with everydayness precipitated by the mechanical nude image is a "step outside the everyday without actually leaving it: it shocks, it seems brutal, and yet this effect is superficial, pure appearance, leading us back toward the secret of the everyday—dissatisfaction" (230). This description seems just as apt to describe the elements of violence in *GTA:SA*. It can be both shocking and brutal: decapitating non-playable characters with a shotgun blast, sneaking up and slitting the throat of an unsuspecting victim, or, the atrocity most emphasized by those against violence in video games, soliciting a prostitute and killing her to reclaim the money. At the same time, all this violence is the pure appearance of a fantasy world that exists only as long as one keeps playing. Game violence is not real life violence; its fundamental appeal being precisely its non-everydayness. Devoid of sensuality, the brutality of the acts lacks palpability and is thus itself merely simulated. Furthermore, for the most part, it goes unnoticed by players. It is after all, the everyday of this embellished world where carjacking is as common as driving. The brutal interruption wears off, the fantasy remains just a fantasy, and the everyday resurfaces.

More than simply creating the violently attractive image of a virtual world, players immerse themselves in, feel themselves to be engaged with, this world that seems fundamentally other than their normal world of daily life. Lefebvre observed "a curious kind of 'alienation'" experienced by sports fans who identify with themselves athletes. The fan "participates in the action and plays sport via an intermediary" (231). Convinced that what he witnesses does not happen everyday, "he quivers with enthusiasm, he fidgets frenetically, but he never moves from his seat" (231). Video games make this participation by proxy all the more explicit, for, rather than merely watching, the gamer literally controls the movement of his intermediary. In fact, Lefebvre's description of the sports fan seems just as apt to describe a gamer in session, especially if one were to add "fingers fly across buttons" to Lefebvre's characterization of the sports fan. Gamers identify their actions with that of their avatar and will claim the actions and accomplishments on screen as their own, literally saying "Those cops tried to catch *me*, but *I* shot them all, when in reality they pressed a button on a control pad in reaction to some flashing lights. It is indeed "a curious 'alienation'" as a player misidentifies as his own actions as those simulated in the constructed space of a virtual world.

Such is the power of the new leisure machines to give players the sense that they have been transported to a "violently attractive" spectral world on the deserts of the real everyday. Picking up the controller, players walk through the fantasy San Andreas repeatedly affirming its non-everydayness by testing the limits of their freedom: killing without mercy, causing explosions, stealing countless vehicles, making stunt jumps off ramps on motorcycles, sleeping with prostitutes, dying only to be respawned at the hospital. The everyday cycles of nature and capitalism still apply; players age, go to sleep, consume electricity and probably food, and have to go back to work or school in the morning. Though they have not left the cycle of work and leisure, nor have they escaped the everyday, merely engaging in the quite quotidian activity of playing a game, players identify themselves outside their unfulfilling day-to-day reality. The fantasy they find in this embellished world offers "*distraction, entertainment,* and *repose,*" which "might *compensate* for the difficulties of everyday life" by liberating them from "worry and necessity" (Lefebvre, *Critique of Everyday Life* 229). Thus, no video game will truly deliver players from the everyday; the best it can do is cycle them from work to leisure. But this does not mean that the freedom *GTA:SA* offers players is any less true agency. Michel de Certeau, in *The Practice of Everyday Life,* attempts to reorient the way we view the subject within the complex of social systems that organize late capitalism. Rather than treating him as a passive consumer of modern life, de Certeau redefines the subject as a "user," who actively operates, manipulates, and employs the systems in which he exists. What is important to de Certeau is not the complex of organizational modes and disciplinary mechanisms in place, but how one practices their daily life in the spaces invisible to these modes and mechanisms.

De Certeau differentiates between what he calls "strategies" and "tactics." Very basically, the former constitutes the rules that govern proper behavior for a particular place, the later refers to the actual behavior, full of unique nuances, styles, and inventions, by which one fulfills these rules (35–37). Frasca illustrates the difference between strategies and tactics when he describes how he survived his worst job:

> What do people do when they face repetitive tasks in order to prevent insanity from taking control of their minds? They play. You can bet we did play, too. We played beat-the-clock, of course. "Let's see who can fold more letters in 15 minutes" or "I bet I can print 500 letters without running out of toner" I know it sounds pathetic. It certainly was (Did I mention I really needed the money?). Only play made my burden bearable [Frasca].

Frasca's job in this story constitutes the strategy, for it dictates a particular behavior, printing and folding letters, for a particular place, the office The practice of this prescribed behavior, however, lies beyond the vision of the workplace parameters. Frasca and the other workers invented games by which they still completed their jobs, satisfied the requirements of the strategies in place, but found their own space for invention, freedom, and a little enjoyment. Frasca shares this story to make a point about the structure of the GTA series.

> When teleporting is not an option, most games force players to simply walk or run to their objective. *GTA3*'s great achievement was to allow the player to do what most people with lousy jobs do: turn their dull activities into a game (remember my junk mail job?). When you need to go to the other side of Liberty City, you do not waste your time: you actually enjoy it. The means of transportation is fun: you carjack a nice car and then drive it according to your mood—either smashing other cars, using the wrong lane or being chased by cops. Driving in *GTA3* is a game in itself [Frasca].

What Frasca describes here is the use of tactics in the game play experience. In *GTA:SA*, icons mark out places of strategy on the map, the locations for specified behaviors that will forward the narrative that structures game play. These places are further marked by a red highlighting circle on the exact spot where the specific strategy begins to apply. De Certeau would refer to these narrative locations as the "proper names" on a map. As these proper names "carve out pockets" for the application of strategy, they simultaneously open up spaces where activities are not defined. In the space between the icons, players find open areas for use, spaces to play with various tactics. The strategy of the narrative requires a task to be done, a proper activity, like meet Wu Zi, and marks out the space for that to happen, The Four Dragon's Casino, for example. How that task is accomplished, the practice of that activity in the assigned place, is a tactic which takes advantage of the available spaces and opportunities that happen along the way. So, for example, on the way to the casino, one could steal a car and run off some ramps, run the whole way there to build stamina, or steal a bike to do a bunch of wheelies and stoppies just for fun.

Strategies appear in many more forms than just narrative directions, however. The strategy is the set of rules that define game play, literally creating the place and allowed behavior. In *GTA:SA*, this includes the list of available movements, the physics and properties that governs the integrity or seeming solidity of objects, their movement, and their interaction, system of controls that constitute action, and so on. Strategies constitute the design and structure that establish the place and manner of play that comprise *GTA:SA* and make it the game that it is. But every strategy opens up space for tactics. Despite the fact that the game is itself a complex of strategies, the practice of actually playing the game is tactical. Play takes place under the rule of the game's design and limitations; however the way in which these rules are enacted remains up to the player. So, for example, a litany of rules ordain how it looks when one steals a car, the physics of driving, the way in which gravity affects objects, the properties of pavement. This network of rules does not require or forbid that a player could invoke all these rules simultaneously to drive CJ off a high jump, exit the car in mid-flight, and send him hurtling to his death on the highway concrete. The game is determined by rules, but the choice of how to play is always up to the player.

No matter how limiting a game's design, it can never account for the eccentricities and particularities of a player's particular style and taste. What De Certeau's theories makes clear is that the freedom to articulate one's own experience afforded by tactical space is not solely a characteristic of non-narrative, simulation style, or emergence games. At the level of practice, the distinction between narrative-based and rule-based games drops out, for both are defined by a set of rules that construct a virtual place and associated proper behaviors, and consequently open up spaces for play. Furthermore, at this level, the distinction between leisure and work becomes inconsequential as well. Though the strategic systems that organize everyday life remain unphased, games like *GTA:SA* that offer so many possibilities for play allow players to define their own use of the available space, and thereby break the monotony of the everyday to have fun. As Frasca shows, even work can be a game, if one can find a space to exercise their freedom through practice. At the same time, however, practice can make games come to feel like work.

Even though the simulated events in *GTA:SA* do not constitute a typical everyday revolving around work and consumption, the practice of playing the game generates an everyday in itself. No two gaming sessions are exactly alike, but they never feel or seem all that different. "The days follow one after another and resemble one another," writes Lefebvre, "and yet—here lies the contradiction at the heart of everydayness—everything changes" (*Everyday and Everydayness* 10). When CJ steals a car, for example, the circumstances are never exactly the same, the car maybe a different color or model, there maybe one or more people in the car, a cop may be present or not, but the procedure for executing that command is always identical. The player presses the corresponding button, which sets forth an animation sequence. The individual instances are so similar that differentiating them hardly seems worth it. Even when "borrowing" a car from a fellow Grove Street Family member, CJ still executes the same procedure, tossing his "brother" to the curb. Carjacking is so unremarkable that the extensive list of statistics, which includes everything from number of girls dated to legitimate kills, does not include a stat for number of cars stolen. All the excitement, challenge, and freedom is not in stealing cars, but in what one does with them afterwards. Stealing cars in GTA is as everyday in San Andreas as opening a car door is in the lived world.

Because it is so common as to be considered a part of the everyday, carjacking all but disappears from the experience of game play. According to Maurice Blanchot, "The everyday is always unrealized in its very actualization which no event, however unimportant or insignificant can ever produce. Nothing happens; this is the everyday" (15). But something does happen; a deluge of details, events, and attitudes so common, so unremarkable, and so painstakingly banal, completely slip past our consciousness. These unnoticeable repetitious actions of daily life are thus said to escape, for they are never grasped by consciousness. The everyday is all that passes under the surface of life that is too unnoteworthy to note. Such is the place of carjacking in *GTA:SA*; it happens so frequently, each occurrence almost indistinguishable from the last, it hardly registers at all. Ted Freidman describes a similar process in "The Semiotics of SimCity." Freidman argues that when one is immersed in a game, one adopts the logic of that game, to the point that one reacts without thinking, "And the reason that the decision, and the continuous series of decisions the gamer makes, can be made so quickly and intuitively, is that you have internalized the logic of the program, so that you're always able to anticipate the results of your actions." Carjacking fits into this immersive logic of *GTA:SA*; a player does not have to think about stealing a vehicle, he just does it to get where he wants to go, just as in the real world one does not think about or acknowledge opening a car door when one goes driving. De Certeau talks about a similar adoption of tactical "logic of operation of actions relative to types of situations," which he identifies as particularly prominent in games. As one plays a game, one develops a memory of tactics that worked, practices and procedures for a particular circumstance or situation. For example, in *GTA:SA*, one who catches the attention of a cop while on foot might steal a car to get away. Though this tactic seems extremely rudimentary, its obviousness highlights how everyday these procedures become. Carjacking is a simple matter of procedure, a tactical application of logic in particular situation. As such, it becomes second nature, everyday, and thus blends into the background.

But carjacking certainly is not an everyday activity. It, therefore, occupies an ambiguous position in *GTA:SA*. On the one hand, it is an extraordinary event, outside the real, lived everyday, and thus contributes to the production of a sense of freedom, possibility, and leisure. On the other hand, through repeated practice, it becomes the most banal, regular and everyday activity of the game, and thus it goes almost completely unnoticed. This development is not unique to carjacking, but can apply to any recurrent event in the game. Killing cops, flying in a jetpack, driving a car off a cliff, all slip further into the everyday the more they are practiced. The game can thus be said to generate an everyday out of the non-everyday. Consequently, however, as these practices escape *into* the everyday, so does their capacity for granting players a brutal, fantastic, but abrupt escape *from* the everyday. The repetition of these practices replaces their gruesome and fantastic brutality with familiarity, thereby inoculating their ability to interrupt daily routines and pass players to another world. While carjacking may have initially been so outside a player's typical life experience that its practice in the game offered a sense of leisure and freedom, eventually, the practice becomes so common and banal that they dissolve into the background. A player seeking freedom in leisure must, therefore, look for a more stimulating activity.

Parker, Frasca, and Friedman all praise games like *GTA:SA* with unscripted designs for allowing players the freedom to create their own goals. A player's experience is thus not determined by a plot, but by their own whim and fancy. These goals, however, must necessarily escalate in intensity as practices become routinized and players require novel experiences to feel free from the everyday. Thus, once carjacking becomes a routine, one might try to steal specific cars, a police car, or give up on cars altogether and go after a plane. Killing police officers is just part of the game and can be a mild annoyance if one wants to get somewhere; going to the police station to kill them all, on the other hand, that is something else (it can't be done; I tried). Evading one wanted-rating star gives way to evading two or more until one attempts to see how long one can survive with a five-star wanted rating (there is, incidentally, a statistic for this, as if the designers were anticipating the course of player's relationship with the star system). In this fashion, the everyday usurps common activities and experiences, sneaking in through repeated practices to make portions of even the most interesting games repetitive and boring. It is this trend toward everydayness that gives meaning to the evaluative category of "replayability."

In an industry predicated on planned obsolescence, part of what has made the GTA series so successful is its capacity for providing multiple and various possible practices thereby allowing for game play to be experienced in nearly innumerable ways. While most popular adventure titles released today can be completed in ten to fifteen hours with mediocre replayability, each successive GTA release has increased both the expansiveness of its virtual environment and the variety of its playable content, spanning three cities with countryside and over one hundred and fifty hours of game play just to finish the scripted portions and preordained goals in *GTA:SA*. Moreover, many activities have their own unique control system, so the physical practice of driving differs from that of flying, operating a crane, or playing pool. These task-specific control systems defamiliarize game play, therefore, theoretically slowing the routinization process. With all the possibilities for game play, *GTA:SA* offers players the freedom and variety of choice to stay the intensifying appetite for leisure fueled by the slow usurpation of novelty by the everyday. Even so, dedicated fan sites on the internet are filled with patches, mods, and cheat codes, evidence that players seek more possibilities, more experiences beyond what the game itself offers.

Necessarily, in order to provide the respite that it does, the franchise has, over the course of its development, included more and more of the real world everyday. Take, for example, living in a home, the hub of everydayness. In the original GTA, released in 1998, the main character had no place to live or sleep. The playable avatar simply appeared on the curb. By *GTA3*, the main character had a hide out and moved on to different accommodations as a player progressed through the plot. *GTA:VC* allowed players for the first time to purchase their own property and establish residence all over the map. Finally, in *GTA:SA*, CJ can own both residential and commercial properties, such as the gas station, car dealership, toy store, or casino, thereby establishing the everyday binary of the separate spheres, home and work. Because both can offer CJ jobs or sanctuary, players need not treat the properties differently, driving back to a residence before going to work. But, as I discuss above, the presence of the everyday is not to hold players to regular cycles. Rather, like the natural cycles of day and night and the linear cycles of labor and consumption, which appear in the game without compelling player's attention, the separate spheres of home and work serve as a background of the banal against which a player's activities are defined as novel, exciting, and fundamentally other than daily life experience under modern capitalism. Thus, by bringing more everyday elements into game play, the GTA franchise offers more spaces of practice to counteract the usurpation of play by repetition.

One could at this point accuse GTA of being wholly complicit in perpetuating the cycles of work and leisure, escalating the degree of violence needed to break with the everyday. As one of the highest grossing video game franchises ever, Rockstar and the GTA franchise certainly benefit from the linear cycles of daily life from which it supposedly grants players relief. Furthermore the game in many ways encourages the generation of desire as repetition claims more and more play for the everyday. Even so, GTA also exposes the dialectical nature of the everyday and leisure as they are motored by practice. The everyday is the referent against which novelty, interest, and entertainment are defined. As carjacking and other non-everyday practices lose their fascination and escape into the undifferentiated background, the desire for leisure takes a new form and a fresh practice must make a more brutal break with the everyday. Thus, like *The Sims*, which offers a critique of material culture, GTA levies its own critique of the everyday, featuring it prominently in game play and demonstrating its capacity to usurp the non-everyday. Furthermore, to reduce GTA to a desire producing machine would be to ignore the spaces of creativity, freedom, and fun the game's design leaves open for players to make their own. Though one cannot escape the everyday, at the level of practice, one can at least play it as one chooses.

Works Cited

Blanchot, Maurice. "Everyday Speech." *Yale French Studies* 73 (1987).

De Certeau, Michel. *The Practice of Everyday Life.* Berkeley: U of California P, 1984.

Frasca, Gonzalo. "Sim Sin City: Some Thoughts About *Grand Theft Auto III*." *Game Studies* 3.1 (2003). <http://www.gamestudies.org>.

Friedman, Ted. "Making Sense of Software." *Cybersociety.* Ed. Steven G. Jones. Thousand Oaks: Sage, 1995. <http://www.duke.edu/~tlove/simcity.htm>.

_____. "The Semiotics of SimCity." *First Monday.* 1999. <http://www.firstmonday.org/issues/issue4_4/friedman/>.

Grand Theft Auto III. New York: Rockstar, 2001.
Grand Theft Auto: San Andreas. New York: Rockstar, 2004.
Grand Theft Auto: Vice City. New York: Rockstar, 2002.
Lefebvre, Henri. *Critique of Everyday Life.* Trans. John Moore. London: Verso, 1991.
____. "The Everyday and Everydayness." *Yale French Studies* 73 (1987).
Parker, Kevin. "Free Play." *Reason.* 2004. <http://www.reason.com/0404/fe.kp.free.shtml>.
Pong. New York: Atari, 1972.
Smith, Jonas H. "Does Gameplay Have Politics?" *Game Research.* 2004. http://www.game-research.com/art_gameplay_politics.asp>.
Stallabras, Julian. "Just Gaming: Allegory and Economy in Computer Games." *New Left Review* (1993). <http://www.stanford.edu/class/history34q/readings/Cyberspace/StallabrasJustGaming.html>.

9. Cruising in San Andreas:

Ludic Space and Urban Aesthetics in Grand Theft Auto

ZACH WHALEN

Perhaps no video game series so far has garnered both as much notoriety and as much praise as Grand Theft Auto (GTA), and the controversy arising around the most recent manifestation, *Grand Theft Auto: San Andreas (GTA:SA)*, has no doubt indelibly changed the public perception of video games. On the one hand, the games and their allegedly prurient content garners much of the criticism aimed their way, but on the other, their innovative approach to narrative in relation to space amounts to a significant development in the representative capabilities of video games. Beginning with *Grand Theft Auto III (GTA3)*, players encounter a rich, traversable world supporting a branching narrative structure which effectively amounts to an entirely new genre for gaming,[1] so much so that new game releases frequently describe their content in relation to GTA. *Gun* (Activision/Neversoft, 2005), for example, is often characterized as "a cowboy version of GTA" (*ContactMusic*) and more generally as "a sandbox-style GTA game" (Raymond). This free-ranging narrative format is coupled with (and relies heavily on) a three dimensional space that the player can explore freely, and understanding the constitution of this space is crucial to accounting for the continued influence of the game idea and its significance in relation to the player's experience of it. In other words, if GTA games take place in a sandbox, the meaning of GTA depends heavily on the character and nature of that sandbox, and because the spaces of these games so closely mimic heavily mythologized American cities, the game's aesthetic merit extends chiefly from an understanding of its spaces in terms of the aesthetics of the urban environments being referenced. Specifically, Los Angeles is a dominant feature of the American landscape. For a variety of reasons, it is a focal point for many critics and authors who write about postmodernity in relation to urban environments. The idea of mediality (the sense in which the act of representation is always already caught up in the rhetoric of the media which carries the representation) is a principle concern in these studies, so the fictive Los Santos of *GTA:SA* provides an interesting corollary to these studies of the real Los Angeles. Moreover, understanding the cognitive maps city dwellers use to navigate their space sheds interesting light on the construction of Los Santos and raises the question of whether Los Santos is primarily a medial space (existing primarily as a parody of Los Angeles) or a ludic space (existing for the purpose of conducting play).

A number of authors have considered the problem of space and spatiality[2] in games within a variety of contexts. In "Space in the Video Game," Mark J.P. Wolf takes the most comprehensive approach in outlining a taxonomy of spatial forms,[3] and Steven Poole offers an interesting perspective in *Trigger Happy* in linking the character of the spaces in question to their function in relation to the physical characteristics and abilities of the player-character (212). Particularly with *GTA:SA*, however, the question of space becomes entangled with the more complicated notion of the city—especially since its juxtaposition of urban and rural spaces presents for the first time in the GTA series a circumscribed experience of urban space that can critically engage with notions of the city as a formal and semantic unit separate from "the country." In other words the degree to which the city itself is a character on which the space of the game depends for its presentation bears upon the broader understanding of the game space's relation to the player and the player's understanding of that space within an aesthetic context. Moreover, given Johann Huizinga's definition of play as fundamentally involving boundaries, the rules of that urban environment extend at least in part from its status as a separate semantic unit. So in analyzing the cities of GTA, it is worthwhile to consider whether their construction depends more on these principles of play or on the equally problematic concept of urban aesthetics.[4]

In linking these two trains of thought, Kevin Lynch's *Image of the City* provides valuable insight into the organization of urban space by way of pathways and edges given. Lynch's study of Los Angeles is, of course, particularly appropriate for the present discussion, but his ideas about the city as a conceptual network apply well to virtually any instance of a simulated space in connecting the "virtuality" of the medium with the "virtuality" of the everyday mental images that govern an individual's understanding of her city. Not surprisingly, Lynch's work has also been influential in the design of user interfaces, so San Andreas seems an ideal conflation of these conversations in that it must be responsible both to the idea of creating an aesthetically pleasing (and navigable) cityscape as well as a legible gaming experience.

Edges, Borders and Thresholds

In approaching *GTA:SA*, my primary focus will be on the central city of Los Santos and a chief concern within this analysis will be that fictional city's relationship to the real Los Angeles. Generally, one finds in the correlation not an exact geographical representation, but rather an aesthetic corroboration that aims more at capturing the spirit or soul of this particular space while at the same time conveying that structure as a navigable game experience. It is this latter concern that applies most generally to the problem of spatiality in the video game and its formal relationship with the history of games and play. Sociologist Johann Huizinga, in framing his classic discussion of culture considered as play begins by reflecting on the spatial conditions of play. He describes a "magic circle" as the play-ground in which the rules of play stand in place of normal rules for behavior. Entering into the physical or psychic space of place amounts to complicity in the rules of the game; therefore, it is useful to begin by considering Los Santos in light of Huizinga's magic circle.

In setting the characteristics that define play and separate it from normal behavior, Huizinga conceptualizes play as happening at a temporal and spatial remove from everyday life: "The arena, the card-table, the magic circle, the temple, the stage, the screen, the tennis court, the court of justice, etc., are all in form and function play-grounds, i.e. forbidden spots, isolated, hedged round, hallowed, within which special rules obtain. All are temporary worlds within the ordinary world, dedicated to the performance of an act apart" (10). One can draw several key features of these spaces from this brief passage, and in the context of GTA, it is worthwhile to note that the initial delineation of this space automatically implies formal rules which ascribe qualities to the status of the individual—whether he is "inside" the circle or "outside."

It is notable as well that within Huizinga's list, the magic of this circle is as much sacred as it is profane—it is both "forbidden" and "hallowed"—and the deviance of play is from the beginning of this analysis pre-supposed in the properties of the space in question. Though GTA games are often criticized for their depiction of graphic violence, play is always deviant to a certain extend in that it is non-productive. It is not surprising, therefore, that the illegal and immoral behavior often cited by critics is more likely to occur in the realm of possibilities provided outside of the game's missions but within the bubble of the game's rules (for example, the notorious ability to hire prostitutes and then kill them to get one's money back). This play is not fundamental to success in the game, so it exists within the boundaries of the play-ground but outside of the "hallowed" ground of the play itself, exploiting its possibilities without being responsible to its objectives. In other words, the space within the circle exists to serve the rules of the game, so within this "forbidden" zone, space is already involved in the taboo of play itself. Outside of the objectives of play, diversionary or subversive play can be truly deviant in that it eschews both the rules of the game and the rules for normal behavior.

Similarly, the space of cities also operates on a peculiar and separate system of rules unfamiliar to outsiders (hence, "When in Rome, do as the Romans"), and as a conceptual object, the city supplies opportunities for engagement on multiple levels. The city, furthermore, can be thought of in terms of aesthetics and legibility, providing a correlating poetics of space that informs and influences the behavior of its inhabitants. The operative question in approaching the cities of GTA, therefore, is the basis and effect of their forms—whether their structure depends more on satisfying rules of play or on overriding metropolitan rules of engagement.

The city of Los Santos is the first of three major cities one encounters in the fictional state of San Andreas, and its clear referent is Los Angeles. Even though the in-game cities are programmatically and discretely defined as separate from one another and the surrounding countryside, the player's experience of Los Santos mimics the geography of Los Angeles successfully enough that, like the real city, finding the boundary of Los Santos is not as straightforward as one would hope. The Mulholland area in particular seems to be a liminal area which is itself separate from the Downtown district and the countryside. Because it exists on top of the Vinewood ridge, this area is itself a boundary between Los Angeles proper and the surrounding area. In this way, Huizinga's magic circle could apply to the spatiality of Los Santos at potentially several "depths"—the literal programmatic space of the city as the first "level" of gameplay or the geographic representation of the city as it corresponds to Los Angeles. The former includes a great deal of the surrounding area that would not, in the latter consideration, be considered part of Los Angeles, and the latter depth invokes the city itself as the justification designating the game space as a play-ground. In other words, the status of the magic circle's boundary depends somewhat on the type of play being circumscribed.

Along these lines, Katie Salen and Eric Zimmerman offer three conditions under which a game operates as a closed system, an open system, or a combination of the two. It is significant that in setting up a discussion of play in opposition to the problem of defining a game, Salen and Zimmerman initially contrast game space with the open-endedness of a child's varied degrees of interaction with a toy, alternately picking it up and putting it down to wander off. "A game of Tetris, on the other hand, provides a formalized boundary regarding play: the game is either in play or it is not. Players of Tetris do not 'casually interact' with it; rather, they are playing a game" (95). In deciding where to draw the circle around Los Santos, the question of permeability therefore also bears on the type of interaction preferred by the game. Considered as an open-ended "sandbox," Los Santos-as-city more closely resembles the toy or simulation, whereas Los Santos-as-game-level corresponds better to the closed system of Tetris described by Salen and Zimmerman. Clarifying this distinction in terms of the boundary of play, the authors define three schemas or frameworks under which the closure of the system obtains in specific ways: games as a set of rules establish a closed system, games as play offer permeable borders, and games considered as culture are completely open (96–97). Given these definitions, the game presented in GTA demonstrates most closely the definition of play (permeable borders), as does the city of Los Santos itself. Above all, it is a play-ground in which one of its games is the decision of whether or not to engage in the missions, mini-games, and objectives outlined as the content of *GTA:SA*. In this way, it is a reflexive space that contains modalities of play and the freedom to select between them as its overarching structure. By creating the space in which various toys and games are available to the player, GTA's landscape offers a magic circle that seems to depend on the aesthetic concept of Los Angeles as an abstraction on which to build its particular ludic spatiality.

Considered as an abstraction or exaggeration of urban form, it is clear that within Los Santos, distinctions exist between the various urban, suburban, and rural environments in the game and that accordingly different formal rules apply as the player engages with and navigates these spaces. This separation is most clear, for example, toward the conclusion of the game's narrative as Los Santos undergoes a riot, and the normal rules of engagement for city-play are suspended. This further sharpens the distinction between the city and the country and clarifies those boundaries with visual and formal (ludic) differences. Among other changes, the sky turns a yellowish hue, and nearby pedestrians all become potential attackers. Meanwhile, the external countryside of Red and Flint Counties remains peaceful and relatively idyllic, temporally and spatially separate from the reassigned rules and aesthetics of play established within Los Santos itself.

Still, the determination of "in" or "out" in relation to Los Santos seems to extend significantly from a general sensibility. One simply knows whether one is inside the city or not. Therefore, whatever the nature and exact boundary of Los Santos's magic circle, its existence and designation is not tied merely to its function but rather to an aesthetic sense of place arising from other factors defined by the city itself. Approaching Los Santos from the North, one encounters a clear physical and psychological barrier, neatly encapsulated in the Mulholland overpass, which separates the Mulholland neighborhood from Richman (Bel-Air) and occupies a position looking down at the Market district of downtown Los Santos, effectively separating both Mulholland and Richman from the "real" Los Santos.

This area creates a barrier in three important senses. First, the physical boundary of the hill creates a geographical separation that reinforces the visual difference during the riot periods. Looking down on the valley, one can see the yellow haze indicating that the city is burning, but pedestrians nearby may or may not be in "riot mode." A second sense of a boundary comes by way of the overhead street itself. This is significant particularly in relation to Los Angeles because Kevin Lynch's research on mental perceptions of Los Angeles found that subjects tended to think of the streets and major highways of LA more as boundaries than pathways (65). In this way, Los Santos behaves aesthetically like Los Angeles. And finally, these boundaries reinforce the underlying and critical sense of class segregation. The Mulholland district, modeled after its eponymous counterpart in LA, is a region defined as more affluent than the "ghetto" of Ganton (Compton), which is the center of the game's narrative and action.[5] Considering these three types of boundaries, it is interesting to note a precedent in this kind of thinking regarding the definition of cities. Ford Madox Ford, in his meditation on London, finds the boundaries of the city space similarly problematic, arbitrarily designating three Londons: psychological, administrative, and natural. In the course of describing these Londons, he variously considers and rejects a series of boundary designations: "Is it where the glow on the sky is no longer seen that 'the country' ends and the influence of London begins?" (25); " London begins where tree trunks commence to be black" (26); "the 'question' of London, seen from one point of view, resolves itself into that one of highways" (27). In Los Angeles as well, highways prove to be significant edges that reinforce both natural and 'psychological' edges of the city as well as separating the interior into districts and neighborhoods, and all of these ideas make similar appearances in Los Santos.

Natural edges are perhaps the most obvious, especially since three sides of Los Santos are edged by the ocean and the north side is occupied by a long ridge. Roads, furthermore, play a major part in limiting players from accessing areas not yet unlocked by the game. When the game starts, players are restricted to exploring only the greater Los Santos area, and this formal, ludic boundary is "narrativized" most naturally in the form of roadblocks. This serves a ludic purpose in encouraging the player to complete game objectives, and works well to define the relative immensity of the Los Santos space. But most importantly to this discussion, the use of roads to provide edges initiates a psychological border that further extends into the interior of the city to define neighborhoods and districts. The result is a fragmented city identity that is a mosaic of discrete spaces, many of which function autonomously in the sense of having their own shops and restaurants. Furthermore, the Johnson boys' gang is identified principally with its home street—the "Grove Street Families" or GSF—and during the "turf wars" game mode, rival gang territories are blocked into a grid formed by streets.

In all of these ways, edges are employed to define geographical, social, and aesthetic boundaries, and within the overall ludic framework of the game's magic circle, the city's aesthetic and psychological edges also come to signify various ways of understanding play spaces in relation to the city. The idea of space as ludic depends in this sense both on the spatial properties outlined by game play as well as the created sense of enclosures, but returning to the central question of this paper, thinking of the city space in terms of its boundedness seems to privilege reading the space as primarily mimicking the structures of the city. In this reading, the ludic space of the city depends on the aesthetic or psychological sense of the city created by the association of Los Santos with Los Angeles. Another, more subjective way of approaching the city space privileges navigation as the formal construct of the space in question.

Paths, Streets and Freeways

In Lynch's studies of the conceptual mapping of cities, he lists paths as an idea even more powerful than edges in determining a city's constitution and delineation into separate areas (49). Other writers have pointed to the notion of navigation and, more importantly, travel in outlining the experience of digital, virtual space portrayed in three dimensions. There is an interesting contradiction, however, in the role realism plays in depicting three-dimensional environments. Writing in 2000, Steven Poole complains of the rigorous geometric realism in games: "The spatial aesthetics of videogames are still stuck in the conservative line of the eighteenth century, because geometrically, it seems, truth is easier than interesting fiction" (225). The alternative he is proposing includes the geometric experimentation of artists like M.C. Escher, and one would assume a game like *American McGee's Alice* (2000) with its bizarre, twisting landscapes might be a gesture toward this alternative. This experimental approach is anticipated, Poole believes, by the distortions of space and physics that players take for granted in normal game play. It seems that the need to believe in a genuinely coherent physical space is suspended in place of the overriding need for identifying consistency in the experience of game play. Still, even while praising a kind of "iconic realism" (i.e. the privileging of ludic coherence over physical consistency), Poole envisions a future where games can depict cities without the arbitrary simplifications common, for example, in racing games which, at least until 2000, had attempted to portray "realistic" cities with "painted on" doorways and hedges (227). *GTA3* presumably fills this void by supplying a greater degree of interaction with the city environment, and as the most recent game in the series, *GTA:SA* is clearly the most effective in providing a rich variety of ways to interact with the environment. GTA games are, after all, racing games, so it is important to note that in Poole's terms, racing games are the most successful at portraying space because in them, the arbitrary simplifications forced into the game world fly by at blistering speeds. The compression of space players take for granted in racing games couples with a more finely granular or "ornamented" environment in GTA to create an intensely iconic and focused experience of the city. In other words, designers of racing games have found that creating a sense of a city space becomes more effective when it is oriented around navigable paths which, as Lynch notes, are already strong visual and spatial clues for inhabitants of real city space.

Gonzalo Frasca's comparison of *GTA3* to *Shenmue* also seems to reflect this duality of realism (compression and ornamentation), and Frasca similarly notes the effectiveness of travel at overcoming this apparent paradox. Whereas *Shenmue* bewilders the player with microscopic granularity,[6] *GTA3* succeeds by providing the right balance of variety in interaction so that the space can either be experienced at high speeds as in a racing game or on foot as in an adventure game (Frasca). Significantly, in both Poole and Frasca's discussion, the existence of paths with which the player can rapidly and quickly navigate the space strengthens the player's ability to identify the city as a cohesive unit. In other words, the successful implementation of comprehensive paths helps to elide the incoherencies of arbitrary simplifications otherwise necessitated by hardware limitations.

This observation, however, does not necessarily obviate the question of aesthetics in San Andreas, for, as Lynch observes, cities that make effective use of paths already rely essentially on this same principle. In fact, in interviewing citizens of Los Angeles, he found the use and knowledge of the city's major roads to be a stronger reference system than visual cues like landmarks and geography. The passage is worth quoting at length, but also reveals a surprisingly ludic preoccupation within travel:

> Automobile traffic and the highway system were dominant themes in the interviews. This was the daily experience, the daily battle—sometimes exciting, usually tense and exhausting. Trip details were full of references to signal lights and sights, intersections and turning problems. On the freeways, decisions had to be made far ahead of time; there were constant lane maneuvers. It was like shooting rapids in a boat, with the same excitement and tension, the same constant effort to "keep one's head." Many subjects noted their fears on driving a new route for the first time. There were frequent references to the overpasses, the fun of the big interchanges, the kinesthetic sensations of dropping, turning, climbing. For some persons, driving was a challenging, high-speed game [Lynch 42].

In general, there is a strong sense in which masterful knowledge of the city's space comes by way of superior skills in negotiating these large paths, and the sense of play and performance corresponds strangely to the same types of values attributed to successfully rendered, virtual cities. Noting this same trait in Los Angeles, other writers, critics, and artists have characterized the freeways of Los Angeles as a kind of ludic space, even if that is conveyed frequently in negative terms.[7]

Paths, it seems, ameliorate disorientation in both real and virtual spaces, and it is not entirely figurative to suggest that Lynch and his respondents see the city as something of a virtual space—creating stronger impressions in general or metaphoric terms rather than geometrically precise dimensions. Purely considered in terms of its spatial geometry, San Andreas merely provides a generally faithful representation of a three-dimensional network of spaces, but in optimizing its structure for high-speed navigation, the game provides an opportunity for player engagement at a level that provokes a deeper identification of the city structure and provokes the kinds of play behavior cited by countless reviewers who describe the pleasure of "just driving around" in Los Santos.

In order to achieve this objective, the space is clearly optimized for vehicular exploration, and following Poole's description of video game space as conforming chiefly to the physical capabilities of the player-protagonist (212), it seems that much of the city's spaces are designed for exploration by car. Stairways are far wider than necessary for pedestrian traffic and often are conveniently placed at one end of a straight road to serve as a launching off point for vehicular acrobatics; gaps in fences are often just wide enough for a four-wheeled vehicle to squeeze through (or run over); and major freeway arteries provide relatively clear lines of travel between points of interest (e.g. safe houses and mission starting points).

Besides creating the ludic impetus of the game's iconic engagement with physical space, transportation systems have always played an important role in defining the spaces of Southern California. Michael Dear documents the development and succession of transportation systems (first electric rail, followed by automobile freeways) as a trajectory of thinking that results in the current status of LA as a quintessentially post-modern urban space. The excess of road development (beginning at roughly the time of Lynch's analysis) corresponds to a desire for control in the development of a comprehensive "master plan" for the city's core "Centropolis" (109). The resulting space is a collective palimpsest of transportation systems, overwritten by successive developments and competing master plans for transportation (107). If pathways of travel are dominant paradigms with which a city dweller identifies the demarcations of her urban space and LA "appears to be a city without a common narrative, except perhaps an iconography of the bizarre" (11), then Los Santos as a ludic simulation of that space might be described as literally post-structural, taking as its play-ground the failed paradigm of the original master plan and re-inscribing it with a master plan that responds overtly to ludic principles.

Conversely, Greg Singh has argued that the illusion of freedom presented in *GTA:SA* is really another system of control in which creators of the game anticipate and therefore prescribe behavior patterns on the user. I believe that overplaying this aspect of control overlooks, perhaps understandably, the distinction between genuinely subversive play (play that subverts and circumscribes intended play purposes) and normative play that simply offers an overwhelming variety of options for play, some of which appear to subvert one another.[8]

Travel is also important to the sense of aesthetics available to Los Santos in presenting its condensed overview of Los Angeles. In optimizing its content for negotiation at high speeds, Los Santos' designers had to find a balance between the simplification Poole discusses and the rich complexity of photorealism. The compressed spaces in this sense rely on an exaggerated, iconic aesthetic of place that creates a particular orientation toward the player. Building on Poole and Aarseth's ideas of ludic space, Margit Grieb offers an insightful comparison of the film *Run, Lola, Run* to *Tomb Raider* in which she compares the film's Berlin setting to a standard video game landscape; "the urban setting of Berlin, a place commonly loaded with ideological meaning for other German films, has become a virtual setting; a city that never had a Reichstag, a Wall, or a Cold War 'evil twin'" (163). The perspective of the film, which self-consciously references videogames in its repeating structure, depends almost entirely on Lola's point of view as she navigates the space. Berlin, therefore, is reduced to paths and nodes, connected or traced solely for the purpose of transporting Lola through her journey. In this way, Grieb argues, the spaces of the film and, by implication, video games, are best thought of as defined by movement rather than architectural structure. Applying this principle to city design, something like the Los Angeles traffic that residents frequently complain of might emerge: a layered fiber of millions of discrete subjectivities competing for mutually exclusive lines of travel.

Along these same lines, Espen Aarseth has discussed the fundamental importance of subjectively perceived space to video games, stating, "computer games, finally, are allegories of space: they pretend to portray space in ever more realistic ways, but rely on their deviation from reality in order to make the illusion playable" ("Allegories of Space" 169). And the work for which he is most well known, *Cybertext: Perspectives on Ergodic Literature,* configures its approach to new media texts in general by considering the over-arching category of path-oriented literature, a unique type or property of text in which the reader navigates the experience of reading by the non-trivial action of making decisions about which paths to follow. In hypertext narratives, paths operate at the level of narrative, creating branching structures out of story sequences that are contingent upon prior decisions supplied by the reader. In terms of space, paths again appear as the threads of navigable space connecting information blocks into a legible network. Successful renderings of three-dimensional virtual space operate simultaneously on both of these principles, connecting both the literal paths of the geometric space with the contingency and exploration motive inherent in ergodic stories. The dramatic tension of a storyline compels the reader forward along a particular path, and in *GTA:SA*, exploration is further motivated by a vast area of objective-oriented pathways, for example, traveling to another part of town to start the next mission and find out what happens.

In this way, paths in *GTA:SA* function crucially both as spatial maps of the city's space, providing conduits for the ease of travel that amounts mastery of the space, and also as temporal threads connecting the narrative together. This "threading" effect in the narrative is significant in that it corresponds as well to the compression of space necessitated in the makeup of the game world. The fact that this double notion of path-orientation takes place on top of a city-framework succeeds in part by building on similar techniques of compression and goal-orientation already "built into" Los Angeles by its planners. Since Los Angeles is, as Dear and others have noted, a city without a master plan (or more cynically, a series of failed master plans), and residents report difficulty in creating mental maps of the city's spaces in relation to each other, it would seem that Los Santos would provide an opportunity for a more orderly structure centered around the clearer objectives of play. In fact, as Singh has argued, *GTA:SA* designers had the ability to "re-make" the city according to whatever image they chose, and in the interest of productive game play, many of the avenues certainly seem built for rapid traversal.

The districts and neighborhoods one travels to and through in Los Santos correspond to programmatically specific locations which are even further delineated by labels and (during Turf Wars) colored outlines. In this sense, the city's character seems to correspond more closely to what Dear refers to as the "High Modernist" period of transportation design in Los Angeles, when a proliferation of traffic networks converged to create a densely layered city of roads (107). Following that analogy, perhaps "Neo-Baroque" would also be an accurate label for the conceit of spatial compression and ornamentation in Los Santos,[9] but I believe that an even more important concept of spatiality gets at what Ford might call the "psychological London." Freud's concept of "the uncanny" provides a valuable framework for approaching the nature of spatiality, especially as it relates to one's identification with one's home and neighborhood. This particular observation about space in turn projects a certain sense of spatiality that in a virtual context evokes a particular aesthetic idea. In this context, it is particularly important to note the issue of repetition which in *GTA:SA* applies not only to the formal repetition of missions in order to complete them satisfactorily, but also to the experience of getting lost in Los Santos, in other words, failing to master the system. Despite the presumably rigid structure underlying the programmed space of Los Santos, the subjective experience of defining it by moving through it is in fact composed of superfluous repetitions which, when considered aesthetically, invoke the concept of the uncanny.

Nodes, Neighborhoods, and the Unheimlich

Family is a strong theme in motivating the redemption story of the game's narrative, and as noted before, Carl Johnson's gang identifies itself specifically with its neighborhood. While the idea of the uncanny has recently been a topic of scholarly interest, critics have only recently begun to extrapolate its effect into the digital sphere of virtual spaces. Still, the relationship of the uncanny to the spaces of experience is undeniable, especially as video game technology increases its appeals to photorealistic representation. In his seminal essay giving the term its present theoretical meaning, Freud unpacks the etymology of the German term "*unheimlich*" (literally "unhomely") noting in its multiple meanings the resonance of relationships to (or estrangement from) a feeling of home.[10] While Carl's home space is probably not strong enough of an association for players to identify it with a home-like sentiment, it and other save spaces in the game provide nodal points of connection for narrative and spatial sequences. In this way, safe houses in the game do demonstrate the character of repetition, one of several classes of experience Freud describes as uncanny. In this type of experience, a situation, number, person or space is encountered in an unexpected sequence and the observer finds that repetition to signify a peculiar relationship between the observer and universe. Repetition is so fundamental to game play that it may, in a sense, be taken for granted as the default manner of interaction, but considered aesthetically and in terms of spatiality, repetition provides a fruitful avenue for understanding the psychological character of Los Santos.

Freud also makes a list of the primary classes of experience that can be described as uncanny, and among those, he supplies an anecdotal illustration of the idea of repetition which will be immediately applicable to Los Santos:

> As I was walking, one hot summer afternoon, through the deserted streets of a provincial town in Italy which was unknown to me, I found myself in a quarter of whose character I could not long remain in doubt. Nothing but painted women were to be seen at the windows of the small houses, and I hastened to leave the narrow street at the next turning. But after having wandered about for a time without enquiring my way, I suddenly found myself back in the same street, where my presence was now beginning to excite attention. I hurried away once more, only to arrive by another *detour* at the same place yet a third time. Now, however, a feeling overcame me which I can only describe as uncanny, and I was glad enough to find myself back at the piazza I had left a short while before, without any further voyages of discovery [Freud 144].

This scenario demonstrates the effectiveness of public space at conveying a sense of the uncanny through repetition, and by linking it here to the notion of disorientation in an unfamiliar environment; the explorer navigating a virtual urban environment easily finds herself in

Freud's situation of disorientation. In either case, it is the surprising *sameness* of the environment that interrupts the normality of the experience, shifting the encounter into the territory of the uncanny and, in Freud's case, precluding further exploration. When the predominant activity of the game or environment in question is "voyages of discovery," introducing the uncanny would seem to be a counterproductive measure, but framed within the ludic context of the magic circle, the specific avoidance of repetition is the explorer's goal. One plays through a mission multiple times, but at its most basic, the player's goal is complete the mission so that she does not have to continue repeating it. In this way, the effect of the uncanny is displaced from the experience of repetition to the experience of the familiar within the place of the repetition. In other words, players learn to take repetition for granted, but in the specific and familiar-feeling atmospheres centered on significant nodes in Los Santos, the uncanny returns as a function of the spaces where repetition occurs. The power of the game's graphics engine (though it is now considered relatively modest) is such that renditions of spaces can be generally realistic, and this mimicry coupled with the functional repetition of encountering the same nodes repeatedly links the psychological space of Los Angeles, itself an uncanny palimpsest of repetition and disorientation, to the ludic space of Los Santos.

Nodes are an important feature of Lynch's study of Los Angeles, and it is not surprising that some of the key nodes he identifies make appearances within Los Santos. Lynch's participants frequently mentioned Pershing Square as a clearly imageable node within Los Angeles, though significantly, "for all its importance in the city image, Pershing Square seems to float a little" (37). In other words, subjects had a strong idea of what Pershing Square looked like, but had a difficult time relating to it in terms of its relationship next to or near any other nodes or paths. The function of Pershing Square in Los Santos (it is one of the few place names that is not changed in the game) is similar. Its location in the grid-like downtown area makes it difficult to locate, but it plays an important role in the repetition aspect of the game. The square is immediately adjacent to the Los Santos Police Department, so players who are "BUSTED" in the vicinity of that station restart their game facing Pershing Square. In this sense, the Square's function as a ludic node within the playing of the game is more important (and more commonly encountered) than its position as a nodal space within the layout of the city. Its status as a location of the uncanny, however, does not necessarily depend on a visual recognition of its iconic characteristics, though *déjà vu* is listed among Freud's unheimlich classes of experience.[11] Instead, the Square's dual function as structural node (i.e. as it functions in relation to gameplay) as well as a visual node places these modalities in opposition and creates instead a threshold state of mediality. In other words, Pershing Square in Los Santos has more to do with a mediated version of Los Angeles than the real Los Angeles itself. Los Santos is the Los Angeles of the Rodney King riots and films like *Get Shorty* and *LA Confidential*, and its immersive rendering of otherwise mediated spaces creates a distorted sense of perspective in which thresholds are established visually by way of exaggeration. Los Santos is, by proportion, a proliferation of landmarks in a city that is famously lacking in icons that immediately identify it to outsiders. The effect of this proliferation is the erasure of thresholds, and at the rapid speeds one traverses the cities, neighborhoods and districts quickly become more important psychologically as transition states indistinguishably fading into one another.

As a question of aesthetics, the pattern of repetition and recurring or overlapping medialities falls into what Torben Grodal calls an "aesthetics of repetition" when he states, "In several respects, video games provide an *aesthetic of repetition,* similar to that of everyday life.... In everyday life ... we repeat the same actions over and over in order to gain mastery" (Grodal 148). By contrast, film and other media have a difficult job creating a pervasive sense of three-dimensional space in part because repetition in those media has an immediately alienating effect. Still, this aesthetics potentially carries with it the baggage of *déjà vu* in the specific aesthetic sense it creates. So in constructing its iconic outlay of the visual space of the game, it is as though game designers have skipped a step in the chain of mediation: Los Santos is a simulacrum of sorts, an iconic template composed of surfaces borrowed from film and other media that has been glued onto the ludic framework required by the game. Because the discrepancy between the signifier (Los Santos) and its signified (Los Angeles) still allows for recognition, players experiencing moments of identification within Los Santos come in contact with the urban uncanny.

Deviant Play-grounds

Considering *GTA:SA* as a play system, the most obvious reading of its multifaceted game play approaches the imposing alterity of the game's allowances as subversive. Returning to Huizinga's magic circle, play that occurs within the formal structure of the game but eschews the game's given objectives can be described as subversive. This is different from cheating, which retains the value of the game's objective but in some way violates the given formal structure of play. Both subversive play and cheating honor the sanctity of the circle, but recalling that the content of the circle is both sacred and "forbidden," subversion becomes a more complex question when the play objectives themselves are considered immoral by an external system of morality. Because GTA games allow players to commit acts of gratuitous (and relatively graphic) violence, the game designers build in a play mode which seems subversive (in that game objectives have been suspended momentarily) but is in fact a key feature of the game's marketing. Singh uses this point to object to common assertions that the game allows for unparalleled freedom on the part of the player, but it is also important to note that so-called subversive play (e.g. initiating a killing spree simply to see how many "wanted stars" one can "earn") generally engages the game environment in a more literal and naturalistic way that comes in contact with Grodal's aesthetics of repetition. In other words, the game is most like a sandbox in this sense of providing a backdrop for whatever kinds of play the gamer chooses, and in this capacity, the game's aesthetics are most relevant to the player's experience. Moreover, this "playability" offered by the environment suggests a particular moral configuration which aligns interestingly with Anthony Vidler's comments about the version of LA that provides the setting for *film noir*. Expanding on Fredric Jameson's discussion of Raymond Chandler's fiction, Vidler offers the following comparison of the status of objects in film noir as opposed to earlier detective fiction:

> These objects, then, have lost the fetish character of clues, and certainly no longer carry the fetish character of their status as products, but instead gain, in their generalized dissemination through the space of the novel, an overwhelming aura of criminality *per se*, as if every beer bottle, cigarette, ashtray, and car were invested with a potential seediness, as if even the spaces in which they are set, the run-down motels, the nondescript bars, the diners, were carriers of a low-grade criminal infection that has transformed the entire city into a scene of perpetual and undifferentiated crime [130].

To apply this comment to Los Santos, the freedom of movement granted to the player and the amoral narrative context which subversive play departs from yields play that engages directly with the criminal "aura" of the city. This criminality is, moreover, closely linked to the generality of the play-types offered to the game player.

By contrast, Graphic Adventure Games that require players to solve puzzles or collect clues follow the "detective fiction" model in fetishizing these play objects. Often this is accomplished by causing "important" objects to be hot spots on the screen, so that a player knows when she is accessing an important object because the cursor will transform (for example) into the given tool for interacting with that object. In this way, objects that become fetishized are separable from their environments, and the setting remains sterilized and characterized aesthetically or morally by the overriding story provided by the game narrative. An environment like San Andreas that offers gratuitous interaction, however, allows the gratuity of those interactions to circumscribe the otherwise dominant narrative of the game's given content to the extent that the setting takes on not the character prescribed by the dominant narrative, but the "aura" extending from the nature of the available interactions. In the case of Los Santos, the effect is, like Chandler's Los Angeles, essentially a scene of "perpetual and undifferentiated crime," but in a game like *The Simpsons: Hit and Run* that mimics the play structures of GTA within a comic setting, different values can be inserted into the equation for different effects.

The aesthetics of spatiality presented in Grand Theft Auto games extends from two primary frameworks: systems of play and systems of representation. The structures of these two frames in many ways mimic one another or succeed on parallel criteria, and in the overlap between the ludic and the medial systems, emergent resonances fall under the purview of the uncanny. The case of Los Angeles is especially problematic for this analysis because it is in many ways a city of contradictions: it is a dominant feature of the American mythos, and yet it contains relatively few iconic structures. Its imagined version, therefore, falls by default into an impression of surfaces and paths which have nevertheless formed a prominent image in the backdrop of American mediality.

Notes

1. I have argued elsewhere that the generic frameworks employed by video game media operate on two competing criteria for evaluating their generic categories. These criteria correspond loosely to the syntactic/semantic dialectic of genre theory outlined by Rick Altman in *Film Theory*. In my analysis, these competing typologies in game genres might loosely fall under the terms "form" and "content" (Whalen 290). For example, labeling a game a "Third-Person Shooter" labels both a structural aspect ("third person") as well as its content (shooting). GTA covers so many forms of play and so much varied content that it is difficult to label it with any of the conventions. "Sandbox" neglects the sense in which GTA is in fact driven by narrative, so calling a non–GTA game "GTA-like" actually communicates a great deal about the game in question.

2. "Space" and "spatiality" are obviously two closely related terms, so it is worth distinguishing the two terms in the context of this discussion. "Space" refers specifically to real, three dimensional space, whereas "spatiality" refers to impressions or representations of space. Video games aim for a kind of spatiality that creates a particular kind of illusion of space, so while it is easy to slip between the two terms, spatiality is a more accurate label for the creation and use of spatial forms in virtual environments.

3. Wolf's essay enumerates eleven distinct spatial structures that appear in

videogames, but these might be better labeled as spatial apparatuses in that they deal more with spatiality (approaches to representing space) that include both the inherent, simulated qualities of the represented space (e.g. that it is three-dimensional), as well as the phenomenal aspects of the player interacting with that space (e.g. that it is accessed through a two-dimensional screen).

4. To clarify, the two threads of criticism I'm hoping to connect discuss play on the one hand and aesthetics on the other. In the first case, critics like Huizinga, Caillois, Aarseth, and Frasca discuss the types of formality and rules that apply in the successful construction of spaces for play. These play-grounds contain certain rules for their construction that can be generalized into an aesthetic sense surrounding these spaces. In the other case, writers since the mid and late 19th century have paid particular attention to the nature of urban dwelling, and some critics have explicitly addressed the aesthetics of the urban environment as definitive of the modern or postmodern human condition. What I find in this analysis is that when both criteria are applied to study environments like Grand Theft Auto, a surprising conflation occurs between the two, and the emergent criticism that develops has unique challenges to face in defining itself.

5. Though it is beyond the scope of this essay, *GTA:SA* presents a complex notion of race that walks a fine line between parody and exploitation. An analysis of racial themes in San Andreas would do well to note the use of iconic visual markers to delineate space along race and class lines.

6. Here and elsewhere in this essay, "granularity" refers to the degree to which a space can be interacted with in discrete units. A space with higher or finer granularity employs smaller discrete units than a space with larger units.

7. Steve Martin's *LA Story* comes to mind, and Frasca, writing well before the release of *GTA:SA* uses Los Angeles as an example of a GTA-style complex space: "As anybody who has attempted to drive in Los Angeles knows, the problem with space is that it takes time and other valuable resources to go from point A to point B" (Frasca). My own experience of traveling within Los Angeles has thankfully been as a passenger, though the experience was no less exhilarating when mediated through the admirable skills of a taxi driver.

8. To be clear, Singh's analysis touches on a complex notion of control within a well-articulated sense of player agency. His presentation is an attempt to problematize the hyperbolic praise and marketing hype of GTA-style games, which do tend to exaggerate the "free" aspect of play. While this is a valuable criticism, it is possible to understand the practice (or perhaps illusion) of freedom in aesthetic terms because of the necessarily subjective perception of agency in the game. Singh's analysis is also useful in introducing the dialectic of mediation, which I address in the third section of this paper.

9. Neo-Baroque in this sense follows Angela Ndalianis's discussion of the proliferation of baroque ideas within new media and cyber culture generally. In her analysis, qualities of the Neo-Baroque include labyrinthine meta-narratives, mixed-media ornamentation, and serial or branching narrative structures (35). All of these could potentially apply to Grand Theft Auto, but the implications of applying this analysis for the present argument are too lengthy to explore here.

10. However, since the significance of spatiality in GTA has to do with its subjective perspective, I should point out that I have experienced a twinge of nostalgia in returning to Grove Street after spending several hours of game time pursuing wealth in Las Venturas.

11. The function of déjà vu in place identification within videogames certainly warrants a detailed study of its own, but it is worth noting here in the context of the uncanny that I've known several individuals who have reported déjà vu in playing Grand Theft Auto games. I recently taught a media studies section in which students had the option of playing through a video game and blogging their progress as it related to other content in the class. One student who chose *GTA:VC* happened to be from Miami, and she frequently commented on the familiarity of the setting:

"Though Grand Theft Auto's depiction of Miami is one of [*Miami Vice*] and *Scarface* its basic foundation is similar to that of today's Miami Beach. The hotels are exactly the same-neon lights and all. Every time I drive down Ocean Avenue I think of home. The only visible difference is the amount of people." Similarly, an acquaintance of mine reports playing *The Getaway* simply for the opportunity to "visit" the London street where he lived for a semester abroad.

In my own experience, the sensation has been the opposite. On a recent visit to Los Angeles, I found myself recognizing certain neighborhoods and landmarks and finding them eerily familiar from my knowledge of playing Los Santos.

Works Cited

Aarseth, Espen. "Allegories of Space: The Question of Spatiality in Computer Games." *Cybertext Yearbook 2000*. Ed. Markku Eskelinen and Raine Koskimaa. Jyväskylä: U of Jyväskylä P, 2001.
_____. *Cybertext: Perspectives on Ergodic Literature*. Baltimore: Johns Hopkins UP, 1997.
Altman, Rick. *Film/Genre*. London: British Film Institute, 1999.
American McGee's Alice. Redwood City: Electronic Arts, 2000.
Dear, Michael J. *The Postmodern Urban Condition*. Malden: Blackwell, 2000.
Ford, Ford Madox. *The Soul of London: A Survey of a Modern City*. Ed. Alan G. Hill. London: Everyman Library, 1995.
Frasca, Gonzalo. "Sim Sin City: Regarding *Grand Theft Auto III*." *Game Studies* 3.1 (2003). <http://www.gamestudies.org/0302/frasca/>.
Freud, Sigmund. "The Uncanny." *The Uncanny (The New Penguin Freud)*. Trans. David McLintock. New York: Penguin, 2003.
Grand Theft Auto III. New York: Rockstar, 2001.
Grand Theft Auto: San Andreas. New York: Rockstar, 2004.
Grand Theft Auto: Vice City. New York: Rockstar, 2002.
Grodal, Torben. "Stories for Eye, Ear, and Muscles: Video Games, Media, and Embodied Experiences." *The Video Game Theory Reader*. Ed. Mark J.P. Wolf and Bernard Perron. New York: Routledge, 2003.
"Gun—Review Xbox." *ContactMusic.com*. 2 Dec. 2005. 18 Jan. 2006 <http://www.contactmusic.com/new/home.nsf/webpages/gunreviewxboxx02x12x05>.
Gun. Santa Monica: Activision, 2005.
Huizinga, Johan. *Homo Ludens: A Study of the Play Element in Culture*. Boston: Beacon, 1955.
Lynch, Kevin. *The Image of the City*. Cambridge: MIT P, 1960.
Ndalianis, Angela. *Neo-Baroque Aesthetics and Contemporary Entertainment*. Cambridge: MIT P, 2005.
Poole, Steven. *Trigger Happy: The Inner Life of Videogames*. London: Fourth Estate, 2000.
Raymond, Justin. "GUN Review." *GameZone*. 29 Nov. 2005. 18 Jan. 2006 <http://gamecube.gamezone.com/gzreviews/r26881.htm>.
Salen, Katie, and Eric Zimmerman. *Rules of Play: Game Design Fundamentals*. Cambridge: MIT P, 2004.
Shenmue. Tokyo, JP: Sega, 1999.
The Simpsons: Hit and Run. Los Angeles: Vivendu Universal Games, 2003.
Vidler, Anthony. *Warped Space: Art, Architecture, and Anxiety in Modern Culture*. Cambridge: MIT P, 2000.
Whalen, Zach. "Game/Genre: A Critique of Generic Formulas in Video Games in the Context of 'The Real.'" *Works & Days* 22.44 (2004): 290–303.
Wolf, Mark J.P. "Space in the Video Game." *The Medium of the Video Game*. Ed. Mark J.P. Wolf. Austin: U of Texas P, 2001.

10. Experiencing Place in Los Santos and Vice City

IAN BOGOST AND DAN KLAINBAUM

The Grand Theft Auto (GTA) videogame series puts the player in large, semi-realistic urban environments. Despite their apparent credibility, these environments are not re-creations of real urban locales, but rather remixed, hybridized cities fashioned from popular culture's notions of real American cities. Locality, the sense of being in a specific city, is especially predominant in Rockstar's recreation of Miami and Los Angeles, those familiar yet fictional streets of Vice City and Los Santos.

By focusing on popular culture's mediation of contemporary American cities instead of directly mapping physical terrain, the GTA series embodies a highly playable (though geographically incorrect) translation of real places. In this context, *translation* refers not only to the physical treatment of each city's local architecture and atmosphere, but also to a rendition of the spirit of these cities as they exist in popular culture. *Grand Theft Auto: Vice City (GTA:VC)* is more representative of the 1980s television cop drama *Miami Vice* than of the city of Miami, and *Grand Theft Auto: San Andreas (GTA:SA)* is more representative of the 1990s film *Boyz in the Hood* than of the city of Los Angeles. By leveraging these popular notions with existing spatial conventions, Rockstar creates an amalgam of real and mediated places resulting in hybrid virtual cities whose cultural rules prove more salient than their physical geography.

Space, Place, and Presence in Videogames

Speeding down *Grand Theft Auto: Vice City's* beachfront strip—the game's representation of South Beach's Ocean Drive—creates an experience analogous to driving in Miami. This same experience is recreated when cruising down *Grand Theft Auto: San Andreas'* equivalent of the Pacific Coast Highway. Understanding how this locality is achieved requires an exploration into the theoretical notions of space, place and presence.

Space is an abstract concept with a broad and varied set of definitions. In Grand Theft Auto games, as with most contemporary videogames, space is defined in the Newtonian sense; as an absolute grid within which objects are located and events occur (Curry 5). This is a popular definition of space, intuitively understood in our contemporary world. The development of computer graphics is a visual implementation of this definition through the use of Cartesian geometry as the screen's coordinate axis representing this absolute grid.

The recent GTA games represent space on the screen primarily through 3D graphics, a method of visualization derived from landscape painting and perspective drawing. Space is also represented through cartographic representation to help the player in navigation. These two methods are aligned with the Newtonian definition of space as an absolute grid and are part of this lineage of western spatial representation.

The history of spatial representation in videogames (Fernandes-Vara, Zagal, and Mateas 8) shows an evolution from abstract 2D space in early games such as *Pac-Man* towards 3D representation in contemporary game worlds that exist beyond the confines of a single screen such as in *GTA3*. Three-dimensional space in gaming is a full realization of Newtonian space and remains the dominant representation in games today. The conventions of this mode were established in the early 1990s with *Mario 64* (Nintendo). Starting with *Grand Theft Auto III (GTA3)*, the series takes its cues on representation of space found in the early Mario classic.

Like space, the term place also has numerous definitions and interpretations when applied to videogame theory. We can begin with the equation, "place = space + meaning" (Harrison and Dourish 1). More specifically, the humanist geographer Yi-Fu Tuan defines place as space with 'history and meaning.' Where space is abstract, place is concrete: space is a grid that can be overlaid on all places, like the city of New York. In videogames we can perceive space as the abstract conception of 3D space, and place as the specific game world we experience such as *Zelda's* Hyrule or *Grand Theft Auto III's* Liberty City.

What is the process of representing Los Angeles and Miami as places in the world of GTA? How are experiences like driving down Melrose Avenue or Ocean Drive recreated in the virtual city? The ways in which GTA accomplishes this feat seem central to the success of their game worlds. If players do not experience presence, a sense of being in these cities, in the places of Vice City and San Andreas, then the act of transgressing the social norms within these cities will not be as appealing to players. The pleasure of the games' so-called "open play" likewise depends on a richness of spatial meaning. The series' success is the achievement of this locality, the presence created for the player.

Presence is a popular notion in the field of Virtual Reality (VR); it frequently describes a user's sense of being in an environment. In third person perspective games such as *GTA:SA*, presence is achieved by the embodiment of Tommy Vercetti, the player's avatar, in the virtual world. The player's agency in that world is expressed through driving cars, going into buildings, engaging in gang fights, and so forth. The Grand Theft Auto games and most other contemporary videogames employ similar techniques for representing 3D space. Scenes in linear perspectives visually immerse the player in the game's action, while map screens are used to navigate the space. These representations are based on notions of Newtonian space.

While extensive research exists on techniques for creating presence in general Newtonian spaces such as hospitals and cities, inquiry into the role of specific places goes largely neglected. Questions of how different cities each create a unique type of presence go mostly unanswered. This void points to a focus on the generalities of spatial experience in lieu of creating presence in specific places, leaving out an important element of our lived geographic experiences. Game developers parallel this trend, providing players with an infinite amount of general game spaces. Setting GTA apart is its ability to create compelling fictional places based on real American cities. These representations exploit the power of place combined with a player's agency in the game world, contribute to a high level of presence for the player.

Perceiving the Urban Landscape

How do we perceive the cities we inhabit? GTA games create a sense of presence in urban landscapes by operationalizing a fundamental understanding of how we perceive the very real cities we live in. Tuan articulates two registers to describe this process of understanding human perception of cities (Tuan 224). The first level is through our intimate daily experiences: the streets we drive on our way to work, the corner on which we find our favorite grocery store. These are specific nuances that are as unique as the individuals who hold them. They are the mental maps we maintain that allow us to function and understand where we live (Lynch 7). The second level of perception is through the abstract notion of a particular city as symbol or image. This image is created by the popular imagination through television, news, radio, and other media.

Designing virtual cities for the first level of perception is difficult and unproductive. It is an impossible task to capture the nuances of a city such that a wide audience of players can relate their personal understanding of that place to its virtual equivalent. While the dream of complete physical verisimilitude pervades popular fantasy fiction (*Star Trek*'s holodeck) and contemporary consumer electronics (HTDV, "next-gen" consoles like Xbox 360 and PlayStation 3), total realism in digital representation remains elusive. The time and energy it would take to map out an entire city's nuances would be a never ending project—it would require an absolute replica of the city at any, or every, given moment in time. When players find themselves in a familiar virtual city, they always attempt to visit the places they know. Inevitably, failure to find a favorite coffee shop results in a breaking down of immersion for the player and makes the virtual environment less meaningful. Likewise, for those who are unfamiliar with a city, nuances such as these would prove less meaningful. Placing such a great emphasis on mimicking the real city compromises the experience for the player in the virtual city when their specific knowledge of a real place goes unrewarded.

The second level, symbolic representation, is where the GTA series excels. San Andreas and Vice City are built on the symbolic perceptions of Los Angeles and Miami respectively. GTA builds its virtual worlds from the perceptions of these cities as they exist in popular culture, instilling a sense of presence in fictional, yet familiar, places. In doing so, GTA brings these virtual environments to life.

If symbolic elements are more significant than bricks-and-mortar representations in creating presence, to what extent are these elements successfully combined? Understanding Los Angeles and Miami as symbolic places made up of cultural and social elements allows Rockstar to create the compelling, playable worlds of San Andreas and Vice City. In the remainder of this chapter we will look closely at the real and symbolic elements of a virtual city in GTA. In particular, we will expose the importance of creating virtual worlds not as re-created places but as spaces that properly attenuate human cognitive functions, with an emphasis on how cities are perceived rather than on their objective realities.

San Andreas as Los Angeles

From Fredric Jameson's famous account of its architecture (Jameson 107–119) to Mike Davis's accounts of its racially striated structural scaffolding (Davis) to Jean Baudrillard's pessimistic meditations on its cultural depravity (Baudrillard 51–64), Los Angeles has often been the subject of critical reflections on nature of postmodern urban experience. One theme that recurs by necessity in such accounts is the automobile, both the pleasure and the curse of Angelenos' daily routines.

Given the series' penchant for adaptations of actual cities, it is perhaps surprising that it took until the fifth installment for the Grand Theft Auto series to tackle Los Angeles. Liberty City, star of its first and now infamous third titles, with their *Godfather*-like gangster motifs, bears closest cultural similarity to New York or perhaps Chicago, both cities in which trains and sidewalks are commoner means of transportation than automobile. *GTA:VC's* focus on Miami as it was represented in the 1980s TV series *Miami Vice*, made automobiles a more plausible focus; that show went to great lengths to showcase exotic cars, large motorboats, and other examples of vehicular excess. But the series title seems particularly suited for Los Angeles, a city famous for its carjackings, freeway shootings, high (and low)-speed chases, and its generally unrivaled car culture.

The *reductio ad absurdum* of this principle was showcased in *L.A. Story*, when Steve Martin's character Harris K. Telemacher drives two doors down to visit his neighbor. There is some truth to this parody; many Angelenos have little experience of their city on foot, even in their own neighborhoods. Scarcity and expense of real estate dictates underground parking at many apartments, condos, and commercial districts (including most supermarkets). Angelenos thus often descend from their residences to their cars in the morning, then from their cars to their workplaces and back again without setting a foot outdoors. As William J. Mitchell says of the city, "It never feels quite right to walk around Los Angeles. It's not just that the streets aren't pedestrian friendly; it's also that you can't get to know the city that way. The scale is too large, you're moving too slowly.... You need a car—preferably air-conditioned, with a good sound system" (Mitchell 153). The primary experience of the city comes at the wheel of the automobile.

The expanse of sprawl that constitutes L.A. and its surroundings frequently tie the cultural value of the city directly to its streets: Hollywood Boulevard, the Sunset Strip, Santa Monica Boulevard, Rodeo Drive, Laurel Canyon, Mulholland Drive. Many of these streets share their names with films and pop songs (some about the streets, others not), reinforcing the tie between the cultural and the cartographic. The association of cultural codes creates a temptation to recreate the topology of such spaces in simulations.

One such game is *True Crime: Streets of LA (Streets of LA)*. The design is significantly and clearly influenced by the Grand Theft Auto series, casting the player as a Los Angeles cop who can choose to uphold the law or break it. In GTA style, the player can "acquisition" vehicles to traverse the environment. And environment is precisely how *Streets of LA* attempted to distinguish itself from GTA. The game claims to realistically map and texture-map 420 square miles of the actual topology of the city Los Angeles.

Streets of LA focuses on the real elements of the city in an attempt to recreate Los Angeles as a credible location for either mission-based or open-ended play. As a former Angeleno, Bogost was most interested in the latter—experiencing a simulation of the city rather than a simulation of crime or crime-fighting. But the demands of cartographic verisimilitude quickly break down, revealing the problems with bricks-and-mortar representations.

The game begins in downtown LA, and after two short training missions the player is allowed to ignore the missions and wander freely throughout the city. Bogost, who lived in Los Angeles for ten years, was eager to explore old residences and old haunts, and he set out west from Grand St. toward the 110 freeway. After a strange mishap in which he somehow embedded his car in the fascia of the Bonaventure hotel, he "acquisitioned" a large SUV, a more culturally appropriate vehicle for the city.

The cartographic accuracy of *Streets of LA* is remarkable. The game scatters real landmarks like the Bonaventure in their proper cartographic positions in an attempt to facilitate way finding, the use of familiar landmarks as a means of self-orientation, a point to which we will return shortly. Every street is in just the right place, with each turn and intersection properly oriented on all three axes of Cartesian space. Bogost's muscle memory of the map of LA was enough to guide him to the freeway onramp, which twisted around from 2nd St. and Figueroa in precisely the manner a regular downtown commuter would expect. So far, *Streets of LA* would seem to offer a credible recreation of the City of Angels.

But this reliance on cartographic accuracy quickly breaks down. While culturally eminent waypoints like the Bonaventure, the Santa Monica Pier, or the Beverly Center mall insure the coarsest level of common experience of the city, the principal waypoints in everyday practice are much less culturally charged. The symbolic representations of familiar places guide our experience of place much more so than the logic of cartography.

Consider Bogost's experience visiting the simulation of Los Angeles in *Streets of LA*. Soon after merging onto the 110 freeway, which heads south from downtown LA toward south central, inconsistencies and rifts in the topographically verisimilitudinous environment quickly emerged. First appeared a freeway exit marked Blaine St., an exit which in fact does not exist. After merging onto the westbound 10 freeway, another spectral exit appeared, 20th St. / Koreatown. Bogost decided to drive first to the Miracle Mile area of the city, where he lived for many years. He was further surprised to see a textual overlay, "Miracle Mile," on the screen at the Crenshaw exit—later this confusion would be amplified by the game's declaration that Wilshire and Fairfax, the heart of Miracle Mile, was in fact West Hollywood.

Small, seemingly irrelevant details plagued the game's attempts at cartographic realism. Traffic lights were missing at the 10 freeway Washington onramp and at the corner of Airdrome and Fairfax. A Shell gas station Bogost frequented at the corners of Fairfax, Olympic, and San Vicente was reduced to an empty asphalt lot. Fairfax offered two lanes rather than one (a rush hour traffic nightmare) between Pico and Olympic. His old apartment building across from Hancock Park was transformed into a supermarket, and the eminently middlebrow Marie Callendar's restaurant down the street was replaced by a nudie club (nudie clubs seemed to pervade *Streets of LA*'s version of the city). These and similar structures offer scarcely little general cultural relevance, but they provide the perception of intimate daily experiences. For Bogost, the absent chain restaurant and the missing gas station were far more disruptive to immersion than cartographic inconsistencies would have been.

This discrepancy also extends to the more culturally prevalent landmarks represented in *Streets of LA*. While the Bonaventure hotel, the Santa Monica Pier, the 3rd Street Promenade, the Beverly Center, even the Frank Gehry-designed Santa Monica Place mall earn detailed and convincing recreations in the game, other LA landmarks are missing. Hancock Park is present but the La Brea Tar Pits are absent. The garden-clad, gold building that houses Variety magazine and producer Aaron Spelling's offices is in its proper place, but the Los Angeles County Museum of Art (LACMA) is nowhere to be found. Driving up Westwood Blvd. through Westwood Village, Bogost was startled to be brought to a halt by a concrete barrier where his alma mater UCLA should have been; the barricade extends around the entire campus, prohibiting entry. USC's fate was even worse: residential neighborhoods sit where the campus should have been. The university's central pedestrian walk, Trousdale Parkway, was just another row of south central-styled houses.

Including even the most endemic landmarks proves an insurmountable task.

Despite the game's failure at cartographic realism, it does enjoy some success at recreating Los Angeles as place. While low-resolution and utterly devoid of meaningful interaction, the architecture throughout the city is designed to adopt a credible style for each area. Miracle Mile boasts characteristic art deco storefronts. Its residential streets are lined with Spanish-style homes. Westwood and Brentwood boast colorful, modern condos, and South Central its large, Victorian homes and small stucco shacks. These architectural abstractions proved among the more successful supplements to *Streets of LA*'s cartographic logic. Despite chasms in tangible credibility, the blending of player expectation at specific intersections and aura of the abstract architecture yields a sometimes-evocative sense of presence. Nevertheless, the game's focus on the cartographic over the symbolic makes the city feel technical, designed rather than alive.

Grand Theft Auto: San Andreas takes a decidedly different approach to the representation of Los Angeles, that of city as place instead of map. As with the previous games of the series, the era is explicitly established (early 1990s for *GTA:SA*), but the locations are knowing representations of real cities. The city of Los Santos is fictional, yet obviously meant to represent Los Angeles even in name—the Spanish name, the transposition of angel with saint. The city itself is very large, but it bears no cartographic resemblance whatsoever to the real topology of Los Angeles.

Taking the place of cartographic realism is a significant extension and deepening of the symbolic representation featured in *Streets of LA*. Rather than devoting resources to the intricate recreation of roadways— hollow, empty spaces that all look the same in the final analysis—*GTA:SA* creates equivalent, yet abstract representations of key Los Angeles spaces.

Consider the starting point and home base for the game, a neighborhood called Jefferson. Its geography and position in the city bears no relation to the Compton neighborhood it is based on, yet the architecture and microgeography of the area matches that area precisely. Nearby neighborhood Idlewood's riffs off the real community of Inglewood, giving the player macroscopic clues about the cultural relevance of these parts of the city. Small name changes help set the player's symbolic expectations throughout Los Santos. The Latino neighborhood of East LA becomes East Los Santos; the upscale Beverly Hills becomes Rodeo, named for the real neighborhood's signature Rodeo Drive. Santa Monica becomes Santa Marina Beach, and the Sunset Strip nightclub district becomes, amusingly, Sunrise.

These name shifts are not merely clever attempts to remedy the city's arbitrary layout. Whereas *Streets of LA* relies on real street names as the primary means of player orientation, *GTA:SA* uses the names as symbolic markers that set up an abstract, received cultural expectation. This approach makes the city much more credible to players familiar and unfamiliar with its real-world referent. Los Santos makes no promises to recreate the cartographic reality of Los Angeles; instead, it deploys abstractions of its culturally relevant neighborhoods to recreate the symbolic and social reality of that city. This focus on the simulation of space makes Los Santos a more accurate simulation of Los Angeles.

The game partly makes good on that promise. Its story revolves around the player-character, CJ, and his attempt to reform and rebuild his neighborhood gang, Grove Street. Rival gangs occupy nearby neighborhoods—Ballas in Idewood, Varios Los Aztecas in East Los Santos. The player must infiltrate, undermine, and even overpower these gangs by force and, more importantly, by garnering respect. Ironically, the game offers less functional distinction between the inner-city neighborhoods and those upscale ones cross-town. The architecture, vehicles, and dress in Rodeo or Santa Marina match their real-world equivalents much more precisely than do the actual neighborhoods in *Streets of LA*, but the game imbues these regions with few meaningful behaviors. Perhaps most notably, race and class differences are all but ignored by the game's upscale non-player-characters (Bogost).

But for players who merely wish to explore the city in accordance with the game's much-celebrated open-ended style, Los Santos serves as a surprisingly convincing simulation of Los Angeles. With the many inconsistencies of cartographic realism averted, Los Santos invites players to fill in the details of its symbolic abstractions with their own experiences. Importantly, these experiences can be real and personal—like Bogost's and other Angeleno's intimate, daily experiences with the city— or they can be fictional and received—like viewers' experience of *Boyz in the Hood*, *LA Story*, *Heat*, or other filmic and televisual representations of Los Angeles.

Vice City as Miami

GTA:VC's recreation of Miami echoes the symbolic perception of the city as represented in 1980s film and television. This symbol of the violent paradise existing between the streets of New York and the jungles of South America presents Miami as a glamorous tropical gateway. Miami is a city teeming with guns and money, straddling the under-developed manufacturing countries of illegal narcotics and the over-developed cities that consume these goods. The fascination with this urban landscape exploded in the 1980s due to high profile developments of corrupt police officers involved in the drug trade, an era of celebrity cartel bosses, as well as highway tourist slayings.

Creating a virtual environment based on the popular image of the city of Miami, *GTA:VC* exploits the sensibilities of the player living in a media saturated world. Influenced by the mobster movie *Scarface*, the television show *Miami Vice*, and news media coverage of Miami in the 1980s, Vice City is a composite of the imagery from these earlier media artifacts; a media representation based on previous mediated representations of the city of Miami.

Miami is not only the land of guns, drugs, and money; it is also the city of immigrants and transplants. In *GTA:VC* we embody the character of Tommy Vercetti upon his arrival in town seeking both revenge and fortune in the drug trade. Tommy is a composite of *Miami Vice*'s Ricardo Tubbs, the New York detective seeking revenge for the murder of his brother in Miami, and *Scarface's* Tony Montana, the Cuban Mariel refugee seeking fortune far from Castro's communism. All three characters are found arriving into town in the opening shots of their respective mediums.

GTA:VC exaggerates the symbol and myth of Miami, making the filmic space of *Scarface* and the televisual space of *Miami Vice* playable. Although some elements of the layout of Vice City echo the real layout of Miami, they are not implemented to create immersion and serve only as satirical antidotes for those familiar with the real city's streets. Upon his initial playing of the game it didn't take long for Klainbaum, a Miami resident for over 12 years, to abandon any attempts at finding personally meaningful landmarks (while driving his Ferrari). The overall urban layout mimics that of Miami, connecting the glamorous beaches to the mainland neighborhoods of Little Havana and Little Haiti, as well as the skyscrapers of downtown.

Game play in *GTA:VC* begins in Tommy's apartment located across from Ocean Beach, the game's recreation of Ocean Drive. This is the prime destination in South Beach with beachfront art deco hotels and bars. The location of Tommy's apartment bears resemblance with the same spot which Tony Montana narrowly avoided death by chainsaw in *Scarface*. Similarly, the Vercetti Mansion is a close replica of Tony Montana's mansion, complete with grand staircase, red carpets and walls, as well as stacks of surveillance monitors in the office. The mansion is appropriately located in Starfish Island between the mainland and the beach. Starfish Island is the stand-in for the real Star and Fisher Islands, where celebrities like Madonna, Shaqueil O'Neil, and Sylvester Stallone have resided in recent years. Adding to the symbol of glamour and violence in Vice City, Escobar International Airport is named by combining one of the most famous drug lords in recent times, Pablo Escobar with the real Miami International Airport.

Creating presence by exploiting a player's expectations of a virtual environment is called "priming"(Nunez and Black 107). Priming demonstrates the important role of cognitive psychology in creating virtual worlds. *GTA:VC* primes its players for immersion in Vice City first by developing a virtual environment based on pre-existing imagery of popular culture. Then it primes its players through marketing and advertising materials that familiarize the players with a consistent presentation of the game. Rockstar Games adamantly self-publishes all materials related to their games, ensuring consistency and proper priming of their players. Using these two techniques, expectations of what players will find in Vice City are established well before the game is loaded on their consoles. When a player's expectations of a virtual environment are met, they experience a heightened presence within that environment.

Other techniques borrowed from Hollywood include spatial overlapping and off screen audio. By presenting a scene first through a wide shot and then through a close-up, the characters in the close-up are contextualized within an environment. In *GTA:VC*, the opening shots of the landscape place the game action in a city very similar to Miami. This is the same technique exhibited in the *Miami Vice* TV series with its famous introductory credit sequence. Off screen audio is also commonly used to create televisual and filmic space. Sounds created from people and objects outside of the frame enlarge a scene and help place it in a spatial context. *GTA:VC's* use of sirens, CB radios, and random pedestrian conversation help establish a sense of presence in a living city for the player. The use of accents in the conversations contributes to a sense of cultural presence.

Comparing *GTA:VC* to the *Miami Vice* videogame exposes two distinct games derived from the same source material. While *GTA:VC* seeks to create an engaging virtual environment, *Miami Vice* places the player in an episode of the popular television show. *Miami Vice* presents a linear storyline with sections adapted for game play in specific scenarios; the drug lord mansion, an art gallery, and the port. On the other hand, *GTA:VC* is an amalgam of similar locales each imbued with a life of their own. Traversing the levels of *Miami Vice* is monotonous; each level is a re-skinned rendition of the others. *GTA:VC* achieves a level of authenticity in its implementation through the attention to detail employed making each environment rich and compelling. *GTA:VC* allows for exploration and rewards players with surprises that are consistent with the overall perception of the city; whereas *Miami Vice* does not allow players to stray from the linear game path, making for a constricting experience. This constriction decreases the level of presence in a virtual environment, as players cannot freely move within the perceived physical space.

Miami Vice the videogame also places emphasis on the ability to embody the popular characters, Crocket and Tubbs, from the original show. A unique game play feature allows players to dynamically switch between these two characters to best match the skills required in a given situation; Tubbs is stronger and can knock down doors, Crocket is agile and can climb walls. By avoiding the use of pre-existing characters, *GTA:VC* emphasizes the exploration of the virtual environment as the selling point of the game. This exploration encourages players to inhabit the city in unique ways.

While many licensed games such as *Miami Vice* implement plot lines and characters from their source artifacts, *GTA:VC* places emphasis squarely on the virtual environment. For *GTA:VC*, drawing players into the game is primarily about creating a rich and open-ended game world and allowing players to inhabit it. This technique is compared with that of the *Miami Vice* game of recreating a series of plot events and allowing the player to embody the celebrity characters as these pre-defined plots are executed.

The success of *GTA:VC* points away from the use of pre-canned narratives and personalities as successful elements in videogames to those of compelling spaces and engagement with processes. Although a linear storyline is available in *GTA:VC*, it is the rich world and the ability to explore it that draws players in. This exposes a productive method for game design of creating compelling and engaging virtual environments, aligned with a player's expectations of that environment.

Driving as Mediating Experience

A powerful technique for the creation of presence in GTA is the re-creation of driving as a mediating experience. In the developed world the urban landscape is predominantly experienced through the distancing mediation of the automobile. A car's windshield can be compared to the television and computer screens by which we experience much contemporary interaction; separating passengers from the world outside and creating a separate space within the automobile. The single source of communication found in GTA cars is the stereo. The decision to allow switching of radio stations greatly aids in the creation of presence for the player. As Mitchell suggests, driving through a city and flipping through the radio tuner defines the contemporary experience of the American urban landscape. The re-creation of driving and simulated radio in GTA promotes a presence in the game worlds of *GTA:VC* and *GTA:SA*.

Furthermore, the content of the radio stations contribute to the mood and era GTA is trying to establish for its players and are of the specific city. In *GTA:VC*, 80s pop music and in *GTA:SA* early 90s gangster rap further place the player in their cities. Interestingly, the television show *Miami Vice* was influenced by the popularity of MTV's mixture of music and images to create moods. *Miami Vice's* use of popular music as ambient soundtrack proved to be a cutting edge implementation in television of the time. Tuan describes the audio as a sense-medium that "encompasses and surrounds" (Tuan 8) the listener, immersing them in an environment. This has a distinct affect as the distancing that visual media afford. As opposed to imagery, sound comes to us from all directions, engulfing the listener. In addition, music has the power to spark memories in people. By using music from a specific era, GTA further immerses the player in the time of its setting and contextualizes the virtual city.

Creating Place

The perceived and known world can be expressed through the media of painting, cartography, photography, storytelling, or videogames (Casey 246). A successful artifact allows people to experience the place represented in a new way. In order to express the complex notion of place, such an artifact should not solely focus on the physical attributes of a place, such as specific buildings or streets, but should also express a more complex understanding of place that includes cultural codes and popular symbols.

Western culture's insistent custom of representing space and place through media can be traced throughout history from the development of linear perspective techniques in painting to the promise of contemporary videogame consoles that put you "in the game" or invite you to "play in their world." In videogames, this practice has been mostly limited to the representation of places as visual re-creations, neglecting many of the sensual and cognitive ways place is experienced. GTA games accomplish a highly expressive representation of Los Angeles and Miami through the digital medium. Building on existing game conventions and popular culture's notions of these cities, GTA creates the compelling game worlds of *GTA:VC* and *GTA:SA,* respectively. These virtual cities combine existing notions of real cities with fictional elements to maximize the experience of locality for the player.

In its success, GTA is a critique as well as an affirmation of the influence of media on people in the developed world. In our increasingly mediated society, what is perceived as real and what is mediated are notions that are becoming blurred. Rockstar's ability to create a compelling place lies in its awareness of these contemporary cultural shifts. These games are designed with a deep understanding of the layered representations that define our media-saturated world, giving GTA games their popular appeal. In essence, Rockstar has created an expressive virtual environment highly influenced by the contemporary tradition of mediated artifacts.

In GTA, players find themselves in compelling translations of American urban landscapes—compelling and controversial virtual environments are a poignant satire of American culture. Lost in the many denunciations of the game's violence is recognition of the sophisticated symbolic spatial representations that pervade Liberty City, San Andreas, and Vice City. The power of symbolic spatial representation and the sophisticated sense of presence created by GTA cannot be overlooked. GTA has exposed the capabilities of these new techniques, pointing towards a future of captivating, entertaining, and powerful places yet to be experienced.

Works Cited

Baudrillard, Jean. *America.* Trans. Chris Turner. London: Verso, 1989.
Bogost, Ian. "Frame and Metaphor in Political Games." *DiGRA 2005 Selected Papers.* Ed. Suzanne de Castell and Jen Jenson. Vancouver, BC: Simon Fraser U, 2005.
Casey, Edward S. *Representing Place: Landscape Painting & Maps.* Minneapolis: U of Minnesota P, 2002.
Curry, Micheal R. "On Space and Spatial Practice in Contemporary Geography." *Concepts in Human Geography.* Ed. Carville Earle, Kent Mathewson, and Martin S. Kenzer. London: Rowman & Littlefield, 1996. 3–32.
Davis, Mike. *City of Quartz: Excavating the Future in Los Angeles.* New York: Vintage, 1992.
Fernandez-Vara, Clara, Jose Pablo Zagal, and Michael Mateas. "Evolution of Spatial Configurations in Videogames." *Changing Views—Worlds in Play.* Vancouver: Digital Games Research Association, 2005. 8.
Grand Theft Auto III. New York: Rockstar, 2001.
Grand Theft Auto: San Andreas. New York: Rockstar, 2004.
Grand Theft Auto: Vice City. New York: Rockstar, 2002.
Harrison, Steve, and Paul Dourish. "Re-Place-Ing Spaces: The Roles of Place and Space in Collaborative Systems." *Computer Supported Cooperative Work.* Cambridge: ACM, 1996.
Jameson, Fredric. *Postmodernism, or the Cultural Logic of Late Capitalism.* Durham: Duke UP, 1991.

L.A. Story. Perf. Steve Martin. Film. 1991.

Lynch, Kevin. *The Image of the City.* Cambridge: MIT P, 1960.

Mario 64. Nintendo, 1996.

Miami Vice. Davilex Games, 2005.

Miami Vice. Perf. Don Johnson, Anthony Michael Harris. Television. 1984.

Mitchell, William J. *Placing Words: Symbols, Space, and the City.* Cambridge: MIT P, 2005.

Nunez, David, and Edwin Blake. *Conceptual Priming as a Determinant of Presence in a Virtual Environment.* Rondebosch: U of Cape Town, 2003.

Scarface. Perf. Al Pachino. Film. 1983.

True Crime: Streets of LA. Santa Monica: Activision, 2003.

Tuan, Yi-Fu. *Topophilia: A Study of Environmental Perceptions, Attitudes, and Values.* New York: Columbia UP, 1990.

11. Positioning and Creating the Semiotic Self in *Grand Theft Auto: Vice City* and *Grand Theft Auto: San Andreas*

JOHN A. UNGER AND KARLA V. KINGSLEY

According to C.S. Peirce, one of the founders of semiotics, "If we seek the light of external facts the only cases that we can find are of thought in signs…. The only thought, then, that can possibly be cognized is thought in signs. But thought that cannot be cognized does not exist. All thought, therefore, must necessarily be in signs" (Peirce, *The Essential Writings* 81). This process of creating a sign to plan, organize, categorize, and/or remember, thereby *mediating* human activity, is known as *signification* (Vygotsky, *Mind* 74). Vygotsky illustrated this process with the example of tying a string around one's finger to remember something; the string is transformed into a sign. The string as sign *mediates* the act of remembering.

How many times do humans go through this process of using a sign to mediate one or more activities in a day, a year, or a lifetime? How is this process of signification related to our ability to perceive and complete goal-directed activity? If "all thought," as Peirce said, "must necessarily be in signs," how does this relationship between signs, cognition, and perception unfold in a world that is totally represented through signs, such as the world of video games? These questions have guided the first exploratory phase of an investigation of two very popular games video games: *Grand Theft Auto: Vice City* (*GTA:VC*) and *Grand Theft Auto: San Andreas* (*GTA:SA*). *GTA:VC* and *GTA:SA* are two in a series of six digital video games that began with the first *Grand Theft Auto* (*GTA*) game released in 1997; this was followed in order by *GTAII*, *GTA3*, *GTA:VC*, and *GTA:SA*, which was released in October 2004. In 2005, *Grand Theft Auto: Liberty City Stories* (*GTA:LCS*), which is a continuation of the GTA series, was released.

The overall purpose of this chapter and the ongoing research is to gain insight into the relationships between signs and cognition, how these relationships develop, and how the relationships between signs and cognition in video games can be used for educational purposes, such as K-16 literacy and language arts contexts. Although the educational value of the Grand Theft Auto series is not immediately apparent, scholars are increasingly suggesting that video games, including those with violent, racist, misogynistic, or other themes for mature audiences, can provide fertile ground for initiating discussions about gender and ethnic stereotyping and/or violence in general (Gee).

Guiding the current research is a synthesis of Vygotsky's ideas with related scholars (e.g., Bakhtin; Cole, Harré and Gillet; Harré and van Langenhove; Wertsch; Wells). This chapter presents applications of these theories to specific segments of participant interaction with *GTA:VC* and *GTA:SA* and suggests possible avenues for further research.

The Process of Signification

The overriding theme of the entire Grand Theft Auto series is for the gamer to assume the role of a criminal whose goal is to "jack" cars (a term almost all participants in the study used instead of "hijack"). The graphics, geographical settings, and physical prowess of characters in *GTA:VC* and *GTA:SA* are more sophisticated and complex than those featured in earlier games in the GTA series (Gertsmann; Kasavin). Both *GTA:VC* and *GTA:SA* feature characters with enhanced abilities and skills that facilitate faster and more complicated physical movements within their respective worlds, with the main character in *GTA:SA* even having the ability to swim under water. Another enhancement to *GTA:SA* is the capability to add a second PlayStation 2 (PS2) game controller, allowing an additional player a brief and very restricted role in the game (Kasavin). In the current study, only one participant reported using this option.

One of the most notable changes from *GTA:VC* to *GTA:SA* is the ethnicity of the main character. The protagonist in *GTA:SA* is Carl Johnson (CJ), an African American male in his early twenties who is attempting to move back to his hometown of Los Santos (modeled on

Los Angeles) from Liberty City, a location from earlier versions of GTA. Moreover, as he progresses through the game, CJ's narrative, physical abilities and characteristics, and situational contexts change much more radically than that of Tommy Versetti's character in *GTA:VC*.

In *Grand Theft Auto: Vice City* the gamer assumes the role of Tommy Vercetti, a square-jawed, husky, Caucasian male. Tommy has just been released from prison and is immediately positioned by the game-narrative as a victim of circumstance (a cocaine deal gone badly). To avoid deadly retaliation, he must complete a variety of missions for an array of humorously cliché mob-characters; one mob-boss even offers a slice of a horse's head from a silver hors d'oeuvre tray. In *GTA:SA*, Carl is *victimized* into returning to his prior life as a gang member through a series of unfortunate events, including the opening scene where corrupt policemen illegally seize Carl's money, and then frame him for murdering a cop. It is interesting to note that in the game narratives of both *GTA:VC* and *GTA:SA*, the main characters do not seem to be personally responsible for resuming their law-breaking behavior.

In both games, players are positioned as victims of corrupting circumstances who are forced to work their way up the social hierarchy of mobster wealth and power. *GTA:VC* takes place in a Miami-like setting, while characters in *GTA:SA* live in a California-sized place. In both games, the main character must jack cars and other vehicles in order to proceed forward in the game. In *GTA:SA*, the main character's strength, sex appeal, and stamina are more visible, more precisely measured, and are more directly affected and controlled by player choices than in *GTA:VC*. In other words, Carl (CJ) has a much more complex semiotic physiology than Tommy Vercetti did in *GTA:VC*. For example, in *GTA:SA* there are consequences for eating too many burgers and not exercising; sex appeal can be increased by acquiring particular tattoos, hair styles, or facial hair patterns.

In both games, players control character movements with the hand-held PS2 controls (see fig. 11.1), the entry point into the textual world of GTA and other video games designed for the PS2 platform. Data for this study indicate that players' interactions with the PS2 controls are central to the process of signification. This process of signification, and moments when this process is clearly linked to player perception of choices, is of particular interest for the present research.

Interdisciplinary Framework

Recall the Vygotskian example of tying a knot to *mediate* the act of remembering. This notion of mediation is foundational to recognizing the nature of human thinking as revolving around signs, which both Peirce and Vygotsky emphasized. Vygotsky's example of tying a knot is worth repeating here:

> Tying a knot as a reminder, in both children and adults, is but one example of a pervasive regulatory principle of human behavio r, that of *signification*, wherein people create temporary links and give significance to previously neutral stimuli in the context of their problem-solving efforts [Vygotsky, *Mind* 74].

Mediation is the process of creating a temporary link between the mind and the world of objects. In this example, the link between the *intermental* world, the world between people, and the *intramental* world, the embodied world of signs that is the self, is established through the introduction of an auxiliary device (Lantolf; Vygotsky, *Thought*; Wertsch, *Voices*), such as the string in the example. These auxiliary devices, also known as *psychological tools*, (Kozulin) include "mnemonic devices, algebraic symbols, diagrams and graphs, and most importantly, language" (Lantolf 418). The transformational process of signs becoming psychological tools is an additional focus of the current research.

Before moving to specific examples in the data, it is necessary to present some related theories on signification from *positioning theory* and *discursive psychology*, along with other foundational concepts that make up the interdisciplinary approach used to interpret the data. This foundation includes ideas from Russian philologist and literary critic Mikhail Bakhtin (1895–1975). Three of these ideas from Bakhtin that are particularly important for the present study are the concepts of *speech genres*, and his view of a *dialogic, authored self* (Bakhtin, *Creation*; Clark and Holquist; Holquist).

Bakhtin argued that individuals exist as events in a dialogic, always responding to and interacting with the self as *other*, as well as other individuals. According to Bakhtin, even when people are involved in activities in which they may consider themselves physically alone, there is always an other involved in a continual dialogic activity of authoring the self (Bakhtin, *Creation*; Clark and Holquist). This notion of a dialogic was clearly evident in the data when participants' movements and activities were in response to the actions of, or information gained from other players that participants' knew and/or characters in the game, information from a strategy guide or the internet, or reflections on earlier moments of play in which participants assigned meaning to a specific sign.

In expressing this dialogic nature of the self, Bakhtin was greatly influenced by Einstein's theory of relativity (Clark and Holquist;

Holquist). "Dialogism, like relativity, takes it for granted that nothing can be perceived except against the perspective of something else" (Holquist 21–22; see also Gibson for a more ecological perspective). Bakhtin emphasized that no two objects can occupy the same place and time simultaneously. From here it follows that one can only position oneself in terms of a synthesis of other(s) and situational contexts that are constraining or affording the enacted event which creates our *being* (Clark and Holquist; Holquist).

Indeed, in *Grand Theft Auto: Vice City* and *Grand Theft Auto: San Andreas*, Tommy and CJ's existence are dependent on the background of "something else" (Holquist 22); that is, a collection of signs signified by participants/players through a sociocultural/historical process. Tommy and CJ always exist as a co-constructed semiotic event prompted by the game narrative and player perception of prominent signs during game play. It could be argued that the biomechanical nature of signification during game-play (see Meyers), which is grounded in the computerized and structural nature of the game, exists in a dialectic tension with the social nature of signification; although with the data presented in this paper, the emphasis is on the social nature of signification.

This view of the self as an enacted, authored event embedded in dialogic activity (Bakhtin, *The Dialogic*; Bruner; Wertsch, *Mind*) is important for understanding the interactions between players and their characters in the game (i.e., CJ and Tommy). Some participants in the current study reported collaborative game activity, usually through conversation, with a spouse or group of friends in order to complete a particular mission. Players also reported how they authored their in-game selves through prior out-of-game activity with the Internet or with other media (e.g., a strategy guide) to gain cheat codes and/or strategy ideas.

For the current research, moments of play can be temporarily and conceptually *bound* (see Merriam) for analysis using Bakhtin's notion of *utterance*. An utterance can be a word, sentence, paragraph, movie, scientific paper, and a novel, which all have in common

> an absolute beginning and an absolute end: its beginning is preceded by the utterances of others, and its end is followed by the responsive utterances of others (or although it may be silent, others' active responsive understanding, or finally, a responsive action based on this understanding) [Bakhtin, *Speech* 71].

Furthermore, the utterance is bounded by "a change of speaking subjects" (meaning the speaker) and "the possibility of responding to it" (Bakhtin, *Speech* 71). In communication, these boundaries of an utterance are most easily identifiable by observing direct oral communication, where gesture and general posture can be observed (see also Kendon). Bakhtin identified the utterance as a practical unit of analysis that could illustrate the spontaneous nature of meaning and the intricacies of language usage in a variety of contexts (Bakhtin, *Creation*; see also Wertsch, *Mind*).

When considering the physical posture and mental activity of those who are engaging in communication, Bakhtin pointed out the importance of the listener as an active respondent to the utterance. As listeners engage the utterance, they begin to formulate a posture toward the utterance, and a response, where they will be agreeing and disagreeing according to where they are positioned and where they position themselves in the exchange. Speakers also adjust the tone of their utterances according to the effect they observe or infer from what is implicitly or explicitly indicated through the unfolding listeners posture/position to the utterance (Bakhtin, *Speech*). This dynamic view of the utterance is particularly significant in getting away from very passive and mechanistic views of communication (Wertsch, *Mind*).

One of the most important features of this dialogic sense of the self and utterance is that "any utterance is a link in a very complexly organized chain of other utterances" (Bakhtin, *Speech* 69). Meaning found in any oral or written text is very much related to past meanings, although the sociocultural/historical nature of meanings may often be obscured. In the Grand Theft Auto series, the oral and contextual landscape is rich in meanings and images from popular culture, purposefully highlighted to prompt consistent, perhaps predictable significations.

The meaning of utterances is additionally affected by other voices (e.g., multivocality) (Bakhtin, *Creation* 143), often with authoritative voices positioned in a specific manner during specific moments of interaction, such as the ever-present authoritative voices in the pronouncements of priests, judges, school administrators, and government officials. "Words in discourse always recall earlier contexts of usage otherwise they could not mean at all. It follows that every utterance covertly or overtly, is an act of indirect discourse" (Bakhtin, *Speech* 24). This indirect discourse is the remnants of words from earlier times.

One example that clearly demonstrates a link to prior utterances in *Grand Theft Auto: San Andreas,* which some participants mentioned, is Ryder's (one of the main characters) resemblance to rap star Easy E. Other examples of the game designers tapping into prior social utterances include using the voices of Ice-T and James Woods to portray criminals in the game. In addition, Samuel Jackson provides the voice of Officer Tenpenny, the corrupt LA cop at the beginning who positions CJ as criminal. Each of these well-known actors' voices are clearly intended to influence players.

For the theoretical framework applied to the data, the point is that the process of signification in videogames is neither solely a structural, biomechanical nor only a sociocultural activity: it is always both. This dynamic view of the utterance is also effective for understanding video-game play as a *genesis* of semiotic activity; that is, as Vygotsky and others described, semiotic events can be seen as unfolding before our eyes (Vygotsky, *Mind* 61; Wells; Wertsch, *Vygotsky and the Social* 55). This includes participant engagement with new or already learned signs from the controllers and the game as a semiotic *genesis*. A number of examples from *GTA:SA* and *GTA:VC* illustrate this genesis of semiotic activity and how this relates to the authorship of the self in the game.

In a very concrete, sign-oriented manner (characters in the game are all signs), Tommy or CJ move one way or another and other characters in the game respond; characters are mutually responsive to each others' significations (Can we call this signs signifying to signs?). Of course, these sign-to-sign significations are structurally computer programmed *self* and *other* movement; however, this programmed movement does not occur without player engagement with signs.

The in-game character movements express *answerability* (Bakhtin, *Creation*) to the context, other in-game and out-of-game selves, and the in-game and out-of-game selves as others. Individual characters in videogames, like Tommy and CJ, exist as possibilities of responding, possibilities of being, in a sociocultural/historical dialogic to other selves (Clark and Holquist 67); the authored, in-game self becomes *semiotic resource* and *semiotic potential* (Van Leeuwan 4–5). Closely related to the concepts of answerability, utterance, and the authorship of players' selves, is the idea of relatively stable spheres of utterances known as *speech genres*. A speech genre can be understood as "a particular function (scientific, technical, commentarial, business, everyday) and the particular condition of speech communication specific for each sphere give rise to particular genres, that is, certain relatively stable thematic, compositional, and stylistic types of utterances" (Bakhtin, *Speech* 64).

In a book about video games and literacy, Gee produced a similar definition that extends some of Bakhtin's earlier ideas. Gee uses the term *semiotic domain* to mean:

> any set of practices that recruits one or more modalities (e.g., oral or written language, images, equations, symbolic sounds, gestures, graphs, artifacts, etc.) to communicate distinctive types of meanings. Here are some examples of semiotic domains: cellular biology, postmodern literary criticism, first-person-shooter video games, high-fashion advertisements, Roman Catholic theology, modernist painting, mid-wifery, rap music, wine connoisseurship [Gee 18].

Of course, participant memberships in specific semiotic domains greatly influence the process of signification. A car mechanic listens to a car differently than an accountant does. A roofer looks at a house differently than a painter. Players have access to different out-of–game resources depending on membership in a variety of semiotic domains. Membership in a specific group is a complex synthesis of how individuals are *self* and *other- positioned* as individuals and members of *communities of practice* (Wenger). To understand this dynamic relationship between the social and individual nature of *positioning* oneself to signs, it is necessary to turn to *positioning theory* [Harré and van Langenhove].

Positioning theory, which was influenced by Bakhtin's and Vygotsky's ideas on signification, is effective for looking at the larger sociocultural/ historical significations that take place inside and outside of game-play, such as signifying our memberships and/or *affinity* (see Gee) with specific ethnic, social, and gender groups outside the game. Positioning theory can be used to examine how players' social and ethnic positioning of the self and other during game-play and out of the game affects their creation of the self.

Positioning theory involves "The study of local moral orders as ever-shifting patterns of mutual and contestable rights and obligations of speaking and acting...." (Harré and van Langenhove 1). More specifically, the study of and the term *position* has come to mean:

> the analysis of fine-grained symbolically mediated interactions between people, both from their own individual standpoints and as representatives or even exemplars for groups. In this technical sense a position is a complex cluster of generic personal attributes, structured in various ways, which impinges on the possibilities of interpersonal, intergroup, and even intrapersonal actions through some assignment of such rights, duties and obligations to an individual as are sustained by the cluster [Harré and van Langenhove 1].

In the authoring of their quasi-individual selves, participants in this study were continually positioning themselves to signs and groups through utterances. These sociocultural and historical acts of positioning and repositioning themselves through utterances demonstrated how individual subjectivity is synthesized and co-constructed through group/community influences (Wenger). To investigate the social creation of the self, it is useful to supplement Vygotsky's definition of signification with Harré and Gillett's use of the term. This allows for a kind of *analytic dualism*, as suggested by Sawyer; that is, to gain a more accurate view of an individual embedded in a community, it is necessary to try to look both at the individual and the community simultaneously. Harré and Gillet use signification to indicate the active role of meaning in structuring the interaction between the person and a context so as to define the subjectivity of that person in the situation and their positioning in relation to certain discourses implicit in that subjectivity ... [23–24].

In this definition, *subjectivity,* "expresses the way things appear to be or are signified by the speech and action of a person seen in relation to a discursive context" (Harré and Gillett 35). This subjectivity becomes inseparable from signification and identity.

The final important piece of the interdisciplinary framework applied to the data is Burke's Pentad, a well known tool from rhetoric that has been suggested as an aid to analyzing human interaction (Wertsch, *Mind* 13). Very briefly defined, the Pentad is: Act (the what), Scene (the where), Agents (the who); Agency (the means), and; Purpose (the why) (Burke 139). Although, not explicitly labeled in each segment of data presented, the data were analyzed by using these terms as flexible reference points to understand the developmental tensions between the agents (the participants/players) and mediational means (the controls, participant knowledge and use of signs) displayed or reported by the participants as they learned and used signs to play GTA (see Wertsch, *Mind*).

The following data segments illustrate acts of responding to utterances and the authorship of the self within the game as simultaneously a response/creation of the self through outside-and inside-game semiotic influences. Most important, the data illustrate the inseparability of perception, signification, and cognition.

Data Collection

The data presented here were collected over a two-year period as the first author worked with research participants in exploring a variety of segments and conditions with *GTA:VC* and *GTA:SA*. About half of the data were collected before *GTA:SA* was released and integrated into the study. Two of the first participants in the *GTA:VC* data collection period returned for game-play sessions in which *GTA:SA* was introduced into the data collection protocol.

All of these data, and the theoretical framework applied during this first phase of the ongoing research, will provide the foundation for further inquiry into *GTA:VC, GTA:SA,* and other video games. Of course, the data interpretations presented in this chapter have numerous limitations. Ultimately, this chapter raises more questions than it answers. Moreover, these data interpretations are intended to introduce readers to how Bakhtin, Vygotsky, and a variety of related theorists can be used to understand and investigate the powerful possibilities that videogames might offer for literacy and language arts learning contexts.

In this initial phase of the research there were eighteen participants: fifteen males and three females. All of the participants were Caucasian, and most were in their early to late-twenties (one was close to forty). Of these eighteen, fourteen engaged in recorded game-play and two participants who previously had played *GTA:VC* returned to play *GTA:SA*. Sixteen sessions of game-play were recorded: eight only involving *GTA:VC*, and a second series of eight game-play sessions that followed the release of *GTA:SA*. In each of these second game-play sessions, participants played one segment of *GTA:VC* followed by one segment of *GTA:SA*.

Most interviews were conducted immediately before game-play, with the exception of the first few interviews conducted early in the data collection period. Interviews mainly covered participants' general histories and habits with video games, their background knowledge and opinions of *GTA:VC* and *GTA:SA*, and what they thought were the most memorable and/or important symbols and events in the game.

The data used for this chapter included audio and video recordings of game-play and semi-structured interviews (Fontana and Frey; Schensul et al.). Game-play was recorded on a television videocassette recorder and an analog video camera mounted and aimed at the television for the first seven sessions of game-play. In order to more closely examine players' use of cheat codes and specific characteristics of player use of the PS2, the video camera was shifted from pointing at the television screen to a top-down perspective of players' hands working the controls. An audio tape recorder was also running during all sessions. As mentioned previously, the PS2 controls proved to be a crucial place for player interaction with the first of many layers of signs in the game.

Figure 11.1 displays the PS2 controls. During the game, the player's right hand is on the left side of the figure where the top of the PS2 has a square, a triangle, a circle, and an X. The X-key was a salient feature in most data segments. Also, note the R at the bottom of the figure above the two buttons labeled 1 and 2. These buttons are normally pushed by the index finger and the second finger of the right hand. The right knob at the top of the figure is usually controlled by a player's right thumb. The left side of the controls, which is located on the right side of the figure, is set up exactly the same, except the four buttons on top of the PS2 have four different arrows. During game play, when the player is prompted by the game to use these buttons, or when the player wants to use a cheat code, these arrows are signified as Up, Down, Left, and Right. As in the right side, there are two buttons on the left-front of the

PS2, which are labeled as L1 and L2. Note the L, which appears on the top of the left, front side of the PS2. As with the right hand, most participants used their left index finger and second finger of the left hand to control the L1 and L2 buttons, and they used their left thumbs to control the left knob. For the description of participant game-play, the three small buttons in the center of the controls are not important. These buttons prompt the starting of new games, change the specific view the player might gain of the action in the game, and a variety of other game settings. To those unfamiliar with the PS2 controls and video games in general, it is worth noting here that the controls can be set to vibrate in the players' hands when they drive off the road into bumpy terrain. Participant knowledge and use of the signs and buttons on the PS2 is crucial to successful completion of missions.

For the first example of data, as with most segments of data, it was found that a specific symbol, the X symbol, on the right hand side of the PS2, clearly influenced participant perception of choices and successful completion of missions when it became necessary for their characters (i.e., Tommy or CJ) to move quickly. This use of the X symbol was found to be particularly important in a segment from *GTA:VC* called, *Road Kill*, in addition to segments of *GTA:SA*. When players move on foot in *GTA:VC* and *GTA:SA*, they repeatedly press the X button to enable Tommy Vercetti and CJ to run faster than they normally would if a player simply pushed the knob pre-set as the *move-forward* sign. Not all participants knew they could increase their speed by repeatedly pushing the X button.

Some of this knowledge of the controller is also presented to the gamer community in what are called cheat codes. Cheat codes are a specific sequence of buttons that are pushed to prompt a specific result in the game. For example, to gain all of the top weapons in *GTA:SA* the sequence is R1, R2, L1, R2, Left, Down, Right, Up, Left, Down, Down, Down. Cheat codes are available on thousands of Internet sites and are available for most video games produced. The process of using these codes emerged as an issue of interest during the research. Some participants demonstrated an extensive knowledge and use of cheat codes, which is the focus of the second example of the data presented for this chapter.

For all segments of data from *GTA:VC*, including those segments in which participants also completed a mission from *GTA:SA*, the participants' mission was to kill Carl, the Pizza Delivery man. In this mission, Tommy Vercetti (the participant/player) leaves a hotel (after the interviewer/researcher told them to) and proceeds to a phone icon displayed in a circular map located on the bottom left-hand corner of the video

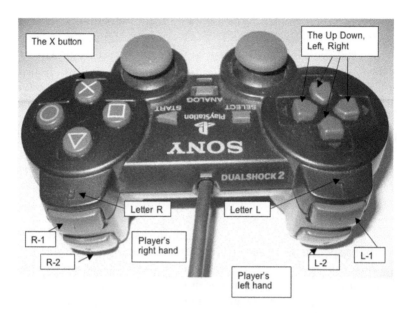

Figure 11.1—A front view of the Sony PS2 hand held controls, as if sitting opposite the player.

screen. Tommy can jack a car or other vehicle, or walk and/or run to the phone icon. When Tommy gets relatively near the phone icon, the phone can be heard ringing, and he steps into a pink highlighted circular area. The screen then shifts to a game narrative where the player has no control over Tommy's actions beyond skipping the narrative instructions (also prompted by pushing the X button).

When the player steps into the pink area, the following utterance is heard and displayed at the bottom of the screen: "Mr. Teal, your help in eradicating those out-of-towners was invaluable to business. I have more work for you, with a more hands-on approach. Your next job is taped under the phone." Writing then appears at the bottom of the screen that says "Carl Pearson, Pizza Delivery Man. Kill him before he completes his deliveries." This utterance is immediately followed quickly by the phrase, *Deliveries Left*, which appears onscreen in blue under the vital statistics icon. Next to the phrase a blue number begins counting down from 50 as the yellow dot on the map, which represents Carl on his scooter, zips through the city. The players' game-intended responses to the utterance that are bounded by Carl's deliveries are to *kill Carl any way they can* before Carl completes his 50 deliveries. Carl is a very fast delivery driver, obnoxiously racing around the city on a pink scooter that looks exactly like a Vespa.

With regards to the genesis of a semiotic self in this mission, there are numerous utterances to which players are responding: the out-of-game utterance requested by the interviewer/researcher to go to the phone icon, the utterance with instructions using a "Mission Impossible" narrative, and the utterance of *Deliveries Left*. In addition, as would be expected, many of the players mentioned the number of blue police stars as important signs, along with their life points and the circular map at the bottom of the screen to track Carl and know which way to turn. Because the successful completion of *Road Kill* was not necessarily dependent on the amount of money the player had, the money signs did not seem to be as important to players in this mission.

Whether or not participants successfully killed Carl and how quickly they accomplished this task was generally related to participants' experience with the game. In many of the examples, collisions occurred during the process of chasing Carl, or participants were noticed by the police and needed to evade the police either after having killed Carl or during the chase. Using the X button to make the character move faster was a factor in most of the participants' missions. That is, whether Tommy was killed by an explosion caused by an accident, busted by the police, or was able to get close enough to Carl to kill him after knocking him off his Vespa, successful completion of all of these missions was generally affected by participants' knowing that pushing the X-button would increase Tommy's running speed.

This knowledge of the X-button to increase running speed is one of many examples in the game where participants' prior knowledge of signs shaped their perception of future choices of action. Most of the experienced players were able to run faster in order to successfully kill Carl; players perceived the option of *running fast* through a sign similar to a hunter perceiving the rustle of leaves or the flight of birds as meaning something for the hunt (Wartofsky). In the same way that a string can be transformed into a cognitive tool for remembering something, participants transformed the X button into a tool for running faster, and this became a perceived choice for future activity; participants planned for future activity by using the X button as a sign.

Another salient example of the transformation of signs into cognitive tools for mediating perception of future activity was found in participants' knowledge and use of cheat codes. Many of the experienced players discussed the use of cheat codes and how easy they are to use and find. On the other hand, two participants specifically prided themselves for not using cheat codes.

During his game-play with *GTA:SA*, Dan (a pseudonym), an experienced male player, undergraduate in his early twenties, demonstrated how he used cheat codes as signs that mediated his current activity and perception of future activity. Dan asked the interviewer/researcher if he could use cheat codes for *GTA:SA*. During the data collection before the release of *GTA:SA*, where participants only played *GTA:VC*, none of the participants had ever asked to use cheat codes, though cheat codes were used by the researcher to pre-load certain weapons, money, and health conditions. After Dan asked, he was given permission to use cheat codes to complete an episode called *Drive-Thru.*

In this episode, the main character, CJ, drives his friends to a fast food restaurant called the *Cluckin' Bell.* As they are leaving, another car filled with members of an opposing gang (The Ballas) drive by and the passengers in the car begins shooting at CJ and his friends. CJ's job is to chase the car down and destroy it to prevent the Ballas from shooting up his home turf, Grove Street in Los Santos.

On the videotaped data, Dan's hands can be seen quickly punching in what appears to be two sets of codes on the PS2. The codes increased CJ's money, health, and gave him a selection of the most powerful weapons. In the post-play interview, Dan mentioned that he obtained the cheat codes from the Internet. He also identified the Internet as being the most important resource for his success at a variety of GTA games (the GTA series was also his favorite video game series).

After the interview with Dan, the researcher quickly reviewed the video tape, and after a search of the Internet, it was determined that the codes Dan probably used to increase his money amount, weapons, and health points were as follows:

1. For the best selection of weapons R1, R2, L1, R2, Left, Down, Right, Up, Left, Down, Down, Down
2. For full health, armor, and money: R1, R2, L1 , X, Left , Down, Right, Up, Left, Down, Right, Up
3. For lowering the police interest (wanted level): R1, R1, Circle, R2, Up, Down, Up, Down, Up, Down [Gamespot].

During game-play, Dan used cheat codes to increase his health points and reduce the wanted level so the police would not pursue him as aggressively while he completed the mission. The fiery explosion of the opposing gang members' car, and a return to a fellow gang member's house (Sweet) signified Dan's successful completion of the *Drive Through* mission. What is particularly interesting about Dan's use of the cheat codes is that he has internalized a sequence of signs that altered his perception of future activity. As he played the game and was pursued by the police, he simply pushed a sequence of signs to avoid being "BUSTED." Dan's knowledge of the cheat codes to gain health points and money essentially enabled him to become invincible and complete the entire *GTA:SA* at his own pace. Through this process of signification, Dan's perception of future activity was seen through the sequence of signs, such as using the X button to make CJ run faster. The data clearly support the idea that signs and cognition are inseparable, particularly the strong link between sign-driven cognition and perception of future action (i.e., choices).

Equally interesting was the way Dan described the process of learning cheat codes; that is, the process of signification. He reported that it took him about 15 repetitions to learn the codes, and he explained that if he was asked to write them down, he would be unable to write down the sequence of numbers and letters (i.e., R1, L1, Up, Right etc.) immediately. Rather, Dan said that he would need to slow down and think about the sequence, breaking it down step-by- step, in reverse order to transform the codes into their original form: numbers and letters. Dan's use of signs was transformed from a sequence of written signs into automatic physical movement that mediated other signs. The process of signification was completed by the letters and numbers, which became inseparable from perception and activity. In other words, the letters and numbers had to be recontextualized in order to become explicitly separate from the cognitive process (see also Wertsch, *Vygotsky and the Social*). Although the original process of signification occurring "right before one's eyes" (Vygotsky, *Mind* 61) was not directly observed, this internalization of the cheat codes will be one of the focal points of future research.

Another participant, Ken, described cheat codes for a particular strategy before he was actually holding the PS2 in his hands; however, he illustrated the cheat codes with his hands held as if they were holding the controls. He was momentarily using his Bakhtinian self as other, positioning his imaginary self holding an imaginary PS2 to mediate the remembering of the codes.

Two male participants, Sean and Martin, reported collaboratively playing video games with their wives. Martin reported trying the two-person mode in *GTA:SA*, but he found that in this mode the screen view was angled in such a way that when his wife pushed her controls, Martin's driving view was lost and he would crash his vehicle. Martin and his wife originally got the idea of trying the two-person mode to date one another in the game; that is, they intended to shop, visit discos, and engage in other activities as in real-life (the topic of sex in the game was not discussed).

Another interesting feature of Martin's wife's interaction with the game was her use of the GTA games to plan virtual trips away from the rural area where they lived. Martin reported that his wife "... wants to go to these places. She wants to see, you know, she wants to see the Giant Pyramid in Vegas, she wants to see the Hollywood sign, you know, she wants to see all the stores and the shops." He described how she really liked the virtual experience of going to the beach and driving expensive cars. He went on to describe a time when his wife was pregnant and they did not own a car; they devoted many hours together learning to play *GTA:VC* with a map taped to the wall.

Throughout Martin's interview he spoke of his GTA activity as being a leisure activity shared with his wife. He explained how she enjoyed traveling around in the game much more than engaging in violence. That being said, Martin reported going to work one day at 7:00 in the morning and returning home at about 4:30 in the afternoon, and in that time his wife had amassed over one million dollars in *GTA:SA* by killing all the right people in the game. Together, they had previously identified those with the most money (e.g., drug dealers). After his wife amassed this money, Martin said "we were able to purchase things and do things." Although the interviewer did not find out what specific things they purchased, Martin inferred in other parts of the interview that he and his wife knew how to have fun shopping in the game. During a time in their lives when they did not have outside-game agency to procure material wealth or to travel, they were able to live richly within the world of GTA.

Martin used cheat codes in *GTA:VC*, but did not use them at all in *GTA:SA*. For *GTA:SA*, Martin said a friend gave him a manual. He explained that when comparing the use and non-use of cheat codes he "would rather, literally, as annoying as it would sound, sit there and play six, seven, eight times and die every time and then finally finish it. It's more gratifying." Martin reported that he and his wife used the manual to successfully work through the entire game without using cheat codes.

It is important to note that the manual to which Martin refers is a 272-page manual entitled the *Official Strategy Guide for GTA:SA* (Bogenn and Barba). The guide contains extremely detailed maps, guides to successful mission completions, vehicle descriptions (including planes, helicopters, boats, and tanks), and a variety of weapons. More important, the manual provides detailed information about the sequential series of events in the entire game narrative, as well as outlining the steps to take to successfully move from one episode/mission to another. In other words, almost everything a player needs to know to successfully complete the game is presented by this manual. Martin and his wife successfully completed the entire game two weeks prior to the interview.

It should be mentioned here that Martin was recruited from a remedial reading class (a zero-credit class). He was placed in this class because his score on a College Placement Test was low. This fact is mentioned to place this participant in the larger context of literacy and the educational possibilities of video games. Through their use of the *Official Strategy Guide*, Martin and his wife effectively positioned themselves to signs in a highly demanding literacy activity; they used the guide to mediate successful completion of the game.

Another participant, Sean, a white male in his mid-twenties, also played GTA video games with his wife. It is interesting that when he talked about trying out new games, he used the pronoun "we," referring to himself and his wife. Sean emphasized the game *Return to Arms* as the game he and his wife most often played together. Most of their GTA experiences were with *GTA3*, as *GTA:VC* and *GTA:SA* were still fairly new to them (his father introduced Sean to *GTA:SA*). It was while playing *GTA3* that Sean learned to use cheat codes. When provided with the cheat codes that some of the participants were given on slips of paper during *GTA:SA* game play, Sean observed similarities in the cheat codes. These similarities expressed broad categories of codes. For example, he described similarity in categories as follows: "Yeah, like the weapons code on R2, R2, Left 1, R2, right, down, 2 circles on the directional pad. And then the other one is R2, R2, Left 2, R1, so you just change one stroke. And then the circles. And the other one is R2, R2, Left 1, Left 2, so they don't change very much."

Recall that one of the other participants (Dan) asked to use cheat codes. Dan noted that *GTA:SA* keeps track of how many times players use cheat codes. He reported that "after playing it [*GTA:SA*] for about a week, I noticed that I'd used cheat codes over a thousand times." When Dan described how he memorized the codes, he explained how he had to slow down and list them in reverse order. By contrast, Sean could recite specific in terms of the broader category of the code; still other participants reported memorizing individual cheats. Sean and Dan fundamentally viewed the codes differently. This is revealed in the way Dan learned the codes in a sequence and Sean depended more on categorization patterns than sequence. The different ways that participants learned and remembered cheat codes, and their awareness of the explicit signs they actually used to enact a specific cheat are areas for future research.

Now that specific cases and examples from game play have been presented, it is necessary to return to some of the broader theoretical ideas presented earlier. As the perspective moves from micro-level segments of data to the broader theoretical lens, reflect back on data examples and your own experiences with signs. Notice the inseparability of signs and cognition both at the individual and social levels of interaction (how separate is the social context and individual?). Recall the questions raised by Peirce's quote from the beginning of the chapter and possible K-16 educational implications: Does cognition exist without signs? How can signs in video games and the related social interactions with signs (reading manuals, talking with other players/games, using the internet) be used in formal educational contexts?

With regards to positioning theory, the assignment of rights, duties, and obligations within *GTA:VC* and *GTA:SA* directly affected how Tommy and CJ positioned other characters in the game such as the police, opposing gang members, and hookers and other female characters. Likewise, Tommy and CJ, who in part represent the out-of-game player, were positioned by the other characters in the game, as well as by the player's membership in a variety of semiotic domains outside of the game. In all cases, players positioned themselves as other by responding to bounded utterances. Some utterances were connected more to the structuralist nature of the game, while other utterances, such as participant responses, were more connected to the social/community group that has access to knowledge about a particular game or mission.

During Martin and his wife's activity with the game, the *Official Strategy Guide* became an inseparable part of their semiotic selves in the game. As in an earlier analysis of some of these data (Unger, Troutman, and Hamilton), and in the data presented in this paper, some participants were able to recognize and use the X button to move Tommy or CJ more quickly in a particular scene. This potential of using the X became inseparable from the perception of choices players had. When Martin and his wife used the *Official Strategy Guide* to mediate the act of winning a mission, their perception of choices and their semiotic agency was transformed in much the same as when the X was signified, but at a more complex level. Martin and his wife's semiotic selves were transformed through the literate activity of reading a variety of signs in the *Official Strategy Guide* and interpreting these through the PS2 controls and constant collaborative talk. Their agency became inseparable from the *Official Strategy Guide* as they read the guide and *talked* advice from the strategy guide into their game-play.

With regards to Bakhtin's notion of authoritative voices (see *super-adressee* in Bakhtin, *Creation* 135), Tommy and CJ are positioned as criminals, they are violating the law, the main authoritative voice inside the game, and, of course, a prominent authoritative voice outside the game. Generally, when people approach situations or formal systems of signs (e.g., traffic lights), people often demonstrate recognition of authority and simultaneously demonstrate their individual, social, cultural, and historical positions. People reveal these positions by moving into the speech genre needed for that moment, the semiotic domain in which the interaction will unfold. People position themselves and others in specific ways during specific interactions, though as much as they (their selves) can control. Within the GTA game context, CJ and Tommy have to jack cars outside the view of the police, or else they violate the authoritative voice of the law; that is, the "indirect discourse" (Bakhtin, *Speech* 24) of the authoritative voice (i.e., the law and rules of society) pushes the player to move their in-game character away from the law. However, many participants reported being proud of how many blue wanted stars they could prompt and how they were chased by the police, the FBI, and finally the Army. With some of the participants, a part of their motivation for playing the game was grounded in their desires to push against authoritative voices in the game.

All participants in the research responded to power issues, one way, or another. Most participants liked the idea of being able to do anything they wanted in the GTA games. Participant histories and game-play with GTA seemed to fall into three basic broad categories: they either explicitly pushed back against the authoritative voices in the game, prompting "gratuitous violence" or become embroiled in some confrontation as they were trying to complete a mission, or they talked of spending time just touring around, enjoying the beaches, shopping, jacking different types of cars, and often building a mental map of different routes and safe houses for later game play.

As occurs with out-of-game communication between real-life interlocutors, as Tommy or CJ move around and act in the game, other characters in the game (e.g., the police, gang members, hookers and other females) respond to this movement. Although this movement as a response to Tommy or CJ is not as detailed as real-life interlocutors, and, of course, is mechanistic, the possibility of responding by characters in the game clearly expresses Bakhtin's boundaries of the utterance. As the utterance of a character in the game unfolds, the player becomes an active respondent to the boundary created by the character and the context in which it occurs.

Another interesting feature from the data is the wide difference in participant attitudes and explicit procedural knowledge about cheat codes. Perhaps even the word "cheat" is no longer valid when the code becomes an integral part of the game as it had for Dan. This is in contrast to Martin, who totally rejected cheat codes while playing *GTA:SA*. Sean was able to orally articulate the numbers he could recall from *GTA3*. Dan would have to slow down through a reverse process to recite the specific sequence and sign. As Dan said: "Almost, like it's become a second nature. I don't think about it when I do it, I just think 'Well, I need to put in this cheat code so I don't die." For the present study, players' agencies and subjectivities have been found to be mutually defining and dependent on players' perception of choices, always in response to others, including the self as other.

When players enter into the world of video games such as *GTA:VC* and *GTA:SA*, players create and respond to utterances. Through this complex process of positioning themselves and the game, they are working within specific and general semiotic domains that overlap with the sociocultural histories of past utterances and other semiotic domains. Players position themselves in specific ways as they author their semiotic selves with the game. Players' perceptions of current activity are dependent on the choices that the signs in-the-game represents for future activity. Players synthesize the choices offered by the knobs and buttons on the PS2 console (see fig. 11.1) to influence current action. The authoring and positioning of the self becomes an act of semiotic mediation, which, within the game, is crucial for success or failure.

Interrelations of Signs and Cognition

Of the data presented in this chapter, many features of participants' game-play and the semiotic nature of the self seem particularly important for future research and possible educational applications. However, as mentioned earlier, there are many more questions than answers that can be gleaned from the data thus far. How can the kind of motivation demonstrated by Martin and others who spend hours with video games be brought into classrooms at a variety of levels? What kind of games are adolescents and remedial college-age students playing and how can these be brought into the curriculum? Moreover, is the individual player's control over a situation in the game based solely in either the individual or societal influences? Whether a person is enacting life in or outside the world of the game, is individual agency only and completely residing in the individual, exclusive of the activity of mediating cognition with signs? These are not new questions (see Gee; Shaffer, Squire, Halverson, and Gee). Overall, the data presented here support the notion that the learning of sign systems, such as cheat codes and strategy guides for *GTA:VC*, *GTA:SA* and other video games, express the social nature of learning and the social nature of agency (Wertsch, Tulviste, and Hagstrom). In other words, the learning and use of signs is dependent on social interaction with particular communities and specific resources, and our perception of future activity is dependent on access to these resources. The data from this study clearly demonstrate the interrelated nature of signs and cognition. Indeed, "thought, therefore, must necessarily be in signs" (Peirce, *The Essential Writings* 81).

Works Cited

Bakhtin, Mikhail. *The Dialogic Imagination: Four Essays by M. M. Bakhtin.* Austin: U of Texas P, 1981.
_____. *Mikhail Bakhtin: Creation of a Prosaics.* Ed. Gary Saul Morson and Caryl Emerson. Stanford: Stanford UP, 1990.
_____. *Speech Genres & Other Late Essays.* Ed. Caryl Emerson and Michael Holquist. Trans. Vern McGee. Austin: U of Texas P, 1986.
Bogenn, Tim, and Rick Barba. *Official Strategy Guide: Signature Series.* Indianapolis: Pearson Education, 2005.
Bruner, Jerome. *The Culture of Education.* Cambridge: Harvard UP, 1987.
Burke, Kenneth. "Ways of Placement." *On Symbols and Society.* Ed. Joseph R. Gusfield. Chicago: Chicago UP, 1989. 139–157.
Chandler, Daniel. *Semiotics: The Basics.* London: Routledge, 2002.
Clark, Katrina, and Michael Holquist. *Mikhail Bakhtin.* Cambridge: Belknap P of Harvard UP, 1984.
Cole, Michael. "Cultural Psychology: Some General Principles and a Concrete Example." *Perspectives on Activity Theory.* Ed. Yrgö. Engeström, Reigo Miettinen, and Raija-Leena Punamaki. New York: Cambridge UP, 1999. 87–106.
Gamespot. <http://www.gamespot.com/ps2/action/gta4/hints.html>.
Gee, James. *What Video Games Have to Teach us About Learning and Literacy.* New York: Palgrave Macmillan, 2003.
Gerstmann, Jeff. Rev. of *Grand Theft Auto, San Andreas. Gamespot.* 27 Jan. 2005 <http://www.gamespot.com/ps2/action/gta4/review.html>.
Gibson, James. *The Ecological Approach to Visual Perception.* Boston: Hougton Mifflin, 1979.
Harré, Rom, and Grant Gillett. *The Discursive Mind.* Thousand Oaks: Sage, 1994.
Harré, Rom, and Luk van Langenhove. "The Dynamics of Social Episodes" *Positioning Theory* Ed. Rom Harré and Luk van Lagenhove. Malden: Blackwell, 1999. 1–13.
Holquist, Michael. *Dialogism: Bakhtin and His World.* New York: Routledge, 1990.
John-Steiner, Vera, and Teresa Meehan. "Creativity and Collaboration." *Vygotskian Perspectives on Literacy Research: Constructing Meaning through Collaborative Inquiry.* Ed. C. Lee and P. Smagorinsky. New York: Cambridge UP, 2000. 31–48.
Kasavin, Gregg. Rev. of *Grand Theft Auto: San Andreas. Gamespot.* 27 Jan. 2005. <http://www.gamespot.com/pc/action/grandtheftautovicecity/review.html>.
Kozulin, Alex. *Psychological Tools: A Sociocultural Approach to Education.* Cambridge: Harvard UP, 1998.
Lantolf, James. "Sociocultural Theory and Second Language Learning: Introduction to the Special Issue." *The Modern Language Journal* 78 1994: 418–420.
Merriam, Sharon B. *Qualitative Research and Case Study Applications in Education.* San Fransisco: Jossey Bass, 1998.
Peirce, Charles S. *Peirce on Signs: Writings on Semiotic by Charles Sanders Peirce.* Ed. James Hoopes. Chapel Hill: U of North Carolina P, 1991.
_____. *The Essential Writings.* Ed. Edwin Moore. Amhearst: Prometheus, 1998.
Sawyer, Keith. "Unresolved Tensions in Sociocultural Theory: Analogies with Contemporary Sociological Debates." *Culture and Psychology* 8 (2002): 283–305.
Shaffer, David, Kurt. R. Squire, Richard Halverson, and James Gee. "Video Games and the Future of Learning" *Phi Delta Kappan* 87 (2005):104–111.
Unger, John, Porter Lee Troutman Jr., and Victoria Hamilton. "Signs, Symbols, and Perceptions in Grand Theft Auto: Vice City" *Digital Gameplay: Essays on the Nexus of Game and Gamer.* Ed. Nate Garrelts. Jefferson: McFarland, 2005. 91–109.
Van Leeuwan, Theo. *Introducing Social Semiotics: An Introduction.* New York: Routeledge, 2005.

Vygotsky, Lev. "The Genesis of Higher Mental functions." Ed. James Wertsch. *The Concept of Activity in Soviet Psychology.* Armonk: M.E. Sharpe, 1981. 144–188.

_____. *Mind in Society: The Development of Higher Psychological Processes.* Ed. Michael Cole, Vera John-Steiner, Sylvia Scribner, and Ellen Souberman. Cambridge: Harvard UP, 1978.

_____. *Thought and Language.* Ed. Alex Kozulin Cambridge: MIT P, 1986.

Wartofsky, Marx. *Models: Representation and the Scientific Understanding.* Boston: D. Reidel, 1985.

Wells, Gordon. *Dialogic Inquiry: Toward a Sociocultural Practice and Theory of Education.* New York: Cambridge UP, 1999.

Wenger, Etiene. *Communities of Practice: Learning, Meaning, and Identity.* New York: Cambridge UP, 1998.

Wertsch, James. *Mind as Action.* New York: Oxford UP, 1998.

_____. *Voices of the Mind: A Sociocultural Approach to Mediated Action.* Cambridge: Harvard UP, 1991.

_____. *Vygotsky and the Social Formation of Mind.* Cambridge: Harvard UP, 1985.

Wertsch, James, Peter Tulvisted, and F. Hagstrom. "A Sociocultural Approach to Agency." *Contexts for Learning: Sociocultural Dynamics in Children's Development.* Ed. Ellice A. Forman, Norris C. Minick, and Addison Stone. New York: Oxford UP, 1993. 336–356.

12. Against Embedded Agency:
Subversion and Emergence in *GTA3*
CINDY POREMBA

Since its release in 2001, *Grand Theft Auto III (GTA3)* has flavored academic and popular debate surrounding agency in digital games. At one end of the spectrum, the game has been put forward as a player-empowering freeform game environment—a triumph of design for player agency. However, when it comes to laying blame for the game's antisocial content and amoral possibility space, agency appears to shift rapidly from the player to the game's producer, Rockstar Games. While this kind of inconsistent attribution of agency is nothing new, what was interesting about some of the primary examples informing this discussion—the use of mods and cheats, or the revelation of play strategies involving killing prostitutes—was that they resisted the dominant analytical framework of agency. Their agency was difficult to attribute—lying somewhere in a nebulous region between player, designer and system.

Current interactive theory has popularized a model of embedded agency where the player has agency only within the context of authorial control. This theory is most prominently espoused by Janet Murray, but is echoed in the work of several other theorists (notably Klastrup). Murray positions the agency as an aesthetic pleasure—implying more agency is not only desired by the interactor, but makes for a better experience. This paper uses *GTA3* to evaluate the embedded agency theory, and as a starting point for examining the interplay between three key players in the question of narrative agency in a game environment: the player, the game designer, and the system itself (from the perspective of "emergence"). It suggests narrative agency cannot follow an embedded structure and still allow for player subversion outside that structure, or accommodate a submission to computational control. In fact, this model of agency creates unnecessary conflict and dualism in the interactive experience—a tension that can be rectified with a more unified model of agency.

Narrative Agency

Janet Murray's *Hamlet on the Holodeck* is without debate a highly influential work in the domain of interactive theory. The question of agency is something that is explored in-depth by Murray. In *Holodeck*, agency is defined as the satisfying power to take meaningful action and see the results of our decisions and choices (Murray 126). However, this power is hierarchically defined as an interactor's agency unfolding within the context provided by the procedural author. Murray argues "interactors can only act within the possibilities that have been established by the writing and programming ... all of the interactors' possible performances will have been called into being by the originating author[1]" (Murray 152). Viewing *GTA3* through this lens, we would see the game producer (author) as having true agency for every permutation of the play experience, having accommodated the totality of a player's in-game actions. The game producer has set out the players' context (Liberty City car thief), the scope of interaction (run, pick up, attack), and laid out a series of missions for a player to engage in, in order to succeed in the game (and access new game experiences). The player has the pleasure of seeing their experience unfold, but their "agency" is limited to what the game producer has allowed them. Rather than being full agents, they are more accurately instantiating the agency of a higher-level game author. In most circumstances, this is a fair assessment of the *GTA3* experience. However it is not one that sufficiently accounts for all aspects of the game as it is commonly played.

Agency itself is a broad and rather openly interpreted concept that crosses disciplines from philosophy to narratology, cognitive science and psychology. An agent is generally accepted as the participant who is the subject when there is action. Agents are assumed to possess the capacity to choose between options, and the means to act on their choices (xrefer). In his literature review of agency, sociologist Victor Marshall finds agency defined in four ways: 1) the human capacity to make choice (to be intentional), 2) the resources within the individual or at the command of the individual that can be brought to bear in agentic behavior (more accurately described as resources), 3) behavior of individuals that reflects intention and 4) the social and physical structuring of choices. In interactive theory, we are most often focused on the first definition—the capacity of the interactor to make intentional choices.

Because of its broad scope, agency is usually contextualized (explicitly or implicitly) when used as an analytic tool in interactive media. For example, when we are saying an interactor has agency in an interactive environment, we're not dealing with broader questions of whether humans truly have free control of their actions. The scope is narrowed to the interactive context—what we're really asking is whether the interactor has the ability to affect change in the mediated interactive environment. As this paper looks at agency from the context of the experience of narrative, what we are more accurately discussing is the question of narrative agency.

To place agency in this context, we need a definition of narrative that will allow us to draw the necessary contextual boundaries. The scope of this paper does not allow for a thorough recounting of the debates as to what constitutes narrative in an interactive, (specifically a game) environment like *GTA3*. Instead, I will ground this concept in what I consider to be a broad but useful framework for looking at how narrative works in a game environment from what are defined as "narrative operators." Celia Pearce (*Towards a Game Theory*) finds six such narrative operators in game environments:

> *Experiential:* Emerging for interactors from the inherent conflict of a game in play.
> *Performative:* Emerging for spectators watching and interpreting a game in play.
> *Augmentary:* The supplementary information and context surrounding a game that supports and enhances other narrative operators.
> *Descriptive:* The recounting of the game to third parties (and the culture that surrounds this exchange).
> *Meta-Story:* The narrative framework or genre in which the game operates.
> *Story System:* The possibility space from which players may construct their own narrative content (may or may not be interdependent with meta-story).

I find this framework useful as it recognizes the fundamental dynamic of a game is not story, but play. Explains Pearce:

> Unlike literature and film, in which center on STORY, in games, everything revolves around play and the player experience. Game designers are much less interested in telling a story than creating a compelling framework for play [*Towards a Game Theory*].

GTA3 contains numerous narrative elements, and without question the preferred reading of the game is centered on appreciation of said elements. However, to say the game is about story is untrue—the game itself is primarily about mastering control of the driving interface (as is consistent with the genre of driving game). While there is certainly pleasure to be had in following the storyline or engaging in side activities and mini-games, the emphasis of the game is reinforced by the recurrent reminder you are playing *Grand Theft Auto*. The very first image you are presented with in the opening of the game is that a speeding car; the first tutorial you are engaged in teaches you not how to handle a weapon or pick up items, but how to enter a car and drive. To successfully progress in the game, you have to demonstrate this mastery above building proficiency in other game elements (this is facilitated by the structure of the missions in *GTA3*: progressing from pick-up and delivery, to car-as-weapon, to eventual race and chase scenarios). You can't win by figuring out the plot, exploring more territory, or even through superior marksmanship. Control of your vehicle is the dominant framework for gameplay, and the driving force (if you'll pardon the pun) behind much of the game.

Even if *GTA3* is not primarily about story, we can still look at narrative agency in *GTA3* as the ability to affect intentional change within the context of Pearce's narrative operators. As not all operators are applicable in a single player driving game such as *GTA3* (although I suspect the true milieu for such a game is a group console gaming experience), the particular concepts I will focus on include experiential, augmentary, meta-story, and (although the link is not quite as apparent) story-system operators (in terms of how a player affects meta-story narrative, or how the game designer influences experiential narrative).

From the context of narrative agency, we can now identify elements of the embedded agency model that may fall short of accurate analysis. For example, players may bring in a game mod that allows them to avoid completing the requisite missions in order to advance to certain game locations. In doing so, they are subverting the game designer's intention of how their experience will unfold. Certain interactions between exclusive game rules and behaviors may also lead to emergent narrative that may not be intended by the game designer or the player. Narrative emergence frequently occurs in multiplayer games where the interactions between players fall outside the scope of authorial agency (both these examples we will examine in-detail in the following sections). As games increasingly rely on algorithmically defined systems of game rules and actions, emergent narrative elements that tend to defy clear attribution are sure to become increasingly common. We will take a closer look at both examples in just a moment.

Player Subversion

> CELIA PEARCE: When people do things that you didn't plan on, that seems to be something that you embrace.
>
> WILL WRIGHT: To me, that feels like success [*Sims, Battlebots,* Pearce].

In relation to gaming culture as a whole, the agency of the game designer is relatively guarded in *GTA3*. While the game has been lauded as an open environment for exploration, opportunities for narrative construction (independent of what Henry Jenkins would call a spatial narrative) are limited. The game provides constant reminders (in the form of visual cues and embedded narrative elements) to adhere to a main storyline consisting of a series of missions that follow a traditional narrative arc. One is welcome to diverge from the main storyline and engage in a series of mini-games; each commonly a variant on the traditional driving game, and each providing a mini arc. For example, I may hijack an ambulance and go on various pick up and deliver missions around the city as a paramedic for nominal game rewards (until I get bored and return to the "real" game). These mini-games provide the bare minimum in terms of narrative elements (in particular meta-story, character and plot), although the rewards may keep with the theme of the mini-game (e.g. the paramedic game can earn you health and drugs; the firefighter game can score you a flamethrower). As such, they are not particularly rich resources for player narrative construction.

The main storyline does attempt to develop what would be considered a more traditional narrative (albeit a shallow one), providing meta-story, character (with minor character development), and other dramatic enhancements such as filmic cut-scenes and a gangster-genre aesthetic. However, on the whole, the narrative agency of players is restricted. Missions must be completed in order, player actions often seem to have a weak or non-existent connection to non-player (automated) dialog and system-generated events, and most manipuable objects in the game world are directly tied to mini-games—thus dictating their preferred use and limiting their creative possibilities. While you are able to wander through the game ignoring, for example, an assigned mission, the game does not respond to this decision. In fact, game elements such as text prompts and direction arrows continually remind you of what you are supposed to be doing—instantiating a particular play experience as created by the game designer.

Unlike some games, *GTA3*'s developer (DMA Design) does not provide code or development tools for altering the game (although they do provide an extensive list of "cheat" codes for suspending some of the rules of the game). This is significant, as while there is a large body of tools and mods for the game, it is important to recognize this is more a function of user enthusiasm (and cultural expectation) than it is the handiwork of the game developer. The game is released on two platforms: the PC and the PlayStation 2 console, the latter of which is technically prohibitive to hack and modify. Taking both technical and design issues into account would suggest player actions are necessarily bounded within the context provided by the game designer.

So is *GTA3* a textbook example of embedded agency? The persistence of player mods and hacks would seem to indicate otherwise. These components and modifications are made by players and inserted into the game narrative structure to allow for variations and subversions of the experiential narrative. Tools created by players allow for modification of the game story-system, such as map, character skin and statistic editors. A survey of *GTA3* hack and cheat websites[2] (several of which have been removed over the course of this research) reveals three categories of player modification:

- *Enhancements* (e.g. Sniper Scope),
- *Game Boundaries* (e.g. Breathe Underwater), and
- *Context* (e.g. Stunt Island)

The first category (Enhancement) consists of minor modifications and enhancements to the game that may enrich the meta-story or experiential narrative (for instance, having flames come out of the back of your car instead of smoke may suggest character attributes). The second category (Game Boundaries) serve to extend the game and allow for a wider range of experiences, in some cases subverting the mission queue dictated by the game to uncover new/preferred environments. For example, a Game Boundaries modification may allow players to unlock inaccessible portions of the map, including developer testing areas. The third category (Context) provides players the opportunity to perform actions that fall outside the scope of the game experience, but nonetheless take advantage of game objects or rulesets. This final category moves players more towards using *GTA3* as their own storytelling environment. These modifications range from the relatively expected (creating an island map that facilitates stunt driving) to the bizarre (a game environment set in rural Alberta). To varying degrees, all three categories allow players to subvert the designer's narrative agency and to direct and extend the game according to their authorial preference. Even a minor modification such as adding a sniper scope to a gun changes the way a player has been directed to think about gameplay—perhaps shifting focus away from driving by enriching the experience of shooting.

Subversive narrative here refers to the creation of story clearly outside the preferred meaning of the work. Unlike most contemporary media, the recognition that a game can be hacked or changed can be an integral part of the play experience. Pearce writes that, unlike traditional entertainment industries, the game industry tends to embrace, and sometimes encourage, audience usurpation of authority (*Emergent Authorship*). The boundaries between game designer and player are far more permeable than in any other medium, and this relationship, for the most part, is recognized and embraced rather than being a source of conflict. Wright, Boria and Breidenback, in an analysis of *Counterstrike* player behavior, note:

> Playing with a game's technical features also marks the development of creative responses to the rules created by the developer.... Playing is not simply mindless movement through a virtual landscape, but rather movement with a reflexive awareness of the game's features and their possible modifications.

Subversion need not imply the player has conflicted with the game designer, particularly if said designers are for the most part pleased that players have extended the game outside the scope of their original intention. The word subversive is here used in relationship to authorial intention with regard to narrative. So while the creation of subversive narratives through game modification could be seen as a statement against the authority of the game producer, a confrontational reading of this relationship is not entirely accurate.

The subversion of experiential narrative through the mod phenomenon is one of the strongest arguments against embedded agency in digital games like *GTA3*. A game modification clearly extends the gameplay context beyond the authorial intention and context provided by the game designer. It is impossible for the game designer to anticipate the production of a given mod, and since mod production can fall outside the development environment (and in this case, does), the game player is the sole agent in its production (the interaction between the mod and the environment is another matter). One counter-argument is that players who create game mods are no longer operating within the same game. This privileges a definition of game that limits game scope to authorial intention. This is not an argument I wish to address here, except to state there is ample support for the construction of a game that involves all components of the game experience, including modification (Zimmerman and Salen 565–567).

Emergent Narrative

> One of the greatest pleasures of being a game designer is seeing your game played in ways that you never anticipated, seeing players explore

nooks and crannies of the space of possibility that you never know existed. Understanding how emergence works and creating a design that encourages emergence is one of the ways your games can bring you this pleasure [Zimmerman and Salen 168].

We've looked at an example of player agency expanding beyond the limits of the game designer's intention, and thus outside the scope of authorial agency. What about narrative elements that emerge from other rules and structures within the game, outside the scope of either the game designer or the player's agency? Emergent behavior provides the second exception to the embedded agency model. Our analysis of narrative agency in *GTA3* would be incomplete without looking at one of the most infamous examples of emergent behavior—one that creates a particularly contentious narrative event with regard to agency.

The *GTA3* "hooker cheat" drew attention from researchers, industry critics, and the popular media. This so-called "cheat" is what is more accurately described as a degenerate strategy or exploit (Zimmerman and Salen 241). It is described on a game forum as follows:

> To pick up a hooker you must park your car next to one and wait. After about 3 seconds of talking she will get in the car. Bring her back to your hideout without any cops and park it in the garage (somtimes [sic] it works without the garage). The car or whatever vehicle you have with a top (no convertables, [sic] it dosent [sic] work, i tried) will start to move and your life will go up till 100. Your money goes down too! when you get out the car kill her and get your money back! you can get your life up to 125 with maybe one more or to more hookers. You can get the same hooker twice! ["LowKey," posted on *Monster Cheats*].

The so-called "hooker-cheat" is actually a combination of 2 actions/possibilities available to the player in *GTA3*. The first is that when a player beats up a character, that character drops whatever they are carrying (often money). The second is that a character gains health points by picking up hooker characters and bringing them back to a secluded location for "sex" (the act itself is implied, not shown). The disadvantage of the later is that it costs money to pay the hooker and thus raise health points in this way (this balances the action within the context of gameplay). By combining these two possibilities, players have found they can avoid a game consequence and continuously raise their health levels, which gives them an advantage in the game. Consequently, this strategy creates, on a narrative level, an abhorrent story component that prompts accusations of misogyny and extreme anti-social behavior. Note however on a strictly gameplay level, divorced from narrative context, this is simply a player exploiting the intersection between game elements.

Debate about the hooker-cheat tends to focus on responsibility, which necessitates an attribution of agency in this context. Is this an expression of authorial agency on the part of the game designer ... or an extension of player agency and creativity? On a primary level, one could say it was neither. As the "hooker cheat" is a result of the emergent narrative that results from the intersection of two entirely independent game actions, can we attribute agency to anything other that the system itself? While this seems awkward, let's examine the alternatives.

If this is an expression of authorial agency, this would mean in the creation of the game's rule components (lets say the initial conditions), the game designer retains agency through all actions in the complex system they have created. The problem with this argument is that the game designer's lack of intention (they cannot possibly predict the interaction of all elements in a complex system) speaks against their authorship. To be emergent, an occurrence cannot be authored—it is not constructed, but generated.

Can we look exclusively to the player for agency? The player does combine two elements found in the game to produce the given effect (as would appear to fit Murray's model). However, while it is one thing to be able to manipulate elements and shape the direction of the narrative experience, it is another to combine elements in a given context that creates something entirely new that cannot be predicted from the initial components. This speaks to intention—in an emergent occurrence, the player by definition cannot intend the resulting occurrence (although they may attribute intention after the fact). Such emergence would at very least defy an embedded agency model in that the context provided is not authorial, but computational. The context is algorithmically defined.

The *GTA3* hooker-cheat produces an interesting effect in terms of narrative. First, it creates a micro-narrative that was likely not intended by the game designer (even if the designer could predict the emergence of this event in a complex system, it is extremely unlikely they would allow an element that upset game balance). Second, this micro-narrative (by upsetting game balance) conflicts with the meta-story by changing the nature of conflict (as you can now extend the health of your character, you change the scope of the experiential narrative). Third, in the game context, the emergent micro-narrative falls secondary to the gameplay advantage of gaining extra health points: many players will state this is not intended as a misogynist act, but as a clever degenerate strategy.[3]

Arguably, the hooker cheat is what may be described as weak emergence (Zimmerman and Salen 159), as it is perhaps not entirely inconceivable that the two rules/actions in question could produce this strategy. But as games rely more and more on computational algorithms for gameplay and narrative purposes, the question of agency and emergence becomes more relevant. How would the situation change, for example, if in the above example one of the rules was the product of the game design, but the second was a result of a player modification? Where is the agency in other game genres that rely more heavily on emergence: games like *The Sims* (Maxis, 2000) or *Fluid* (gameLab, 2002)? Can the interconnected narrative produced by players in a massive multiplayer online game (MMOG) reflect the agency of any one player? These scenarios test the validity of an embedded agency model.

New Models for Narrative Agency

Given the limitations of an embedded agency framework, this paper proposes exploring other models for agency that allow that, particularly in a game environment, one cannot always assume the author/game designer has control over the boundaries in which player agency unfolds. Further, an embedded model creates a hierarchy of control within the play experience that implies contention between the game designer and the player: a battle for control, if you will. This would not appear to be the case. Game designers have expressed pleasure in player's creative actions—even ones that clearly go against design intention and extend the boundaries of the game. Conversely from a player perspective, gameplay is often about determining what the game designer wants (i.e. how to play the game), rather than a constant drive for more agency.[4] Further, interactions between game elements produce effects on narrative and gameplay that are not expressly the result of player or designer actions: they are simply emergent. Placing one's vision for a game or in-game experience in the hands of emergent and unpredictable interactions can also be an immersive and pleasurable experience—lack of agency aside. Further work needs to be done to explore new models for agency that accommodate a more complex relationship between game designer, player, and the game itself.

Notes

1. This suggests a kind of extended authorial agency, similar to those expressed by Alfred Gell. Gell maintains artifacts hold a secondary agency that reflects the distributed agency of the artist, part and parcel of a distributed and extended self (Gell 21–22).
2. GTA World, GTA Glitch Vault, Monster Cheats.

3. This speaks to the difference between meaning in narrative and meaning in gameplay.

4. In fact, too much player agency may reduce the pleasure of gameplay (as is the case with having to micro-manage game characters).

Works Cited

"Agency." *XREFER*. Digital Reference Library. 21 Jan. 2003 <http://www.xrefer.com>.

Gell, Alfred. *Art and Agency: An Anthropological Theory*. Oxford: Oxford UP, 1998.

Grand Theft Auto III. New York: Rockstar, 2001.

GTA Glitch Vault. Discussion Board. 18 Jan. 2003< http://www.geocities.com/gtaglitch-vault/glitches.html>.

GTA World. 18 Jan. 2003 <http://gtaworld.nfscheats.com/utilities2.php>.

Jenkins, Henry. "Game Design as Narrative Architecture." *First Person: New Media as Story, Performance, and Game*. Ed. Pat Harrington and Noah Wardrip-Fruin. Cambridge: MIT P, 2002.

Klastrup, Lisbeth. "Texts, Spaces, Labyrinths." Masters Dissertation. U of Copenhagen, 1999.

Monster Cheats. Discussion Board. 18 Jan. 2003 <http://www.monstercheats.com/Playstation 2/*Grand Theft Auto III*.html>.

Murray, Janet Horowitz. *Hamlet on the Holodeck: The Future of Narrative in Cyberspace*. Cambridge: MIT P, 1998.

Pearce, Celia. "Emergent Authorship: The Next Interactive Revolution." *Computer & Graphics Winter* (2002). 31 Jan. 2006 <http://www.cpandfriends.com/writing/computers-graphics.html>.

_____. "Sims, Battlebots, Cellular Automata God and Go: A Conversation with Will Wright." *Game Studies* 2.1 (2002). 31 Jan. 2006 <http://www.gamestudies.org/0102/pearce/>.

_____. "Towards a Game Theory of Game." *First Person: New Media as Story, Performance, and Game*. Ed. Pat Harrington and Noah Wardrip-Fruin. Cambridge: MIT P, 2002. 31 Jan. 2006 <http://www.cpandfriends.com/writing/first-person.html>.

The Sims. Electronic Arts, 2000.

Victor W. Marshall. "Agency, Structure, and the Life Course in the Era of Reflexive Modernization." Symposium on "The Life Course in the 21st Century." American Sociological Association. Washington DC. Aug. 2000.

Wright, Talmadge, Eric Boria, and Paul Breidenbach. "Creative Player Actions in FPS Online Video Games—Playing Counter-Strike." *Game Studies* 2.2 (2002). www.gamestudies.org.

Zimmerman, Eric, et al. *Fluid*. Gamelab, 2002.

Zimmerman, Eric, and Katie Salen. *Rules of Play: Game Design Fundamentals*. Cambridge: MIT P, 2003.

13. Inviting Subversion:
Metalepses and Tmesis in Rockstar Games' Grand Theft Auto Series
WM. RUFFIN BAILEY

The Grand Theft Auto (GTA) series has grown in its ability to confound virtual and real by willfully extending to its user the privileged position of coauthor. Starting as early as the original two-dimensional *Grand Theft Auto,* the series invited gamers to play in an open-ended world where they were free to ignore the game designers' set narratives and, perhaps, simply use the game to go for a virtual Sunday drive. With *Grand Theft Auto III*'s *(GTA3)* move to three-dimensional cyberspace, Rockstar Games' web of connections between its open-ended gameplay with the "real world" institutions of the Internet, film, print, and even other video games grew, consistently making reference to these other media, often quite explicitly. This game borrowed heavily from gangster and "'hood" genres to create what amount to interactive movies (Murray 91). Users explored every nook of *GTA3,* including portions of the game that its designers clearly did not expect to be found.

The designers of Grand Theft Auto anticipated users who would be appreciative not only with these references outside of the game proper, but who would also be savvy enough to rip and replace each game's zeroes and ones. Designers provided interfaces for these users to inject personal touches, from the design of the jacket that appeared on the hero's back to the choice of what songs would be played on the in-game radio. Users were even allowed to insert vehicles and buildings of their own creation into the game. As they added the hooks for this sort of user-created content, Grand Theft Auto's designers provided new outlets for interacting with those users who were no longer limited to a simple phenomenological interaction with the virtual worlds the games created. The groups' interactions and ability to coauthor the game they shared now extended to the digital foundations of Grand Theft Auto's virtual worlds.

Grand Theft Auto: San Andreas (*GTA:SA*) took the lessons learned from the two earlier games in the Grand Theft Auto series as givens. In this game, the designers counted on the capacities users had exhibited in and learned from the earlier games. Users' skills allowed them to uncover content that would never be experienced playing the game "by the book." A few clever hackers found a sexually explicit minigame, popularly dubbed "Hot Coffee," hidden in *GTA:SA*, a minigame whose discovery required the use of highly subversive technical explorations into the game's software code.

It is the goal of this study to trace how Rockstar's Grand Theft Auto series' designers and users have negotiated their way to a more nuanced dialog, and to offer some explanation why designers have chosen to potentially give up so much of their creative control to their users. In order to do so, a number of concepts from the fields of game design and literary theory will be explored in the hopes of creating an informed, multidisciplinary approach for reading the Grand Theft Auto series.

Metaleptic Training

Grand Theft Auto's mediation of the dialog between users and its designers is most striking in its careful usage of what Gérard Genette terms "metalepses." Metalepses takes place when there is a "transition from one narrative level to another" (234). Using Todorov's example of *Thousand and One Nights*, Genette demonstrates an extreme case of narrative levels, where, in one story, "Scheherazade tells that ... Jaafer tells that ... the tailor tells that ... the barber tells that ... his brother (and he has six brothers) tells that..." (214n4), easily indicating five degrees of narration. When the frame of one level of narration is broached by actions from another, if the barber's actions were affecting Jaafer, for example, the breech causes the collapse of the "shifting but sacred frontier between two worlds, the world in which one tells, [and] the world of which one tells" (236), and metalepses occurs.

Genette provides several illustrative examples. He quotes the forced inclusion of the reader with the use of second-person and plural, first-person possessive pronouns as the narrator of Diderot's *Jacques le fataliste* says, "If it gives you pleasure, *let us set* the peasant girl back in the saddle behind her escort, *let us let* them go..." as if the reader's wishes could change the course of the action already written (234). Genette later cites Balzac, whose narrator remarks, "While the venerable church-man climbs the ramps of Angoulême, it is not useless to explain..." though there is obviously no literal lull to be filled while the character is climbing; the book is already printed, sitting in the reader's hands (235).

Espen Aarseth uses Genette's description of metalepses to describe what happens in the Interactive Fiction work *Deadline*. Here, a player finds a book that claims to contain what amounts to a finished transcript of the adventure the user is concurrently experiencing, a transcript they continue to cocreate as they type the action "read book." If a user does choose to read the book, the game forces the user's avatar to kill themselves, apparently out of the depression caused by learning the narrative's Mobius-like outcome—namely that the avatar learns that it will commit suicide!

The Grand Theft Auto series is not, then, unique among digital games in that it is comfortable with metalepses. The concept has been a central force in video games since *Adventure*—both in Crowther and Woods' seminal work of *Interactive Fiction* and in Warren Robinett's game by the same name for the Atari 2600. In Crowther and Woods' *Adventure*, the player can happen onto the game's characters "sleeping like uninitalized variables" (Montfort 90), a description that belies their digital makeup. Robinett's contains a hidden message for gamers, clearly *not* for their avatars, now famous as the first Easter egg in a video game. In the first, the user's separation from the digital nature of the game's characters is stripped, eliminating the narrative distance between the game's code, effectively the game's narrator, and its user's world. In the second, Robinett's digital narrator ignores the conventions of the medieval fantasy being told and directly addresses the user, not unlike what transpires in Ginette's quote from Diderot.

What makes Rockstar Games' Grand Theft Auto fundamentally different is the level of comfort and play metalepses is afforded. There are what would seem to be dummy websites for virtual businesses advertised on the in-game radio, like PetsOvernight.com. This appearance is problematized for users that discover that these sites can be found online, in "real cyberspace," the game's narrative space collapses with that of the users. Similarly, there is also a ticker at the virtual airport in *Grand Theft Auto III* that, upon close inspection, is found to list a web address for game hints. The music playing on the in-game radios are, for *GTA:VC* and *GTA:SA*, tracks from artists that were popular in the time those games were set. That is, except when the music is from the user's own mp3 collection, which, on the version of *GTA:SA* for Microsoft Windows, can be added to a particular folder and played between the DJ's comments. Of course, the music playing in the user's own, "real" car could be coming from one of the fifteen soundtrack CDs that contain the tracks from the in-game music found in the two most recent games in the series, further blurring the "sacred frontier" between virtual narrative and real life. And what if someone who plays one of the games in the series "really" steals a car from a driver listening to one of the games' soundtracks?

In all, *Grand Theft Auto*'s metaleptic play conjures the "uneasiness Borges so well put[s] his finger on: 'Such inversions suggest that if the characters in a story can be readers or spectators, then we, their readers or spectators, can be fictitious'" (Genette 236).

Designer-Sanctioned User Authorship

It is essential to understand Rockstar's use of metalepses to realize that their encouragement of users' subversion of the game's code, its very medium, is no accident. This is particularly obvious with the versions of Grand Theft Auto that play on personal computers running the Windows operating system. Here, players so disposed may quickly learn to modify the game by inserting textures and models that create new vehicles, weapons, even new clothing and building façades. That Rockstar has made hacking the series not only possible, but a relatively simple affair, shows their willingness and desire for gamers to coauthor more than merely the plot of what is already one of the most open, free-flowing game experiences available to date, including its digital content.

There are a number of ways for an anonymous third party to change the conventionally static content of a video game, and one system of classification is to categorize them based on the level of expertise required for each content type's creation. At the simplest level, there are skins. Skins afford players the most straightforward route for personalizing their game experience beyond textual contributions, like avatar names and chat text. The term "skin" comes from games with three-dimensional representational systems. Though the game is displayed on a two-dimensional screen, the game engine does keep track of each object in three-dimensional space. The objects are kept in memory as models made up from vectors, essentially wire frames or skeletons, and each model has a number of animations that it can perform. Some games, notably some later versions of *Descent,* took advantage of the vector-based system and created displays that would appear three-dimensional with specialized glasses. A skin, nothing more than a simple two-dimensional raster image, is draped over the model or skeleton to create, for example, the player's marine in id software's *Quake 1*, the game primarily responsible for introducing gamers to the concept of malleable, interchangeable skins. Altering an object's skin can be accomplished using any image editing software that understands the image format used by the game engine. In *Quake 1*'s case this is .pcx and Grand Theft Auto utilizes .tga, both of which can be translated into a standard bitmap using a number of freeware utilities before being edited in something as simple as Microsoft Paint, a utility bundled with the Windows operating system.

Two-dimensional game engines, like those of the original *Doom* or *Super Mario Brothers*, do not use wire-frame models but flat sprites. The skin logic holds, however. Editing the image that is "placed" on the flat sprite changes the object's appearance. Examples of hacks of two-dimensional games that include sprite-skinning range from the simple hacks listed at I-Mockery.com's "Hacked ROM Reviews" page to Cory Arcangel's complicated total conversion of *Super Mario Brothers* into a fifteen-minute movie, created by using *Super Mario Brothers'* graphics and sounds, the result of which can be viewed only through a Nintendo Entertainment System console or an emulator.

To create or change a skin, then, a hacker need only locate the skin to edit in a game's content, open it in image editing software, make their edits, and then replace the original image. This sort of hack is limited, as the attempts to create female skins designed for the very stereotypically male model, or skeleton, of the marine in *Quake 1*, show (Pomaville). The simple process is, however, also very powerful, and third-party skinners have taken to inserting customized objects into *Grand Theft Auto: San Andreas*, from Tupac Shakur shirts (LaoBoy) to Federal Express and Krispy Kreme trucks (JD 'GunMod'), even a new look for a car dealership (SimonS).

The three-dimensional skeleton of an in-game object is called its model. Modeling requires more expertise and specialized, sometimes quite expensive, software, and is not a task for the casual hacker. New models have been created for *Grand Theft Auto: San Andreas*, including vehicles as varied as the Batmobile from the movie *Batman Begins* (DieselGT) to an easily recognizable Toyota FJ40 (Todd587), as well as new weapons, like a Thompson machine gun (Blue Zircon). An easy to follow example of how to create and skin a new model can be found in Jonn Gordon's "3D Modeling and Animation" site, where he shows how the Marvel Comics character Wolverine was created and placed into *X-Men: Ravages of the Apocalypse*, a commercial game that was built atop the

Quake 1 engine. Rather than simply creating a skin and placing it on an existing panel truck, burly marine, or car dealership building, both the *GTA:SA* modelers and Gordon first created new wire-frame skeletons, animations for each of the actions the games' engines supported for their models, and customized skins designed to fit on the models made for each new object or character. To insert the newly created models, like skins, one must know the location where the game engine expects to find it and place the new files in that location.

Maps—in essence the geographical limits of the worlds created by games—are created in a method similar to any other object. In 3D games, worlds are modeled with wire-frames made up of vectors covered with raster textures, much like skins. The re-textured used car dealership in *Grand Theft Auto: San Andreas* is one example of how world maps closely parallel models.[1] Though the world maps generally do not have the same granularity as high-resolution avatar models, mainly in the interest of quicker authoring times and lower hardware requirements for rendering, similar skills are required for their creation.

The Grand Theft Auto series exposes each of these avenues for user self-expression, from skins to models to maps. Though the amount of time and knowledge needed to create vast changes in the virtual Grand Theft Auto worlds are difficult to come by, the games' designers have seen fan art and objects produced for their past works and have done nothing to discourage such additions in their last two releases. The games invite users to participate in the creation of their experience, and the digital doorways for customization discussed here are natural outgrowths of the open-ended approach the original Grand Theft Auto games exhibited in their nonlinear, open-ended plots.

Eggs and Coffee

Most importantly for understanding "Hot Coffee" is the consideration of Easter eggs, which occur when a designer hides a message or some other metaleptic object addressed specifically to the player that can be discovered from within the game's interface, if only through somewhat dissident play. As a recent example, Microsoft used an Easter egg as part of a marketing campaign for their Origami project, a new platform for portable tablet personal computers. Part of the strategy was to build interest by withholding information, giving only teasers on the project's web site. The site originally only contained an animation that stated questions including, "do you know me? do you know what I can do?" ("hello"). The first hard evidence about what was going on came a week later when a second page was added. This page had a similarly cryptic animation that displayed several landscapes. Within the HTML code for the web page, something most web surfers would never access, was a telling Easter egg that stated, "Origami Project: the Mobile PC running Windows XP" ("hi there"). About a week later, Microsoft and Origami project partners introduced the beneficiary of the strange, Easter egg driven marketing campaign at a conference that centers on discussions of computing hardware.

Easter eggs are not exclusive to digital works, though in print they are much more difficult to create and mediate with the control provided by digital media. Regardless, *UFO 54–40*, the twelfth book from the popular 1980s children's series Choose Your Own Adventure, contains a remarkable print example that serves well as a heuristic entry point for considering the structure of Easter eggs. Though the books of the Choose Your Own Adventure series were distributed as traditional printed texts, bound into codices as any conformist book, the method by which they are intended to be read involves processes much like that used to approach hypertexts found on the Internet. This method emphasizes traversing nonlinear but finite linkages between textual units.

A Choose Your Own Adventure work initially operates like any other book, with its narrative starting on its first page. The clearest indication that the story will not read as other texts is in its quick implication of its reader *as a character* in the book. *Inside UFO 54–40*, for instance, opens with, "It's your first trip on the Concorde..." (Packard 1). The reader's metaleptic participation is not an option; the metalepsis occurs with the text's second word, though the author obviously has no control over who reads the book. The series' texts are broken up into units through the use of demarcations that separate narration from instruction, found at the bottom of some of the stories' pages. The second page of *Inside UFO 54–40*, for example, says, at the bottom of the page below a solid line, "*Turn to page 6.*"

Some of these textual units end with instructions that provide branches or choices. The reader is to select a single direction from the finite list before turning to the page indicated for the corresponding choice, much like a hypertext. As Aarseth remarks, nonlinear hypertext systems that mirror this selection process do not necessarily provide less control than a codex written with the expectation of being read linearly.

A hypertext path with only one (unidirectional) link between text chunks is much more authoritarian and limiting than (say) a detective novel, in which the reader is free to read the ending at any time (Aarseth 47). In a hypertext, the location of the next unit of text[2] is hidden in the link's HTML code, and navigation to that page, beyond the user's initial click, is mediated through a browser, but the parallel with Choose Your Own Adventure is a natural one. Both are authored with strict conventions in mind that attempt to control nonlinear readings.

Furthermore, even when a codex is intended to be approached in a conventional, linear fashion, an author is never able to control where their reader reads closely and where they only scan or quickly skip ahead, which is a phenomenon Barthes explains with his concept of tmesis, or "skipping." Barthes says that this linear yet variable reader is "on the one hand respecting and on the other hastening the episodes of the ritual (like a priest *gulping down* his Mass) ... the author cannot predict tmesis: he cannot choose to write *what will not be read*" (11), giving a well-deserved, hypertextual connotation to linear text.

Aarseth broadens the context of his consideration of tmesis to reincorporate the word's meaning as a method for cutting apart and splicing together words or concepts. In a multidirectional hypertext, as that found on most Internet web sites, the author can, as is argued here, force their reader to complete reading one section of text before clicking a link to proceed to the next. With any codex short of the most experimental, the content of every page of the system is immediately accessible as the book rests in its readers' hands. A hypertext system allows more stringent control precisely because such a system can hide the locations of the vast majority of its textual units. Viewing the initial page's HTML code only reveals the location to the pages reachable through the links that page contains. The total number of pages remains unknown.

Though such control is impossible in a multidirectional codex like Packard's, he takes advantage of this openness to embed a clever Easter egg. Throughout the book, one of the side plots is a quest to locate a place called Ultima, the "planet of paradise," which the book's preface unequivocally claims can be found, but that "no one can get there by making choices or following instructions!" (Packard "Special Warning!!!!") While flipping from one trail in the book to another, some readers may notice a two-page picture in the intermediate pages (102–3), the only such spread in the book. The page before the picture, page 101, clearly indicates that the picture straddling the next two pages is of Ultima.

Unfortunately there is no branch in the story that ever instructs the reader to turn to page 101 of *UFO 54-40*, and page 100 is a dead end; the reader is not supposed to continue from page 100 to the next page where Ultima is revealed. *UFO 54-50* takes advantage of the lack of authorial control within a codex, using page flipping as the interface for the Easter egg's discovery. Though technically no specialized tools are required to discover the pages containing Ultima, the reader does have to resist and subvert the standard interface for accessing the work's content through the use of Aarseth's broadened definition of tmesis-as-cutting. A suspiciously similar reading is required to access *Grand Theft Auto: San Andreas'* hidden minigame, "Hot Coffee."

Hot Coffee and Possible Piltdowns

The skull planted in Piltdown, England may be the most successful of scientific hoaxes, and is certainly the greatest in physical anthropology. Little more than an orangutan jaw placed next to a human skull, the false fossil tricked anthropologists into considering a British human origin story for more than four decades. The Piltdown concept is a useful one for video games, especially when trying to evaluate authorial intent with respect to apparently fossilized content. Are programmers cunning enough to disguise Easter eggs in their games as fossil remnants from previous, unreleased versions of their software[3] in order to trick the gaming public into believing they were left there only as accidents? Rockstar's *Grand Theft Auto: San Andreas* raises just this question.

GTA:SA contains what appears to be just such a stranded fossil, a portion of the game that is inaccessible without some sort of hack or download. The "fossil" is a minigame that allows a gamer to have limited control over relatively graphic sexual scenes between CJ and his girlfriend(s). In *Grand Theft Auto: San Andreas*, CJ's current girlfriend may, at times, invite him into her house for coffee. Without the "Hot Coffee" modification, the girlfriend's house shudders much like CJ's car does when a prostitute enters. With the modification, the camera follows CJ inside the girlfriend's home and explicitly shows them having sex. There is a ludic element to the scene, and the user can control CJ's style of intercourse using the game's controller.

"Hot Coffee's" discoverer, Patrick Wildenborg, says the following about the modification he created to allow other uses to unlock the minigame on his website:

> After reading various discussion [sic] about this mod around the internet, I would like to make the following statement:
> *All the contents of this mod was already available on the original disks. Therefor* [sic] *the scriptcode, the models, the animations and the dialogs by the original voice-actors were all created by RockStar. The only thing I had to do to enable the mini-games was toggling a single bit in the main.scm file. (Of course it was not easy to find the correct bit)* [Wildenborg, emphasis original].[4]

Though Wildenborg discovered the minigame in the Windows version of *GTA:SA*, after his discovery others found the same content in versions for home gaming consoles as well, both on the Playstation 2 and Xbox.

After the discovery of "Hot Coffee," Rockstar very quickly became trapped in a lively controversy, with U.S. Senator Hillary Clinton calling for the Federal Trade Commission to investigate how the game received a "Mature" rating, which recommends its sale to people seventeen years old and older, and not an "Adults Only" rating. An "Adults Only" rating was later given to *GTA:SA* due to the apparent fossil discovery, the game was pulled from mass retailers' shelves, and Rockstar Games, *Grand Theft Auto: San Andreas*' publisher, lowered their company's earnings expectations. A revised version with the hidden "Hot Coffee" code removed was released in October of 2005 as a "special edition" for a number of gaming platforms.

Using a metaphor ultimately quite favorable for Rockstar, Rodney Walker, a Rockstar spokesman, likened fossilized content in computer software to portions of a painting that were later painted over.

> "An artist makes a painting, then doesn't like the first version and paints over the canvas with a new painting, right?" said Rodney Walker, a spokesman for Rockstar Games. "That's what happened here. Hackers on the Internet made a program that scratches the canvas to reveal an earlier draft of the game" [Schiesel].

While it is true that fossilized content can "reveal an earlier draft of [a] game," the metaphor is flawed due to Walker's inattention to the digital medium of *GTA:SA*. A copy of a painting does not include an embedded history. Owners will not discover a sketch of Mary with her left hand to her breast in their copies of mass-produced prints of Leonardo da Vinci's *Virgin of the Rocks*. Every copy of *GTA:SA* has the hidden sex game, and infrared reflectography is not required to discover the content ("The Hidden Leonardo"). It is also possible to erase unused code from a digital product's final version, whereas it is nearly impossible to remove an unfinished draft from below a masterpiece's last layers of paint. Walker's metaphor may have been one of the best of the quick attempts to understand the nature of "Hot Coffee," yet it is one that unjustly favors the publisher in its depiction that ignores digitalism.

Digitalism refers to the fact that computer code is made up of digits, and, as computers are currently implemented, specifically a binary system of zeroes and ones. Changing a "single bit," as Wildenborg remarks, means making the smallest modification possible to a binary file, either changing a single zero to a one or vice versa. With a hex editor, which will be described below, changing such a switch once the switch is found is as easy as changing a single letter in a document using a word processor. When the "Hot Coffee" switch is off, *GTA:SA* plays as if the sexual minigame never existed. When the switch is on, the minigame acts in every way as if it were an integral part of the game's software. "Hot Coffee" could not be unlocked playing *GTA:SA* conventionally. The only way to access the minigame is to modify *GTA:SA'* files with an application external to the game.

Surprisingly, the process by which Wildenborg found the "single bit" that needed to be changed to unleash "Hot Coffee" may not have been quite as close to finding the proverbial needle in a haystack as he makes it sound. With the advantage of hindsight from his discovery and description above, it is relatively simple to hazard a guess to the approximate location of the switch that needed to be thrown to allow the *GTA:SA* engine[5] to access the "Hot Coffee" code.

Just as a text editor allows one to view the text in, for instance, an XML or HTML file, a hex editor allows someone to view the zeroes and ones in any binary file, though the numbers are displayed in hexadecimal shorthand.[6] Using a hex editor to view the "main.scm" file Wildenborg mentions, a key support file that seems to keep track of user preferences and other information in *GTA:SA*, allows a user to view precisely the same information the game's software processes. Though much of the information is an esoteric mess of seemingly random numbers, software designers often use the American Standard Code for Information Interchange (ASCII) format to store text in such files. Though in many ways it is easier for a computer to read numbers rather than text, these ASCII text "signposts" are useful mnemonics for the programmers, making the code slightly less machine readable but much more human friendly. *Grand Theft Auto: San Andreas'* main.scm file is full of such human-friendly signposts, and includes entries like, "TATTOO," "BARBER," "DEBT," and "VENDING_MACHINE." In one section of the file, there are a number of signposts that have the prefix "GF_" followed by "MEETING," "DATE," and "SEX," each followed by a number of "bits," mostly with values of zero in the main.scm file installed by the game by default. Changing one of the bits after the "GF_SEX," or "girlfriend sex," section may unlock the minigame. Now, when CJ reaches his girlfriends' houses, the bit that decides if the camera should follow him inside is switched on, and the sexually explicit content that was already contained elsewhere in the software is displayed.

Without a decent amount of trial and error, it is difficult to know for sure if the "GF_SEX" section represents the site where Wildenborg unlocked "Hot Coffee," but this is the method one would use to find where such a bit might exist. The ASCII signposts represent a virtual gold mine for users wishing to discover other ways to change their experience of *GTA:SA*. Perhaps manipulating the bits in the "BARBER" section could unlock new hairstyles or the "VENDING_MACHINE" section could be changed to give CJ candy bars for free. Finding the hidden "Hot Coffee" section was less startling coincidence or the uncovering of a lost masterpiece than a simple matter of time. Had Wildenborg not performed his exercise in curiosity, eventually some technically savvy user would have unlocked the hidden feature in the Windows version of *GTA:SA*, and their finding would have then led others to unearth the existence of the minigame on millions of copies playing in home consoles across the world.

This method of reading the main.scm file is quite like reading a linear, conventional text. The file may have originally been scanned straight through, with particular attention being given once the reader come into contact with the "GF_" prefixed section, in which case Barthes' version of tmesis is a useful tool for understanding Wildenborg's process. If Wildenborg used the hex editor to search for particular ASCII text, like "SEX," Aarseth's tmesis-as-cutting is more appropriate.

What has changed in the move from printed text to New Media is not the method by which users are reading, but the manner by which they apply their willingness to disobey convention and read what authors never intended them to access. It is impossible to create a piece of software without authoring code for the computer to read and execute. Now those files are being accessed by humans as well, users who are gulping down files that designers, years ago, would have safely considered *"what will not be read."*

Designer Motivations

The question is whether Rockstar, much in the same way Packard expected some readers to find the Ultima pages that fell outside of any track through *UFO 54–50*, anticipated users to find "Hot Coffee." In no small part because of the abundance of ASCII flags in the main.scm file, combined with the liberty with which users have been allowed to coauthor their experience in past Grand Theft Auto releases, it is a reasonably safe assumption to believe some designer, perhaps covertly, was confident "Hot Coffee" would be found. If the inclusion of "Hot Coffee" was intentional on any level, by one or more programmers, it shows a new sophistication on the part of game designers.

But what are their purposes? Why would any designer allow users to so easily and profoundly change the in-game world? Why would *GTA:SA* contain "Hot Coffee" when the inclusion could mean incurring the disdain of politicians and the economic penalties that accompany an Adults-Only rating and parents' lawsuits?

Jerome McDonough's eighteen-month study of designers of three-dimensional virtual worlds and in-game, virtual anthropological observations of participants in one of those worlds, pseudonymed "CyberVille," offer some intriguing answers. McDonough is perhaps most interested in understanding how design decisions inscribe designers' conceptions of potential users into the medium of computer software. Anticipating the type of dialog—and learning—that has unambiguously occurred with users and designers of Grand Theft Auto, he remarks that, "the inscription of the user can be a point of negotiation between designers and the real users of the system, and may evolve over time" (867). He concludes, however, that designers' inscription, in spite of the continued negotiations, is one that will "form a singular vision of their users—an ideal type," (862) and is a process where, "The designers' own conceptions ... [result] in virtual environments designed by a white, middle-class culture and for a white, middle-class culture" (867).

It is in this context of oppression through inscription that McDonough unfortunately reads the motivations of the designers of CyberVille as they discuss adding scripting functionality to the software engine of their virtual world. Scripting allows users to contribute very small snippets of code that use the virtual reality engine as a host; users contribute code without having to invent a world from scratch and without having to become familiar with outrageously large codebases to do so. Adding scripting interfaces is very much like what Rockstar's designers did to allow user-generated models and skins. As a rule, scripting is meant to minimize the investment in the programming skills in general and knowledge of particular bodies of code in particular necessary to create change. Scripting interfaces allow users a safe place to play with the medium of virtual reality worlds, but at the same time creates the possibility of their accomplishing real work and powerful transformations of the system. By choosing scripting as the method for users to contribute to the gaming world and because of the cultural characteristics that stereotypically accompany those with programming skills, McDonough posits that, by offering scripting, "these designers may be unwittingly contributing towards the reproduction of white, masculine hegemony in the virtual environments they are creating" (866).

Parallels with Grand Theft Auto games, including "Hot Coffee," are easily made. Here too, a user has to be exceptionally technically savvy to first find the online forums where the "Hot Coffee" modification was discussed, follow the links to the sites that offered the download that enabled the minigame, download, and install it.[7] Manipulating skins is also a comparatively complicated process for most computer users. Nonetheless, without moving works like Grand Theft Auto away from digital media, opening the software up to user modifications to create a space for true and equal coauthorship will continue to require having the same skills as the designers that who initially wrote the works. Authoring digital media *necessarily* creates a bias for users that are familiar with binary files. Scripting is an excellent, practical means of minimizing that bias.

Contrary to McDonough's claims, developers who extend invitations for coauthorship at the level of those found in Grand Theft Auto or CyberVille's scripting are doing their best to appeal to nontraditional programmers, starting with the fact that these scripters would be programming for "play," not profession. In one sense, the Grand Theft Auto designers have learned McDonough's lesson, providing more nonprogrammatic avenues for game coauthorship, like the ability to play a user's mp3 tracks on the in-game radio. "Hot Coffee" offers an extreme programmatic test case, where users are able to choose to unlock a significant alteration to their experience of the work that brings their phenomenological, in-game experience more in line with the game's cinematic relatives, and they do this unlocking literally by flipping the simplest of binary switches.

Conclusion

The Grand Theft Auto series shows digital scholars that programmers may now count on users to perform the sort of convention-breaking investigations that introduce tmesis to the medium of not only video games, but any binary file. It would seem likely that at least one of the game's designers knowingly counted on players to perform this sort of convention-breaking, tmesis-introducing investigations that they learned while coauthoring their experience over the course of the series' earlier titles. If so, "Hot Coffee" belies a new ingenuity on the part of programmers, who are now playing with established conventions like Easter and fossilized eggs to mask their software's intentions. "Hot Coffee's" hidden, controversial content manages to implicate the gamer every bit as much as the designer through forcing them to coauthor access to the minigame's material. More importantly, Grand Theft Auto has developed the idea of potential texts in ways unlike any other composition, and is uniquely experimenting with digital media in ways other designers are only beginning to understand.

Notes

1. With that said, I have not had first-hand experience of a user-developed map in the Grand Theft Auto series, and those that can be found online have not reached the level. RealGTA3 <http://www.realgta.net> appears to be the most popular, adding real cars, the Statue of Liberty, and a new bridge, among other additions. It is based on the Windows version of *Grand Theft Auto III*, the first of the three-dimensional Grand Theft Auto games.

2. Both Choose Your Own Adventure and common hypertexts include nontextual elements, of course. For the sake of simplicity, I am ignoring those in these cursory explanations.

3. A more thorough explanation of the concept of software fossils is developed in (Bailey).

4. Also interesting to note is that this text, once plainly presented on the home page of Wildenborg's website, can no longer be seen by the casual web surfer. Much like the hidden comment in the code of Microsoft's Origami marketing website, Wildenborg's message can only be read by viewing the source code of his site's front page, mirroring the method of his discovery of the "Hot Coffee" minigame inside of the *Grand Theft Auto: San Andreas* code.

5. A detailed exploration of the concepts of binary code and game engines can be found in (Bailey). Briefly, a game engine is the portion of the game that enforces in-game rules, from gravity to communication to hunger. It stands in contrast to, though it works in concert with, game content, which includes models or in-game music, as discussed earlier.

6. Hexadecimal notation is the use of numbers in base 16 (A,B,C,D,E,F are used for 10,11,12,13,14,15), where each digit represents a number from zero to sixteen, and takes up one-eighth of the space of zeroes and ones. The hexadecimal number EE would represent 1111111011111110 in base 2, a significant space savings.

7. This "technically savvy" unavoidably includes access to a computer and web access as well.

Works Cited

Adventure. Atari. Sunnydale: Atari, 1978.

Aarseth, Espen. *Cybertext.* Baltimore: Johns Hopkins UP, 1997.

Arcangel, Cory. "Super Mario Movie." 6 June 2005. *Cory's Web LOG.* 12 Aug 2005 <http://beigerecords.com/cory/Things_I_Made_in_2005/super_mario_movie.html>.

Bailey, Wm. Ruffin. "Hacks, Mods, Easter Eggs, and Fossils: Intentionality and Digitalism in the Video Game." *University of Florida Game Studies Conference: Playing the Past Proceedings.*

Barr, Roger ed. "Hacked Rom Reviews!" *I-Mockery.com.* 12 Aug 2005 <http://www.i-mockery.com/romhacks/>.

Barthes, Roland. *The Pleasure of Text.* Trans. Richard Miller. New York: Hill and Wang, 1975.

Blue Zircon. "Thompson 1928." 26 July 2005. *Gtagaming.com.* 12 Aug 2005 <http://www.gtagaming.com/pafiledb.php?action=file&id=1180>.

Descent. Parallax Software. Champaign: Parallax Software, 1995.

DieselGT. "'Tumbler' Batmobile." 17 July 2005. *Gtagaming.com.* 12 Aug 2005 <http://www.gtagaming.com/pafiledb.php?action=file&id=1130>.

Genette, Gèrard. *Narrative Discourse: An Essay in Method.* Trans. Jane E. Lewin. Ithaca: Cornell UP, 1980.

Gordon, Jonn. "3D Modeling and Animation." 12 Aug 2005 <http://www.zerogravity.com.au/>.

Grand Theft Auto: San Andreas. New York: Rockstar Games, 2005.

Grand Theft Auto III. New York: Rockstar Games, 2001.

"hello." 24 Feb 2006. *Origami Project.* 10 Mar 2006 <http://www.origamiproject. com/1/>.

"The Hidden Leonardo." *NG London/News & Features.* 2001. 12 Aug 2005 <http://www.nationalgallery.org.uk/collection/news/newsitems/leonardo/default.ht m>.

"hi there." 3 Mar 2006. *Origami Project.* 2 Mar 2006. <http://www.origamiproject.com/ 2/>.

JD 'GunMod.' "High Res Realistic Delivery Trucks Info." 1 Jan 2006. *Grand Theft Auto Files.* 11 Mar 2006. <http://grandtheftauto.filefront.com/file/High_Res_Realistic_ Delivery_Trucks;55929>.

LaoBoy, "Tupac Shirt." 1 Aug 2005. *Gtagaming.com.* 12 Aug 2005. <http://www.gtagaming.com/pafiledb.php?action=file&id=1207>.

McDonough, Jerome P. "Designer Selves: Construction of Technologically Mediated Identity within Graphical, Multiuser Virtual Environments." *Journal of the American Society for Information Science.* 50.10 (1999): 855–869.

Montfort, Nick. *Twisty Little Passages.* Cambridge: MIT P, 2003.

Murray, Soraya. "High Art/Low Life: The Art of Playing *Grand Theft Auto.*" *PAJ: A Journal of Performance and Art.* 27.2 (2005): 91–98.

Packard, Edward. *Inside UFO 54–40.* Toronto: Bantam, 1982.

Pomaville, Leann, ed. *Quake Woman's Forum.* 1999. *PlanetQuake.com.* 11 Aug 2005 <http://qwf.planetquake.gamespy.com/qskins/skinpac0.html>.

Quake 1. Santa Monica: MacPlay, 1996.

Schiesel, Seth. "Video Game Known for Violence Lands in Rating Trouble Over Sex." *The New York Times.* 21 July 2005, late ed.:A1.

SimonS. "Johnson Autos." 28 June 2005. *Gtagaming.com.* 12 Aug 2005. <http://www.gtagaming.com/pafiledb.php?action=file&id=1033>.

Todd587. "Toyota Landcruiser FJ40." 15 Jun 2004. *deviantART.* 12 Mar 2006. <http://www.deviantart.com/deviation/8141143>.

Wildenborg, Patrick. "PatrickW GTA-Modding | Home." 12 Aug 2005. *PatrickW GTA Modding.* July 2005. <http://patrickw.gtagames.nl/index.html>.

14. Playing with Style:
Negotiating Digital Game Studies
DAVID PARRY

I intentionally maxed out CJ's fat and muscle to make him a
great big giant of a man. I kind of change clothes depending on
the stuff I'm doing. When in Los Santos, I have CJ wear green
track pants, a green hoody, and green lowtops to get into the
whole "gang war" thing. When out in the countryside, I have
him wear a combat jacket, woodland camo, dogtags and no
shoes. Of course, the yellow watch and pink hair are standard, I
just love bright colors.

—*Flaneater, posted in GTA Forums*

When I think negotiation, I think of this fatigue, of this without-
rest, this enervating mobility preventing one from ever stopping. If you would like to translate this philosophically, the
impossibility of stopping, this means: no thesis, no position, no
theme, no station, no substance, no stability, a perpetual suspension, a suspension without rest.

—*Derrida, Negotiations*

In his article "Towards Computer Game Studies," Markku Eskelinen
contends that those who study digital games need to resist "colonization" by other disciplines and move towards crafting an independent
area of study (36). In order to distinguish between games and narrative
texts, Eskelinen makes the following observation: "To generalize in art
we might have to configure in order to interpret, whereas in games we
have to interpret in order to be able to configure, and proceed from the
beginning to the winning or *some other situation*" (38, emphasis added).

It is the last part of this statement that is perhaps the most intriguing, this "some other situation," this cast-off phrase that completes Eskelinen's sentence. In what is otherwise a rigorously conceived essay, this "some other" seems an imprecise term. Yet it indicates a place that can move digital game studies past the already played out, dead-end debate between narrative and ludics, to a more complete framework of analysis. In many ways the focus of this scholarly debate has often obscured what perhaps really matters in digital games, a feature brought into focus by the Grand Theft Auto (GTA) series, and bizarrely highlighted by "Flaneater's" yellow watch and pink hair.

Although digital games scholars have begun to produce a substantial body of theory which seeks to open up the questions raised by digital texts, these engagements have been frequently limited by analytic frameworks which divide gamer from game, treating the subject (gamer) and object (game) as discretely separable concepts. Whether narrativist, ludic, or somewhere between these two poles, digital game theory has often hermeneutically engaged its object of study, dividing gamer from game, in an effort to rush to a conclusion about what these texts mean. Whether understanding the game as a subject of configuration or interpretation, it has treated digital games as if they were a completely whole text, its borders fully definable. In the end these approaches have rather vigorously engaged with digital games in an effort to understand what it is that these texts mean, *but this ignores a perhaps more fundamental question of how it is that these texts mean.* What I would like to suggest is that when we take a step back to address this question, a host of problems arise to expose the inadequacy of either the narrativist or the ludic approaches. Realizing that digital games and digital gamers are not preconceived, determinate subjects of study necessitates that we understand the gaming-event as a site of negotiation, a restless interaction where final interpretation or configuration is always reserved for a later moment—which is to say never, in the final analysis, made possible. That is, what comes to matter is not the what but the how, not the ending but the *style.*

Despite its popularity, aside from issues of violence, the Grand Theft Auto series has generated a surprising lack of theoretical analysis. What I would suggest is that this is to a large extent a result of the overplayed theoretical debate between ludology and narratology which has obscured the features of gameplay that make GTA one of the most popular digital games. By shifting digital game theory towards the question of how gameplay is negotiated we can perhaps more adequately come to understand how important the notion of style is to these texts, hyperbolically so with respect to GTA, whose evolution has relied heavily on this concept to maintain its popularity. And so, the focus of this essay: First, an attempt to develop a theory of digital games that understands the gaming as a negotiation, and second, an answer to the question which "Flaneater's" comment implicitly raises as to why that "some other situation," exemplified by pink hair and a yellow watch, is essential to any analysis of the aesthetic of the GTA series.

Perhaps the inadequacy of our current theory begins with early digital games studies (Murray, Laurel) which sought to analyze these games using neo–Aristotelian models of drama or neo–Kantian aesthetic critiques, both of which are wholly inadequate frameworks for engaging "old media," not to mention sites incapable of serving as the foundation for engaging "new media."[1] Even when digital game theorists have tried to move beyond this paradigm, they have often only succeeded in so much as they maintain the belief that a text is absolutely separate from the world (the commonly used substitution of configuration for interpretation betrays this hermeneutic bias). A more careful paradigm of analysis would be one which considers the digital game not so much as an object of study, but rather an *event* of study, and it is this consideration of the gaming-event that would help to explain why that "some other situation" is in fact far more important than the winning it seems to be merely supplementing. While this type of analysis is not breaking any new ground in aesthetic theory or philosophy, it has been surprisingly absent from digital game studies.[2]

Consider the conundrum previous digital game theories have faced in developing a substantial framework for analysis (one which has failed to account for the popularity of games such as those in the GTA series): Where should one begin? With the gamer or the game? What is the status of a game with no one to play? Or, what is a gamer without a game to play? Are we to see the game as the object played by a gamer, or are we to see the gamer as one who plays a game? To be overly reductive: what came first, the gamer or the game? This type of unanswerable question has been central to the study of the digital game. But digital game theory needs to recognize this unanswerable frame and instead begin from the fact that the gamer and the game are, strictly speaking, inseparable. Any analysis which sees gamer and game as separate entities that come together necessarily marches off to answer a host of wrongly conceived questions. While many such as Murray, Atkins, and Laurel would seem to be privileging the Cartesian subject who comes to the game whole and complete, ready to have a mimetic experience of truth and beauty, the other side of the debate would seem to reflect the opposite error, suggesting that the text itself is wholly analyzable object before the subject even approaches. (How would one know if a text is ergodic or not without first interacting with the work? Any judgment about the ergodic quality of a text would have to come after an interaction with the text.) Upon final analysis, both the ludic and narrative approaches share the error of being foundationalist and thus overly reductive.

These frameworks have been responsible for the rather limiting perspectives often imposed on games such as those in the Grand Theft Auto series, an analysis which focuses on the violence one must enact (ludic actions) or the missions (narrative story) without actually addressing the gaming experience in its entirety. Perhaps there is a better way, one which would not see the game or gamer as subject or object in an already completed project, but one which would seek to understand how the positions of gamer and game are produced from the interaction. This tack of analysis would refocus the questions towards a consideration of the gaming-event, which cannot be adequately understood utilizing the current rubric which relies heavily on the ability to reduce the gamer and game to object and subject. In this vein, I would like to suggest that we think of the digital game as a negotiation, an interaction which never fully comes to rest, structured between two poles, game and gamer, but not reducible to either of the two parts. This is why it is never really possible to speak strictly of the game; instead, one must always speak of gameplay. What is really important here, and the key to producing a theory of this gaming-event, is an understanding of the restless negotiation of the digital game interaction, one in which the GTA series serves as a paradigmatic example, not only because of the stylistic variations through which players engage the game, but also because of the ways that these stylistic variations themselves are subject to negotiation outside of the game world.

If we begin by thinking of change and negotiation as crucial concepts for understanding the gaming interaction, we end up with a far more productive theory for digital game studies.[3] That is, digital game studies must come to see negotiation itself as the catalyzing element around which the gaming takes place, from which the positions of gamer and game are produced. But this negotiation itself is a difficult concept, aporetically structured. On the one hand, there must be something to be negotiated in the gameplay, something which itself will undergo change. However, on the other, there must also be something that is non-negotiable, positions which cannot be erased in the interaction; for if the distance between the two positions were collapsed, the negotiation produced by this difference would also be erased. What this means is that there will always be a negotiation on the level of play, as the various participants, human and technological, interact and change, but there will also be a larger framework, that is beyond the negotiation, a non-negotiable structure that creates the space for there to be a game.

So, in the interaction, what is negotiated is the non-negotiable difference between the gamer and game. On one level this negotiation is produced by the rules, a product of the system, but on another it is always a negotiation about the structure, in resistance to the very rules themselves. As long as the structure is maintained, there is a difference within the possible positions, and while one might struggle to overcome this difference (in some cases by winning or losing) the result of annulling the difference would be to collapse the system—ending the negotiation. This is why it is important to displace the concern for winning and losing which are themselves anti-negotiation—they end the interaction, foreclosing any future possibility—and instead move towards that "some other event" which continues the negotiation, the gaming, that which prevents the game-over screen from appearing.

In his attempt to claim unique ground for "ergodic texts," and by extension digital games, Espen Aarseth articulates a distinction he sees between traditional texts and what he will come to define as cybertexts. In the classical text, "The reader's pleasure is the pleasure of the voyeur. Safe but impotent. The cybertext reader on the other hand is not safe, and therefore it can be argued, she is not a reader. The cybertext puts its would be reader at risk: the risk of rejection" (4). While I would ultimately disagree with Aarseth about the distinction between these two types of texts, his analysis brings us closer to understanding the nature of the interaction in the digital game-text. What is at stake is not, however, a one-sided rejection of the reader (the game-over screen), but rather the possibility of an end to the interaction: a rejection of *both* reader and text. The threat is the threat of an end to the gaming that is an end to the negotiation. This threat is always double, and Aarseth's critique seems to miss this point. While there is a threat that the game might "reject" the reader, ending the negotiation (although I would argue that if the game rejects the gamer it rejects itself in so far as the rejection negates the interaction), there is always the risk that the gamer too might reject the text, producing the same result. What is always at stake is the palpable tension between the gamer and game, a relation always subject to negotiation that is consistently threatened by the possibility of closure.

If the digital game is best understood as a mutlicursal labyrinth, as Aarseth contends, with multiple paths to completion, one should consider the game through the criteria of completion, of winning. But closer analysis reveals that it is not completing the maze, or exiting the labyrinth, which really matters; rather, it is figuring out a way to make the maze continually exciting to continue to engage with the text, i.e. that "some other situation." The goal (exit) is only important in so much as it is never attained, for once the goal is attained the negotiation of the game ends (unless one renews the goals and the terms of the game, as often happens in the re-playing of the game).

This is where the GTA series plays a particularly descriptive role, where that "some other situation" comes to take precedence over any single completion. Although certainly not the first example, the GTA series is often held to be one of the premier examples of "sandbox" gaming. While the term "sandbox gaming" has been used fairly broadly, it has most often been used to refer to games with open-ended gameplay where the gamer is given "freedom" to do whatever she wants within the game world. Most sandbox-style games contain deformable worlds which allow gamers "unrestricted" movement within the game world. It is precisely this deceptive notion of freedom to which we will have to return in a moment. (Now, I am not going to unquestionably celebrate GTA here—to be sure, I have a host of concerns about the cultural representations in the game—but also, to be fair, many, including myself, have spent countless hours enjoying negotiating the game.)

A rather basic analysis could suggest that the GTA series does not, in fact, follow this sandbox model. All three of the latest versions, *Grand Theft Auto III (GTA3)*, *Grand Theft Auto: Vice City (GTA:VC)*, and *Grand Theft Auto: San Andreas (GTA:SA)*, present a game which develops across a series of missions, measured by the criminal rating, and in some part by the "percentage complete" stat. However, several factors are important to keep in mind here. First, that it is possible to complete the main story missions of the game without achieving 100% completion; in fact, gameplay suggests just this, as most players complete the main narrative without initially achieving 100% completion. Second, and perhaps more importantly, 100% completion is not 100% completion. Many gamers play the game far after obtaining, or without ever obtaining, 100% completion. The percentage complete stat is just one stat amongst many, given no real privilege within the game. The primary motivation for obtaining 100% completion seems to be either the in-game rewards that completion produces (but why would I need infinite ammo as a reward if the game is truly 100% complete?) or the bragging rights that come with maximizing this statistical category.

The GTA series keeps track of a substantial quantity of information on the statistics screen. A brief perusal of the various stat screens illustrates this point. Take for example *Grand Theft Auto: Vice City*: while there is a collection of stats that seems to relate to the main narrative, depending on where the rolling stats are accessed, one encounters a wider range of stats that have nothing to do with the central story line; rather these stats relate to that "some other situation." (A few of my favorite examples: "tires popped," "best score at keepy uppy beach ball," "seagulls sniped.") This statistical saturation ensures that while a gamer could complete the percentage stat, no true 100% complete is ever possible. Even after maximizing the percentage complete stat, one could always try, as indeed many players have, to continue to change the stats of their game. Indeed, consider how after one completes the "main" quests to the game, credits roll, and following the credits, *gameplay continues.* If winning were the point, the credits would close the gaming. Here the Grand Theft Auto series reflects an often talked about feature of games: replayability. One of the keys to the game is not playability, one straight play through—this would be boring, but rather what is important is the always implied, from the first moment, replayability of the game. Because of the structure of the game, no final playing is ever possible; there is always more to be negotiated, more stats to change, more of the interaction to be developed.

A comparison of the stats tracked across the GTA series reflects the increasing emphasis that Rockstar has placed in developing a game that encourages this restless statistical negotiation, opening up the games to a wide array of stylized playings. *GTA3* logs 35 stats, *GTA:VC* tracks 84, and *GTA:SA* expands this number to 155. Furthermore, while *GTA3* displays one privileged stat ("criminal rating" remains on the screen while the others roll by), the later two GTA games remove this hierarchy, treating all stats equally. Notice also that while some of the stats added in later versions of GTA feature in "winning" the game, a majority of those added measure "some other situation": "headshots," "budgets," "wheelie," "stoppie," "last dance score," "furthest hoop," etc. The later GTAs also feature an expansion of the stats designed to measure how one has played the game ("distance traveled" by particular vehicle, "favorite radio station"). This is why it is important to see the act of gaming as an open-ended negotiation, rather than the product of a subject appropriating an object, or an object determining a subject. For, to simply focus on the winning, losing, or narration of the game, is to ignore substantial amounts of textual evidence that suggest gameplay moves beyond these rather limited categories. What is being negotiated here between the players and the game is the notion of style: what is possible, what is not, what is within and without the bounds of the gaming-interaction—the how of playing.

Indeed, what is intriguing about the stats themselves is their distinct lack of hierarchy. Again, consider *GTA:VC.* First notice that, while often in printed lists of the stats screens the rating and percentage complete occur first, during gameplay the stats are presented in a continuous scroll and no single stat is given prominence over others. The percentage complete stat, or one's "criminal rating," does not appear in a separate stat screen while the other markers are displayed. The only group of stats that is presented in a different fashion (rendered in all caps) is those that are grouped around "INSANE," as if to suggest that the only privileged criteria is insanity. Equally as important to consider is how individual stats themselves can be particularly ambiguous. Is it desirable to have a low number or a high number for "wanted stars obtained"? What about "distance traveled by foot"? Or "auto repair" and "painting budget"? Even the seemingly straightforward stats appear less so upon contemplation. While given the violent nature of the game, one could suggest that it is desirable to have a high number of "people wasted," further consideration suggests the opposite might be the case. Indeed, it is harder (therefore, arguably, better) to play the game killing as few people as possible. What is the minimum number of people one can waste while still managing to finish the main missions? And so here is the point: not only are the stat values always under negotiation by the player, but the *value of the stats* themselves are always under negotiation. In some sense, negotiating the digital text is always about that "some other situation." This is the point of playing with style: to temporarily determine a set of choices that reflect a way of engaging the text, a way that can only be measured in its difference from other playings.

A look at the internet discussions around the Grand Theft Auto series suggests that style is, in fact, the point of playing. Style only exists in terms of hyper-contextualization, a negotiation that produces the meaning and dynamic quality of the gaming interaction. Players often post their statistics on the web and then argue, through extensive postings, why their particular stylistic choices are superior to another. Again, no final resolution is possible, so the negotiation of value takes place not only within the game, but in comparison with others' engagements with the text, as players frequently participate in discourse and debate about what constitutes a superior playing of the game. Thus, what frames the gaming-event is not simply limited to the time and space of the actual playing, but is informed and shaped by negotiation with other experiences of the game. This is a significant development over older style digital games, and perhaps one of the key features that has led to their cultural prominence. While with older games such as *Pac-Man* or *Galaga* stylized play was limited—often all players compared was a score or the witnessing of the same event (the final produced narrative element was always reduced to a rather boring numerical finality)—now the interaction has become far more complex. What is compared is no longer the numerically reduced conclusion of one's gameplay ("I got to level 10, scored 182,004 points."[4]), but rather how one has played the game.[5]

("Not only did I rob all the stores, but I did so wearing an outfit from the Gash wielding a chainsaw.") This is, again, one of the many places where digital games studies has tended to fall short. It is descriptively inaccurate to distinguish between the "game world" and the "real world," for much of the negotiation of what matters in the game world (the rules which constitute the structure of the game) is itself determined by negotiation with the "real world" through discussion forums, what other players have done, prior gaming experiences, cultural preferences—indeed, the list of factors which inform the gameplay is inexhaustible. Meaning in each one of the worlds is clearly infected by and through its interaction with the other, and thus drawing a border between the two becomes impossible. While for the purpose of analysis we might engage in distinguishing between gamer and game, in the end they remain inseparable, for each relies on the other for its continued existence. How these borders are drawn, the locations of determination between the two, is always a question of style: what counts, what does not, how much of the "real world" should factor in the textual negotiation, how much of what happens in the "game world" is allowed to count in the "real world."

Any theory of digital games which mobilizes the neo–Kantian, neo–Aristotelian tradition is doomed to be haunted by dialectic thinking, clearly reflected in much of the rhetoric surrounding digital games studies: rhetoric which often depicts players and games in opposition and thus has failed to adequately explain the popularity of games such as GTA.[6] By focusing on questions of style, one sees the two participants as engaged in a negotiation that produces the meaning, rather than falling into the trap of focusing on the hollow category of winning.[7] In fact, winning is in itself an anti-game moment. What happens when a game is won? The interaction ends, the game ceases to be. Considering the game from the perspective of winning leads to one of only two possibilities, both of which arrest the potential of the gamer-game negotiation: either the gamer is defeated by the game, or the gamer defeats the game. In either case the interaction ends and there ceases to be anything that can be understood as the negotiation of the game. All that one is left with is a narrative of what has occurred, a foreclosure of meaning, rather than an opening to future possibilities.[8] If winning were the final point of closure, there would be with every game one "best" way to play the game, a "perfect" interaction. In this analysis gamers would simply play until this perfection is achieved, and the only point of discussion would be the degree to which the final reading occurred. There would be no discussion, no negotiation, between the gamer and the game; instead the negotiation would have already taken place, programmed from the beginning, a pre-determined occurrence. While gamers certainly play games with the notion of "perfection" in mind (finish all the missions, do so without dying) these notions of perfection are never finally determinate. What constitutes a perfect reading is always, upon final analysis, subject to further negotiation. In contradiction to this thinking, ludologists are in bizarre parallel with narrativists: for the narrativist "complete interpretation is possible," and for the ludologist, "complete configuration is possible." However, the point is precisely the converse: the nature of the digital game dictates that completion (configuration or interpretation) is never possible, that any attempt to fix the meaning produced is, in the first case, never contained within the game, but always in reference to an outside negotiable criteria, and, in the second case, is tentative, subject to further interaction, remaining so as long as the negotiation continues.

This is another area where the extent to which many digital game scholars have rejected contemporary theory is particularly vexing. For, one of the key concepts contemporary theory has developed is a realization of the extent to which any narrative remains forever open, subject to further negotiation. Now, I do not mean to suggest that negotiating a novel, or a film, or a digital game is absolutely the same, but contemporary theory offers much in the way of understanding how textual interaction has always been a form of open negotiation even if it has not always been understood as such. This is perhaps why conservative literary voices have been so quick in their attempt to "colonize" digital game studies: not because digital games are best understood through notions of "truth and beauty," but rather because if digital games cannot be adequately understood through these conservative aesthetic tools (which I would argue they cannot), they threaten to expose the inadequacy of these methods not only for digital games studies but perhaps more threateningly for other media analysis (of novels and films) as well.

To be sure, without the possibility of producing the interpretation or configuration, the game would also cease to have meaning. But the potential to craft another narrative is still always possible based on another ludic negotiation which always remains and undercuts any finality obtained through a "winning." Winning is simply a goal that structures the tension of the interaction. In fact, winning is guaranteed from the first moment of the interaction, as if even the FAQs, walkthroughs, and "Official Brady Strategy Guides" prove inadequate, cheat codes guarantee the end. Now, one could object that many players refuse to use FAQs or cheat codes. But this is precisely the point: it is *how* one engages the game, the *style* with which one plays that truly matters. It is simply not within the style of some gaming-events to use FAQs or cheat codes. But these questions of how to play the game are always under negotiation, even within the same seemingly "coherent" gamer. Consider how some gamers will not use FAQs or cheat codes on the first play through, but on subsequent playings utilize them frequently. Here the style of play has changed and thus the way(s) that the gamers choose to negotiate the game are locally determined, indicating that at some moments the use of cheat codes is clearly understood as part of the style of play. Cheat codes are only "cheating" if they do not fit within the style of play.

While there are FAQs devoted to explaining how to complete each *GTA* mission and obtain 100% completion, there are also entire discussion boards, FAQs, and fan-sites dedicated to cataloging the variation with which gamers play.[9] Players catalog for others how to skydive from the greatest possible height (*GTA:SA*), how to get past the airport metal detectors (*GTA:VC*), or how to obtain a bullet-proof Cheetah (*GTA3*). These FAQs describe various ways players have developed to engage the game beyond the missions written into the game, from the popular motorcycle stunts to human bowling or searching for the best places form which to jump or engage in killing sprees. Gamers have even taken to developing their own missions and publishing them for others to attempt. Perusing the various GTA discussion forums reveals that most of the postings revolve around *this* type of gameplay. After all, only so much can be written about how to obtain 100% completion, but the amount that can be written about various styles of gameplay is inexhaustible. It is these stylized forms of play that drive players to re-play the game, to keep the game world open, rather than structure their respective interactions around the act of winning. In the end, winning becomes merely a tangential concern.

It is this question of how style is negotiated, how style is produced with the game, not against it, that seems crucial to me to developing a theory of digital games. Beginning with "style is what makes the player," a logic of relation will be developed that understands that gamers and games are not autonomous entities and that can resist the trap of seeing the game or the gamer as the determinate element (Massumi 77).[10] Such an analysis simultaneously resists the oppositional analysis that currently holds sway over digital game theory. This is, admittedly, a difficult path to pursue, as the object of analysis, style, will by its nature resist quantification. However, without this focus on *style*, much of the gameplay surrounding "sandbox" style gaming proves inadequate to the task at hand, and fails to address how players negotiate these games.[11] Indeed, the concept of style is something the makers of GTA have clearly understood in their progression of the series. While many series games have utilized expanded platforms and advancement in software development to enhance graphic capabilities of game sequels, Rockstar has selected a different route. Little has changed graphically over the latest three installments of the GTA series. Cut scenes, which have become an industry staple for showing off programmer prowess, are of surprisingly low quality in the GTA series (notice how characters' fingers always look like wood blocks). Instead, Rockstar has expanded the ways through which players are allowed to engage the game, resulting in an increase in the ability of gamers to play in a stylized manner. (This is more complicated than the "complete in-game freedom" often talked about, but more on this later.) For instance, one of the noticeable spatial differences in *GTA:SA* is the addition of elevation change. While *GTA:VC* was relatively flat, *GTA:SA* adds a host of rolling hills, particularly in San Fierro. Although this does little to make the game more challenging, what is added is the increased ability to perform "stunts." When I first was allowed on the island of San Fierro, I spent my first hours there not engaged in accomplishing missions or seeking to increase my criminal rating, but destroying motorcycle after motorcycle while negotiating the hills of San Fierro, attempting to pull off the most INSANE trick possible.

Perhaps the most talked about change in *GTA:SA* was the addition of the ability to change the appearance of the main character, CJ. Players in *GTA:SA* are allowed to select from a wide range of clothing styles (tuxedo, cowboy suit, athletic apparel, gang colors), tattoos (to cover one's entire torso and arms) and hairstyles (pink Mohawk, afro, cornrows), and body types (work out and CJ becomes muscular, eat too much and he becomes fat).[12] While digital game critics often speak of features such as "significant input" or "agency" to explain interactivity, these examples demonstrate that players are not often focused on "significant input." When gamers mod games, one of the first things changed is the "skin," the appearance of characters and the game world, a feature which has no effect on the actual winning of the game, yet represents one of the substantial ways gamers interact with the games. Without focusing on "non-trivial" (Aarseth) interactions, and considering this "some other condition," critics miss the *style* of play, the production which itself structures so much of the negotiation. One only has to peruse fan sites to see how important *style* is to gamers, to see how important the difference of playing is to the gameplay.

As Eric Zimmerman has pointed out, play is possible aporetically, "because of and despite the more rigid structures of a system" (*Narrative* 159). While "sandbox" gaming is often praised for its "complete freedom" and "realism," these phrases miss the point that the games are in no way free or realistic. In the first case, players are not free to do whatever they wish within the game world. In fact, a completely free game world would lack tension, and would mean gamers were completely in control of their experience; hence the negotiation would cease to exist and there would be no game. Rather, it is the play within the rules that creates the game world, play which is, as Zimmerman has noted, free movement within a more rigid structure. (Freedom within a structure is not freedom.) It is also important to take note that we are talking of movement within a rigid structure, not an absolutely determined one. That is, the structure, the rules themselves, are always part of what is being negotiated in the interaction. Rules that are too restrictive often result in hacks, mods, and cheat codes to allow gamers more freedom. Play occurs "in the interstitial spaces between and among its components," one component of which is the player and how she negotiates the text, taking advantage of the "space of possibility" (*Rules* 304). It is only by taking advantage of this space of possibility, understanding the relation of style to the negotiation, that we can develop a theory of digital games. Analysis ought to focus on how this space of possibility is produced: *before one asks what it is that games mean, it is necessary to engage the question of how it is that games mean at all.*

But if Zimmerman's rule-based thinking seems adequate to the task at hand, it in some ways falls short. For in this analysis, Zimmerman and Salen separate the player's experience from the rules "constituting the player experience," a separation that they admit is "artificial," but a separation that "allows us to look at games as formal systems" (*Rules* 121). However, this separation steers us away from recognizing the ways in which rules themselves are always the subject of negotiation: what constitutes a formal written rule? what constitutes an "unwritten rule"? what is cheating? what is acceptable? This is one of the locales of style, on the border of written and unwritten, exploiting the rules themselves to open up a new possibility of the interaction. Rules are not, in fact, separate from what one would describe as "aesthetic qualities," but that which enables the very possibility of their being anything like an aesthetic quality. Perhaps these "artificial," overly formalist distinctions are what lead to the false conclusion that, "Of course, there are plenty of cases of hacking, cheats, and Easter eggs in games, but these interventions only serve to highlight the fact that as a whole, the rules of digital games are indeed fixed and binding" (*Rules* 142). Indeed, the reverse is true: it is only the ability to subvert the rules—the exceptions, the cheats, the bendings of the rules—that enable the existence of the rules in the first place. Certainly, these negotiations often take place within the rules, but there is always the negotiation which cannot be framed solely within the game world: the set of negotiations about which rules are to be followed, when, and how, that in essence produces the différance in gameplay. In one sense, the negotiation is always focused on the rules (the structures) themselves, written and unwritten. If this were not the case, there would be only one "best" playing of each game, with all others measured in reference to its hierarchy, the conclusion guaranteed prior to the beginning, when in fact the reverse is the case. Hence, one of the things the digital text conspicuously puts into play is the hierarchy of rules themselves.

Again, this type of playing clearly informs Rockstar's design efforts, whereby the game world, rather than becoming a space of winning or losing, a completely pre-programmed interaction, becomes a site of restless negotiation, both about the space of play and about the rules which frame that space. Each installment has not only featured expanded stats and an increase in the possible ways that gamers can interact with the game-world, but has also an increased recognition that this type of play takes place. Later versions of GTA offer more options to game players, more paths along which to proceed in their interactions, and not just in the sense of divergent narratives, alternate endings or cut-scenes. More importantly, these options speak to the way that players stylize their gameplay, through selection not only of "meaningful" choices in the game world (which weapon(s) to choose as certain weapons are "better" than others), but seemingly "non-meaningful" ones as well (why does it matter what color hat I wear or what radio stations I listen to most?).

In later version it is these "non-meaningful" choices that dominate gameplay, for which the GTA game designers have included a horde of in-game "rewards" for players who choose to deviate from the missions. These "Easter eggs," which Zimmerman argues are exceptional to gameplay, actually become key features. *GTA:SA* contains a sign on top of a bridge that reads, "There are no Easter Eggs Here. Go Away," a reference to *GTA3*, which contained a sign which read, "You weren't supposed to be able to get here" (*GTA:VC* contained the actual Easter egg). The bridge also contains a sign for those who take the time to read it: "Bridge Facts, length—150.7 m, height—60.3m above sea level, 16000 polygons inc. LODs, 600m draw distance, 11 textures, takes up a staggering 1.27mb of disc space." As the series developed, the designers increased the number of secrets which players who deviate from the main narrative can discover. They are far too numerous to even attempt to chronicle here, but what seems important about this type of game design is the extent to which the designers have realized that this "non-meaningful" play is an inevitable, even desirable type of gameplay.[13] Rockstar has even recognized this type of game playing within the frame of the game: in *GTA:SA*, the third highest pilot rating is "Noops," a ranking in honor of a gamer who flew the dodo of Liberty City for 52 hours.

Often this type of engagement is deemed as "subversive play," but to marginalize this stylized play through terminology is to ignore a crucial aspect that structures these digital games. This play is not subversive, but, more properly speaking, it is the always-there potential that structures *any* engagement with the text. Without the possibility of subversive play, there would be no such thing as non-subversive play. And so here is one of the crucial points: It is often this subversive play, this style itself, which is under negotiation, that is, what is and is not considered subversive, against the rules.

Rather than create a text that appears or attempts to close off resistant readings, digital games open up the possibility for an infinite variation of alternative readings. While initially players/readers demonstrated their skill through absolute completion of the game, which included finding all the Easter eggs, now, on some level, the game has become all "Easter egg." The game world is one giant Easter egg, not built for absolute discovery or mastery, but always a re-invented world: re-negotiated, counter-signed, and re-made in the playing. In fact, this is the way the games are now read: play to see what Easter eggs can be created by the players, ones the "authors" of the digital game did not even "intend." But these are always present in the textual field of play. Resistant readings are not just written in (be the pizza boy, drive taxis) but always already available to the players who craft their own stylized play not anticipated by the authors of the game-world (for instance, drive full speed on the highway into oncoming traffic, line up cars to derail the train into the water, use the purple dildo to kill as many cops as possible in the police station). [14]

As I indicated in the beginning, this reading of digital games is not restricted to GTA (even if GTA serves as one of the primary texts which raises these questions). Indeed, many of the popular games foreground the ability of the gamer to negotiate the text with style. One could certainly include *The Sims, Need for Speed Underground, SSX 3,* and the *Tony Hawk* series. In the final analysis, I would contend that this negotiation is central to all digital games, and offers one of the reasons that on-line games are so popular: they offer a wide range of ways to play. Digital game theory that continues to focus on the question of narrative over ludics or ludics over narrative will continue to miss this mark. For the possibility of a narrative might structure the gaming, might provide the ability to create a stylized play in difference to other already created narratives, but this is only possible through a ludic negotiation with the text. In this way narrative and play are inextricably linked in digital games. Without both narrative and ludics, there is no negotiation of the digital game. Digital games, simply put, foreclose the notion of authorial intent, the idea that a transcendent reading for meaning (configuration or interpretation) is ever possible. In this sense, we always return to that "some other event." There is no final truth or beauty or winning to be had, and any reading with such claims has missed the possibility of another negotiation. The point of reading is to produce/create something not contained within the closed object of the text. That is, to play with style.

Notes

1. In early digital game analysis, it was somewhat common practice to renounce postmodern theory. Notice how both Murray and Atkins begin their works by casting off any contemporary theory, as if it is possible to return to Kantian aesthetics where art is understood as a mimetic representation of truth and beauty (hence Murray's final chapter "New Beauty, New Truth," a regression to Arnoldian criticism). While I am not suggesting that one has to wholly embrace contemporary theory, certainly one must recognize that writings such as those of Nietzsche, Heidegger and Derrida have significantly problematized our ability to delineate the aesthetic domain as representative of truth.

2. For an example of this type of analysis in relation to other media, see Weber's *Mass Mediauras.*

3. I would not want to limit this type of analysis to digital games. Thinking about the artistic interaction between text and reader as an open negotiation is productive for a wide range of mediums. Indeed, upon final analysis, I would suggest that it reforms how we think of all acts of reading.

4. Interestingly enough, as if to highlight the rather limited nature of this type of game play, the GTA series contains these arcade-style games within the game world. Walk into a bar in San Andreas and one can play a range of these arcade-style games where play is easily quantifiable.

5. Yet even here one finds evidence of stylized play, as gamers completed *Pac-Man* levels without eating ghosts, or played *Asteroids* as a racing game. These "subversive" readings are always already available, but as game structures expand the ability to stylize one's play is also expanded.

6. Clearly, the popularity of the game cannot solely be attributed to violence, for there are far more violent and graphic games on the market that have not garnered anywhere near the following that the GTA series has.

7. While it might appear that older digital games focused on the situation of "winning," a game's longevity and replayability were a function of the degree to which the game allowed for various paths, styles, for winning the game. That is, what mattered even in these early games was not the situation of winning, but rather how one went about winning: not if one completed the level but how it was done. I know players who prided themselves in completing certain levels blindfolded, a stylized play certainly beyond the realm of the "original" digital text.

8. The most radical example of this would be Gladitorial combat, where winning is achieved only by eliminating any possibility of future negotiation (death of one of the competitors). Winning is thus achieved by negating the game, and any future possibility of the game. Thus the game, and the negotiation, continues only in so much as winning remains a structural possibility that is yet never achieved.

9. To see examples of these, visit GTAforums.com, where a range of videos can be found including videos of stunts, base jumping, short films and a *Dukes of Hazard* film where gamers modified a car skin to look like the General Lee and engaged in elaborate car chases through the rural areas of San Andreas.

10. As Brian Massumi notes, this type of "logic of relation" might seem at odds with how we traditionally conceive of our subject/object world, but in fact it is an "indispensable step towards conceptualizing change" that resists a way of thinking whereby "everything is given in advance" (70).

11. As a brief aside, this is a concept any sports fan understands. Athletes do not engage in the game for the sake of producing a box score, or even a "W." If this were the case no one would watch these events; fans would only care about the final result. But instead fans want to know how the games transpired. This is why a 500ft home-run is more fun than one that barely clears the fence, despite the fact that they both produce the same result. Or, perhaps equally to the point, a 310ft home run which bounces off the center-fielder's glove might be more fun than the 500ft blast. These questions are always subject to negotiation.

12. This perhaps is one of the reasons I find playing San Andreas so unnerving: much of the stylistic play in the game occurs around racial tropes. While earlier versions of GTA certainly contained these problems, San Andreas magnifies them. That is, the game encourages what David Leonard has called "High Tech Black-face." And although these issues are beyond the frame of this essay, it is important to note how often race is treated merely as a trope to exploit for the sake of style. No consideration of style and game play is complete without engaging these issues as well.

13. For extensive lists on these secrets and alternative play styles, see <http://www.gamefaqs.com>, particularly the hints and secrets FAQs.

14. Two examples outside of the *GTA* world seem worth mentioning here. First, *Warthog Jump*, where a group of *HALO* players figured out that by stacking grenades under vehicles they could launch themselves onto previously inaccessible terrain. Second, *Doom*, where players derived entire vocabularies to describe play such as Buddha-style, completing levels without killing any monsters, or Jason, using only the chainsaw.

Works Cited

Aarseth, Espen. *Cybertext: Perspectives on Ergodic Literature*. Baltimore: John Hopkins UP, 1997.
Atkins, Barry. *More Than a Game: The Computer Game as Fictional Form*. New York: Manchester UP, 2003.
Derrida, Jacques. *Negotiations*. Trans. Elizabeth Rottenberg. Stanford: Stanford UP, 2002.
Ehrmann, Jacques. 'Homo Ludens Revisited.' *Game, Play, Literature*. Ed. Jacques Ehrman. Spec. issue of *Yale French Studies* 41 (1968): 31–57.
Eskelinen, Mark. "Towards Computer Game Studies." *First Person: New Media as Story, Performance, and Game*. Ed. Noah Wardrip-Fruin, and Pat Harrigan. Cambridge: MIT P, 2004. 36–44.
Glass, Randy. "Warthog Jump: A Halo Physics Experiment." Online Video. 11 Dec 2005 <http://www.warthog-jump.com/>.
"GTA Forums, San Andreas Theater." GTA Forums. 11 Dec. 2005 <http://www.gtaforums.com/index.php?showtopic=166423>.
"GTA Domain Forum." GTA Domain. 11 Dec. 2005 <http://gtadomain.gtagaming.com/forums/index.php>.
Leonard, David. "'Live in your World, Play in Ours': Race, Video Games, and Consuming the Other." *Studies in Media & Information Literacy Education* 3.4 (2003). 11 Dec. 2005. <http://www.utpress.utoronto.ca/journal/ejournals/simile>.
Massumi, Brian . *Parables for the Virtual: Movement, Affect, Sensation*. Durham: Duke UP, 2002.
Murray, Janet. *Hamlet on the Holodeck. The Future of Narrative in Cyberspace*. New York: Free P, 1997.

Weber, Samuel. *Mass Mediauras. Form, Technics, Media.* Stanford: Stanford UP, 1996.
Zimmerman, Eric. "Narrative, Interactivity, Play, and Games." *First Person: New Media as Story, Performance, and Game.* Ed. Noah Wardrip-Fruin, and Pat Harrigan. Cambridge: MIT P, 2004. 36–44.
Zimmerman, Eric, and Katie Salen. *Rules of Play: Game Design Fundamentals.* Cambridge: MIT P, 2003.

About the Contributors

David Annandale did his M.A. on the Marquis de Sade at the University of Manitoba and his Ph.D. on horror fiction and film at the University of Alberta. He teaches literature and film at the University of Manitoba. His scholarly work has appeared in anthologies such as McFarland's *Horror at the Drive-In,* and he is a regular film reviewer for *VideoScope* magazine. His novels *Crown Fire* and *Kornukopia* have been published by Turnstone Press. On the gaming front, he is exploring the themes of guilt and grieving in the horror narrative of *Silent Hill 2: Restless Dreams.*

Wm. Ruffin Bailey is a graduate student in the English Department at the University of South Carolina. He has six years' experience as a database administrator and customizations programmer, created the first cross-assembly suite for the Atari 2600 on the Macintosh, and was a contributor to *The Macintosh Bible,* 8th ed. His current projects include the influence of the discovery of the New World on the rhetoric of natural history.

Ian Bogost is a game designer, academic game researcher, and educational publisher. He is an assistant professor at the Georgia Institute of Technology, where he researches videogame criticism and videogame rhetoric and teaches in the undergraduate program in computational media and the graduate program in digital media. Bogost is especially interested in the function of ideology, politics, advertising, and education in games. He is the author of *Unit Operations: An Approach to Videogame Criticism* (MIT Press 2006), *Persuasive Games: Videogames and Procedural Rhetoric* (forthcoming from MIT Press), and co-editor (with Gonzalo Frasca) of *Water Cooler Games,* the online resource about videogames with an agenda.

Mark Finn is a lecturer in media and communications at the Swinburne University of Technology in Melbourne, Australia. He has published widely on various aspects of new media, including the historical development of electronic commerce and the social implications of mobile computing technologies. For the past five years he has been specializing in the social and cultural dimensions of video games, with his most recent work examining the debate over game censorship.

Nate Garrelts is an assistant professor of English at Saginaw Valley State University, where he actively teaches writing and writing intensive courses on digital games and other media. His research focuses on composition rhetoric and media literacy with an emphasis on digital games, film, and instructional technology, and he actively publishes and presents in these fields. He is the founder and chair of the digital game studies area at the Popular Culture Association/American Culture Association National Conference and his book *Digital Gameplay: Essays on the Nexus of Game and Gamer* was published in 2005 (McFarland).

Tanner Higgin is a graduate student in English at the University of California, Riverside. His recent work has focused on rethinking notions of embodiment and disembodiment in digital media and understanding the expression and function of violence in video games. He is co-editor of *The Means* <http://www.the-means.com>, a literary journal that has expanded into a weekly blog and podcast.

Aphra Kerr is a lecturer at the National University of Ireland Maynooth in the Republic of Ireland. Her research is focused on production, consumption and regulatory aspects of digital games, and she is the author of *The Business and Culture of Digital Games* (Sage, 2006). She has had articles published in the *International Journal of Cultural Studies, Convergence, New Media* and *Society and Media, Culture and Society*. A founding member of the Digital Games Research association (DiGRA), Aphra runs an online resource for the games community in Ireland <http://www.gamedevelopers.ie>, is an academic member of the Irish chapter of the International Game Developers Association and is a committee member of Women in Games (Europe).

Karla V. Kingsley is an assistant professor of instructional technology and educational computing at the University of New Mexico. Her teaching and scholarly interests focus on technology-mediated teaching and learning, the use of semiotic resources for constructing knowledge and meaning, digital game-based learning (DGBL), issues of educational equity and social justice, learners with special needs, and critical media literacy. She has published her research in peer-reviewed journals and has presented research and conducted practitioner-based workshops at national and international conferences. She serves as an associate editor for the *Journal of Special Education Technology* and as a review board member for the *Journal of Praxis in Multicultural Education*.

Dan Klainbaum is a digital media researcher and designer. He holds an M.S. in information design and technology from the Georgia Institute of Technology and a B.A. in American Studies from Tufts University. His work can be found at: <http://www.danklainbaum.com>.

David Leonard is an assistant professor in the Department of Comparative Ethnic Studies at Washington State University. He has written on sports, video games, film, and social movements, appearing in both popular and academic mediums. He has completed an edited volume on sports films from Peter Lang Publishers, with another examining race and the NBA scheduled for 2007 (SUNY Press). His work has appeared in *Journal of Sport and Social Issues*; *Cultural Studies: Critical Methodologies*; and *Games and Culture,* as well as several anthologies, including *Handbook of Sports and Media* and *Capitalizing on Sport: America, Democracy and Everyday Life.* He is a regular contributor to popmatters.com and *Colorlines Magazine.* His work explores the political economy of popular culture and globalized discourses of race, examining the dialectical interplay of movements of popular culture, white supremacy, and state violence through contextual, textual and subtextual analysis.

David Parry is a Ph.D. candidate in English studies at the University at Albany. His dissertation examines "negotiations" of reading across a range of textual media, from Nietzsche and Nabokov to hypertext and digital games. He is particularly interested in how contemporary theory can help us address questions concerning the ways in which technology, and language as technology, shape the act of reading, and how knowledge and the university are evolving as media for transmission and archivization become digital. He has taught classes at the University at Albany and at Simon's Rock College in philosophy, literature, and new media. He can be reached at <http://www.outsidethetext.com>.

Cindy Poremba is an interactive arts lecturer in Simon Fraser University's School of Interactive Arts and Technology, Surrey, British Columbia, Canada. Her research explores issues of agency, co-creation and rhetoric surrounding digital media—specifically, digital games and robotics. She holds a master of applied science degree in interactive arts from Simon Fraser and has presented work at the Life by Design: Digital Cultures symposium, Level Up (DiGRA 2003), the New Forms Festival, and Entermultimediale. She has served as one of the conference coordinators for Vancouver's 2003 New Forms Festival and produced the PoV Alternative Games Exhibition for Changing Views: Worlds in Play (DiGRA 2005).

Dennis Redmond graduated in 2000 from the University of Oregon with a Ph.D. in comparative literature. He is an independent scholar with interests in video culture, multinational economics, critical theory, and the process of cultural and economic integration in East Asia and the European Union. He is the author of *The World Is Watching* (2003) and the editor of *Satellite Uplink,* a quarterly webzine focusing on the contemporary videogame culture and the multinational media at <http://www.efn.org/~dredmond/Uplink.html>. Many of his works, essays and translations are online at <http://www.efn.org/~dredmond>.

Laurie N. Taylor, a Ph.D. candidate at the University of Florida, researches video games and digital media, where she is a managing editor of the journal *ImageTexT*. Her articles have appeared in *Game Studies: The International Journal of Computer Game Research; Media/Culture; Computers and Composition Online* and *Works & Days*, and has forthcoming articles in several collections on video games. She also writes a newspaper gaming column, an online gaming column, and radio programs for the public radio program "Recess!" Her research includes a book-length project on the Gothic in video games.

John A. Unger is an assistant professor of English at Northeastern State University in Tahlequah, Oklahoma, and teaches linguistics, grammar and usage, and English as a second language–related courses. He has published and presented papers and workshops on teaching English as a second language, literacy, and multicultural education. His research revolves around different types of semiotic literacies for the completion of specific goal-oriented activity. Before his life in higher education, John spent four years in the U.S. Navy and fifteen seasons on coastal and deep-sea commercial fishing boats in the Northern Pacific, Gulf of Alaska, and Bering Sea.

Timothy J. Welsh is a Ph.D. student at the University of Washington, specializing in media studies and twentieth-century U.S. literature.

Zach Whalen is a graduate fellow at the University of Florida where he is completing a Ph.D. studying new media, video games and digital textuality. His M.A. thesis analyzes formal structures of video game music, and continuing research examines the function of cryptography in new media texts. He has published articles in *Game Studies, Media/Culture,* and *Works & Days*, as well as a forthcoming book chapter on psychoanalysis in *CSI: Crime Scene Investigation*. He serves as managing editor and webmaster for the journal *ImageTexT: Interdisciplinary Comics Studies* and created the blog and Game Studies resource site, Gameology.org.

Index